Voice of the New West

John G. Jackson about 1799. (From a miniature owned by the late Mrs. Grace Duncan Britt. Courtesy of Mrs. Dorothy Davis.)

VOICE OF THE NEW WEST

JOHN G. JACKSON HIS LIFE AND TIMES

Stephen W. Brown

MERCER

ISBN 0-86554-162-0

Voice of the New West
John G. Jackson, His Life and Times

Printed in the United States of America

All books published by Mercer University Press
are printed on acid-free paper
that exceeds the minimum standards set by the
National Historical Records and Publications Commission.

Library of Congress Cataloging in Publication Data

Brown, Stephen W., 1950–
Voice of the new west.

Bibliography: p. 245
Includes index.

1. Jackson, John George, 1777–1825. 2. Legislators—United States—Biography. 3. United States. Congress. House—Biography. 4. Businessmen—West Virginia—Biography. 5. Businessmen—Virginia—Biography. 6. Virginia—Politics and government—1775–1865. 7. West Virginia—Politics and government. I. Title.
E340.J25B76 1985 975.4'03'0924 [B] 85-4991
ISBN 0-86554-162-0 (alk. paper)

Contents

Foreword

One need not be a votary of Thomas Carlyle to recognize that persons other than towering giants may enlighten the history of an era. The "one indispensable element" in a good biography, the late Allan Nevins wrote, is that it relate its subject to history and define his position and significance in the broad stream of events. Professor Stephen Brown has taken the injunction of Nevins to heart. In *Voice of the New West: John G. Jackson, His Life and Times,* he has done much to rescue a deserving but not Olympian American from an undeserved obscurity.

John G. Jackson was a member of the most illustrious family in northwestern Virginia (later West Virginia) politics in the nineteenth century. Yet, of that family only Stonewall, of military fame, would qualify for the pantheon of great Americans. In the 1790s Jackson's father, a local frontier hero, began service as a Virginia legislator and congressman and set the family upon a political course. Jackson's own descendants included a congressman, a governor of West Virginia, and federal judges, but they were only part of the Jacksons who distinguished themselves in public life.

In his own career as a state legislator, congressman, and federal judge and as a frontier industrial entrepreneur, as well as in other aspects of his life, John G. Jackson exemplified the ruggedness, boldness, energy, and restlessness of the New West of the early nineteenth century. Yet he had qualities of mind, versatility of interests, breadth and depth of learning, and a suavity of manner that fitted him for high position and sophisticated society. His first wife was a sister of Dolley Madison and Lucy Washington, and his second wife was a daughter of Postmaster General Return Jonathan Meigs, Jr.

Jackson first began to speak for Western concerns as a young Virginia legislator, and throughout his life he remained an eloquent champion of Western interests in the long sectional struggle between eastern and western Virginia. He consistently called for constitutional revision. In the Staunton Convention of 1816 he led the fight for general as opposed to limited reform, insisting upon extension of the franchise, legislative representation based upon white population, and popular election of state and county officials. He enunciated these views long before they became identified with the democracy of Andrew Jackson.

John G. Jackson's congressional career, which spanned the years 1803-1810 and 1813-1817, affords a useful perspective on politics in the new nation. In the first phase Jackson shifted from strict constructionist views to broader interpretations of the Constitution and began to embrace an economic nationalism that was closely akin to that of Henry Clay. Yet, politically, he retained an intense loyalty to the Jefferson and Madison administrations. During the Napoleonic Wars, when the security and honor of the nation often seemed at stake, he upheld both on nearly every issue of foreign and domestic policy. Had he remained in the House of Representatives in 1810 he would certainly have been one of the most vociferous of the War Hawks. He excoriated Federalist critics of both Jefferson and Madison, and his intemperate remarks drew him into one duel and threatened him with others. He did not spare the Quids in his own party, and more than once he crossed verbal swords with the much feared John Randolph of Roanoke. In the second phase of his congressional career he was widely regarded as a spokesman in the House of Representatives for President James Madison, his brother-in-law.

Had he never sat in Congress, Jackson would be worthy of study as a frontier industrialist and business entrepreneur. Spurred by the needs and opportunities during and preceding the War of 1812, Jackson erected salt works, an iron furnace, carding and fulling mills, tanneries, and other facilities at a site known as "The Factory," about one mile from his Clarksburg home. He took the lead in establishing the Virginia Saline Bank at Clarksburg for the purpose of providing investment and operating capital. His grandest venture was the Monongalia Navigation Company, in which he and his family were the principal stockholders. With state support the company undertook the construction of locks and dams in the West Fork of the Monongahela River. Questions relating to the relative importance of public utility and private gain, the ecological effects of the improvements, and alleged conflicts of interest on the part of Jackson, who was both president and chief contractor of the company, wrecked the plan. Acrid controversy over a proposal of the Army Corps of Engineers to build a dam on the West Fork in the late 1970s suggests the longevity of the public clamor over Jackson's project.

Questions naturally arise as to why Jackson with his great intelligence, learning, skill in frontier politics, and political connections never rose to greater heights in the state and national political spheres. Unfortunately, as Professor Brown makes clear, Jackson had serious shortcomings. For one thing, he was never able to divest himself of extreme partisanship. He not only lacked, but he would have disdained, the spirit of compromise that Clay sometimes used with such beneficial effect. Moreover, Jackson's biting sarcasm and bitter invective in debate often made more enemies than friends. Even the sincerity of his nationalism was often clouded by the suspicion that he sought to make Western interests appear to be true national interests and that he did not have sufficient appreciation of the needs and concerns of other sections.

Professor Brown's study of Jackson is judicious in conception and executed with scholarly discernment. He has recaptured a fascinating figure, with all his virtues and faults, and through him enlivened some of the most important segments of American and regional history.

Otis K. Rice
West Virginia Institute of Technology

Preface

John G. Jackson, Virginia legislator, congressman, and federal judge, is among those American leaders of secondary rank whose lives and careers elucidate the nation's history and add depth and dimension to the broad outlines shaped by the great figures who towered above them. Jackson sprang from the northwestern Virginia frontier (now West Virginia) and often styled himself a "Western man." In his devotion to democratic ideals he was in the mold of Thomas Jefferson and Andrew Jackson, and in his desire to foster and uphold the political and economic honor and power of the new nation, he equaled Henry Clay.

Because of his multifaceted interests, Jackson defies neat categorization. As an ardent Republican, he began political life as a states' rights advocate and an implacable foe of the Alien and Sedition Acts. Over the years, however, he became a staunch nationalist. Throughout his career he made the United States Constitution his polestar, and he spoke regarding it with a knowledge and authority that would have done honor to James Madison himself. Jackson viewed constitutions as living documents, and in Congress he fought for clarifications of the Constitution that would give the federal government unchallenged authority to deal with its expanding problems, aid it in welding the people into a genuine nation, and enable it to assert with force and vigor the ideals and rights of the nation. In Virginia he did battle for twenty-five years to modernize an antiquated and undemocratic frame of government.

His catholicity of interests and broad, deep learning in many fields stamped Jackson as more than a politician. He was one of the first serious agricultural innovators in western Virginia, as well as a bold, discerning industrial and business entrepreneur unmatched in the Western country of his time. His involvement in the everyday concerns of his constituents gave his political life a relevance and meaning that was not always apparent in the buffetings of local and sometimes even national politics.

Jackson mingled with the mighty of his time. His correspondents included Jefferson, Lafayette, Clay, John C. Calhoun, and other prominent men. His first wife was the sister of Dolley Madison and Lucy Washington, and even after her death Jackson remained close friends with the Madisons and her other relatives. As a congressman, he was commonly regarded as a spokesman for President Madison. Jackson's second wife was the daughter of Return Jonathan Meigs, Jr., governor of Ohio and postmaster general of the United States. Two of his closest friends were John W. Eppes, the son-in-law of Jefferson, and Caesar A. Rodney.

In his public career and private ventures Jackson epitomized the spirit of the new, burgeoning nation. His willingness to grapple with great political and economic matters and the fierceness with which he advocated causes often created enemies and even led to a duel between him and Congressman Joseph Pearson of North Carolina. His career, however, illuminates the links between political theory, national goals, and the thoughts and longings of the people for whom government exists. Jackson touched the lives of the people at many points, often with sensitivity and understanding, and thereby made his career worthy of rescue from the near oblivion into which it had fallen.

For me, this study of Jackson has served as a reminder that historical research nearly always carries with its excitements and frustrations deep personal obligations to those who have given assistance or encouragement. Some of my most satisfying experiences are a result of the helpfulness and courtesy extended to me during visits to the Dawes Memorial Library of Marietta College, the Virginia Historical Society, the Virginia State Library, the West Virginia Department of Archives and History, the West Virginia University Library, and the Vining Library of the West Virginia Institute of Technology. Numerous librarians also responded to my questions and my requests for materials in a way that constantly reminded me of the close alliance between historians and librarians. They included the staffs of the Historical Society of Pennsylvania, the Library of Congress, the Massachusetts Historical Society, the National Archives, the National Archives Records Center at Suitland, Maryland, the New-York Historical Society, the New York Public Library, the Ohio Historical Society, Princeton University Library, and the Western Reserve Historical Society.

The two most extensive Jackson collections are the John George Jackson Papers in the Lilly Library of Indiana University, Bloomington, Indiana, and the Meigs-Jackson Papers in the archives of the Blennerhassett Historical Park Commission, Parkersburg, West Virginia. Dr. Otis K. Rice, chairman of the department of history of West Virginia Institute of Technology, made available to me copies of all the Jackson papers in the Lilly Library, which he photocopied several years ago. Dr. Rice also made several useful suggestions during the course of my research and writing. For the use of the Meigs-Jackson Papers, I am indebted to the late Mrs. Florrie Jackson Needham, great-granddaughter of Jackson, and her daughter, Mrs. Caroline Smith of New York City, New York, their former owners, Mr. Edwin Dils and Mr. Ray Swick of the Blennerhassett Historical Park Commission, and Mrs. Betty Radda of the Commercial Bank of Parkersburg. I am also indebted to Mrs. Dorothy Davis of Salem, West Virginia, who arranged for me to visit Mrs. Needham, provided me with photocopies of other materials to which I did not have access, and gave me a delightful, informative tour of the sites in the Clarksburg area associated with Jackson's life. I must also acknowledge with appreciation a grant from the West Virginia Tech Foundation.

This study of Jackson is based upon my doctoral dissertation at West Virginia University. My adviser, Dr. William T. Doherty, transformed what might otherwise have been a test of endurance into a happy experience with his judicious and encouraging comments and his sound advice at every stage of the work.

Finally, my wife, Julia, and my son, Lennie, have borne with patience the days and weeks when they seemed to come second to the research and writing. By their support they have contributed more than they can know.

Stephen W. Brown
26 January 1985

John G. Jackson, His Life and Times in Pictures

President James Madison, brother-in-law and close friend of John G. Jackson. (From Irving Brant, James Madison: The Presidency, 1809-1812. *Indianapolis: The Bobbs-Merrill Company, Inc., 1956, frontispiece.)*

Dolley Madison, sister-in-law and confidante of John G. Jackson. (From Meade Minnigerode, Some American Ladies. *New York: G. P. Putnam's Sons, 1926, frontispiece.)*

Mary Sophia Meigs, second wife of John G. Jackson. (Owned by the late Florrie Jackson Needham. Courtesy of Mrs. Dorothy Davis.)

Return Jonathan Meigs, Jr., father-in-law of John G. Jackson. (Blennerhassett Historical Park Commission, Parkersburg, West Virginia.)

Jonathan Jackson, cousin and protégé of John G. Jackson and father of Stonewall Jackson. (From Mary Anna Jackson, Memoirs of Stonewall Jackson. *Louisville KY: Courier-Journal Job Printing Company, 1895, 13.)*

Joseph Pearson, the North Carolina congressman who fought a duel with John G. Jackson in 1809. (From Lora MacMillan, comp., North Carolina Portrait Index*. Chapel Hill: University of North Carolina Press for the National Society of the Colonial Dames of America in the State of North Carolina, 1963, 176.)*

Clarksburg August 25th 1809

Sir:

By the mail of Yesterday I received your letter of the 7th instant — The remarks attributed to me by the Natl. Intelligencer to which you have called my attention, were [illegible] used by me; and the words I used are not now recollected distinctly: altho' at that time my friend Mr. Eppes at my request reduced them to writing, & furnished me with the paper — But hearing nothing further from you, I either destroyed it, or left it with other papers at Washington. — I am unable to distinguish between the meaning of the words ascribed to me by the paper viz "a groundless & slanderous charge", and a determination (as you & your friend understood me) to oppose "unfounded, declamatory or unworthy charges" produced by your remarks — and therefore if your letter were couched in a less offensive stile, & I had every disposition to terminate this affair to your satisfaction, I could not ask any correction by the Editor

Sir your mo Obt St

J G Jackson

The above is a copy of a letter directed by Col. J.G. Jackson to Joseph Pearson representative in Congress. Salisbury N. Carolina

Jas Pindell

Letter of John G. Jackson to Joseph Pearson prior to their duel. (Blennerhassett Historical Park Commission, Parkersburg, West Virginia.)

Ruins of Monte Alto, residence of John G. Jackson. Photograph taken about 1903. (Harrison County, West Virginia, Historical Society.)

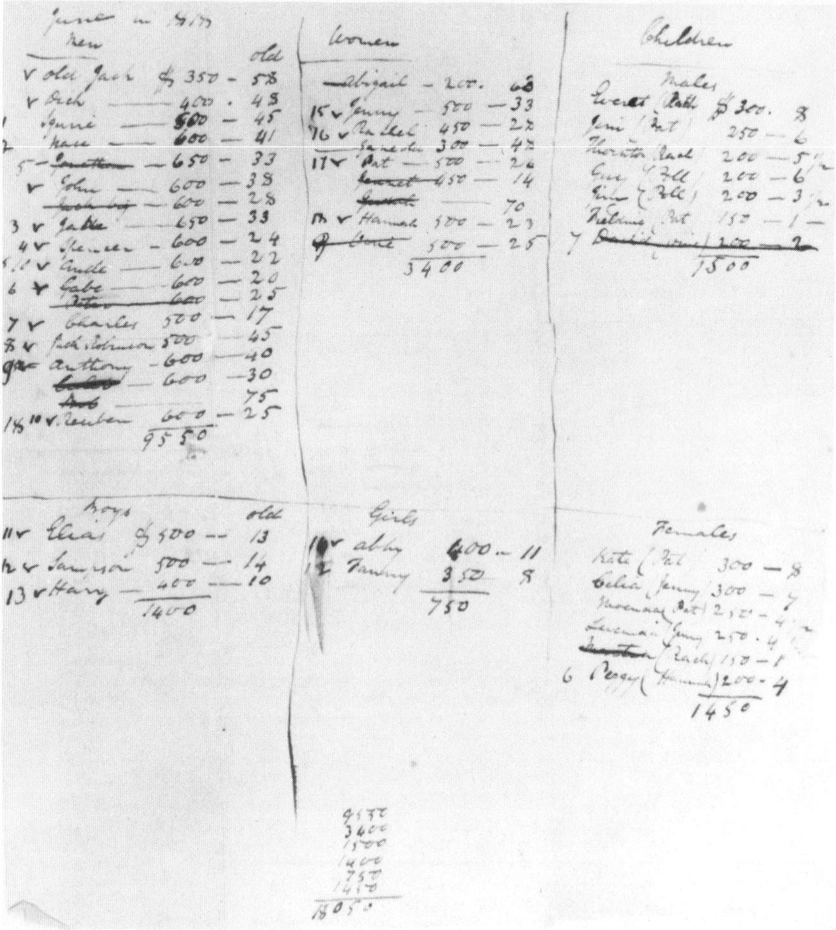
June [illegible] 1818

Men old
old Jack $350 - 58
Dick 400 . 48
[illegible] 600 - 45
[illegible] 600 - 41
[illegible] 650 - 33
John 600 - 38
[illegible] 600 - 28
Jake 650 - 33
Spencer 600 - 24
[illegible] 600 - 22
Gabe 600 - 20
[illegible] 600 - 25
Charles 500 - 17
[illegible] Johnson 500 - 45
Anthony 600 - 40
[illegible] 600 - 30
[illegible] 75
Reuben 600 - 25
9550

Women
Abigail - 200 . 60
Jenny 500 - 33
Rachel 450 - 22
[illegible] 300 - 42
Pat 500 - 26
[illegible] 450 - 14
[illegible] 70
Hannah 500 - 23
[illegible] 500 - 25
3400

Children
Males
[illegible] (Rach) $300 . 8
[illegible] (Pat) 250 - 6
[illegible] (Rach) 200 - 5½
[illegible] 200 - 6
[illegible] 200 - 3½
[illegible] (Pat) 150 - 1
[illegible] 200 - 2
1500

Boys old
Elias $500 - 13
Sampson 500 - 14
Harry 400 - 10
1400

Girls
Abby 400 - 11
Fanny 350 8
750

Females
Kate (Pat) 300 - 8
[illegible] (Jenny) 300 - 7
[illegible] (Pat) 250 - 4½
[illegible] (Jenny) 250 . 4
[illegible] (Rach) 150 - 1
Peggy (Hannah) 200 - 4
1450

9550
3400
1500
1400
750
1450
18050

List of John G. Jackson's slaves, 1818, in Jackson's handwriting. (Blennerhassett Historical Park Commission, Parkersburg, West Virginia.)

Jackson Cemetery, Clarksburg, West Virginia. Stones in the foreground (left to right) are those of Mary Meigs Jackson, John G. Jackson, and Mary Payne Jackson. (Photograph from the collection of Stephen W. Brown.)

1 THE FORMATIVE YEARS

The Jackson family of the Tygart Valley, on the upper waters of the Monongahela, would never forget the autumn of 1777. On 1 September, following the alliance of the Indians northwest of the Ohio with the British during the Revolutionary War, about two hundred warriors attacked Fort Henry, at Wheeling, and killed nearly half of its defenders. For the next three months marauding Indians ranged throughout the region between the Ohio and the Monongahela, and the Jacksons and their neighbors, deprived of the fort's protection, lived under the shadow of "the uplifted tomahawk." Believing that winter would end the Indian forays, the Tygart Valley residents welcomed a heavy snow, which fell about 20 November, as a great blessing and relaxed their vigilance. Unfortunately, the early snow melted quickly, and about twenty Indians, who had remained in the vicinity, emerged from their concealment and wreaked death and destruction upon the picturesque valley.[1]

On 22 September 1777, in the very midst of these perilous times, John George Jackson was born at the mouth of Turkey Run, a tributary of the Tygart Valley River. The family of young John, or John G. as he was later known, was, like thousands of others in trans-Allegheny Virginia, of Scotch-Irish descent. John, the grandfather for whom John G. was named,

---

[1]Harrison County Legislative Petition, 23 October 1793, Virginia State Library, Richmond, Virginia; Alexander Scott Withers, *Chronicles of Border Warfare*, ed. Reuben Gold Thwaites, new ed. (Cincinnati: Stewart and Kidd Company, 1895) 232-35; Otis K. Rice, *The Allegheny Frontier: West Virginia Beginnings, 1730-1830* (Lexington: University Press of Kentucky, 1970) 90-100.

was born at Coleraine, County Londonderry, in 1716. After learning the building trade in London, John immigrated to America in 1748 and settled in Cecil County, Maryland. In 1755 he married Elizabeth Cummins, an emigrant from London. John G. Gittings, a great-great grandson, later described the founder of the illustrious family into which John G. Jackson was born as a "diminutive man," but he characterized his wife as "a stately blonde, nearly six feet in stature and almost perfect in form and feature." Of greater importance, "she was well educated and possessed a resolute, active mind." Another descendant, William J. Bland, claimed that "the Jacksons got all their brains from her."[2]

In the spring of 1758 John and Elizabeth Cummins Jackson began a series of migrations that by the end of the French and Indian War found them living on Howard's Lick Road, about six miles south of Moorefield, West Virginia. There John met Samuel Pringle, who, with his brother John, had deserted the garrison at Fort Pitt in 1761 and had hunted and trapped in the Tygart Valley for several years. Pringle lavished such praise upon its beauty and fertility that the Jacksons, with their sons, George and Edward, and nine other immigrants accompanied Pringle when he returned to the

---

[2]John G. Gittings, *Personal Recollections of Stonewall Jackson, Also Sketches and Stories* (Cincinnati: The Editor Publishing Company, 1899) 5; Dr. William J. Bland Statement, Dabney-Jackson Collection, Virginia State Library, Richmond. See also Elizabeth Cummins Jackson Statement, undated, Meigs-Jackson Papers, Blennerhassett Historical Park Commission, Parkersburg, West Virginia (hereinafter cited as Meigs-Jackson Papers, BHPC); George W. Jackson to M. G. Underwood, 14 May 1866, Roy Bird Cook Collection, West Virginia Collection, West Virginia University Library, Morgantown, West Virginia; Roy Bird Cook, *The Family and Early Life of Stonewall Jackson*, 4th ed., rev. (Charleston WV: Education Foundation, Inc., 1963) 7-24, 106.

Among the numerous descendants of John and Elizabeth Cummins Jackson who gained distinction were their son George and his sons, John George and Edward Brake, all of whom served in the United States Congress. Grandsons of John George who had important political careers included Jacob Beeson Jackson, a governor of West Virginia; John Jay Jackson, Jr., a federal judge; and James Monroe Bland, a congressman from Missouri. George Jackson's illegitimate son, Samuel D. Hays, also served as a member of Congress. The noted Confederate general Thomas Jonathan "Stonewall" Jackson was the son of Jonathan Jackson, the cousin of John George, and the great-grandson of John and Elizabeth Cummins Jackson.

Tygart Valley. The Jackson family quickly acquired numerous tracts of land along the Buckhannon River. Three thousand acres, including the site of Buckhannon, were patented to Elizabeth Cummins Jackson, who paid for them in English gold.[3]

George Jackson, young John's father, had a limited education, but he was endowed with an exceptional native ability and the qualities of leadership needed and respected in a frontier community. His wife, Elizabeth Brake, like Elizabeth Cummins, was a woman of physical vigor and strong character. George gained local renown as an Indian fighter during the Revolutionary War and rose to the rank of colonel in the Virginia militia. Following the war he emerged as a leading political figure. In 1784 he led the movement for the organization of Harrison County and arranged for the holding of the first court of that county at his home. He pressed for location of the county seat at Clarksburg, on the West Fork of the Monongahela, where the Jackson family soon moved, and served as a justice of the peace of the new county. From 1786 to 1790 George represented the county in the Virginia House of Delegates. In 1788 he served in the Virginia convention at Richmond, where he strongly supported ratification of the United States Constitution. He won election to the House of Representatives from the Third District of Virginia to the Fourth, Sixth, and Seventh Congresses. After the death of Elizabeth Brake Jackson, by whom he had fourteen children, George married Nancy Richardson Adams, whom he described as "a poore widow woman" with five children. He died at Zanesville, Ohio, on 17 May 1831.[4]

---

[3]Elizabeth Cummins Jackson Statement, Meigs-Jackson Papers, BHPC; Withers, *Chronicles of Border Warfare*, 121-22; Cook, *Family and Early Life of Stonewall Jackson*, 9-12.

[4]Cook, *Family and Early Life of Stonewall Jackson*, 13-14; Withers, *Chronicles of Border Warfare*, 342-43; Rice, *Allegheny Frontier*, 344-46; Dorothy Davis, *History of Harrison County, West Virginia* (Clarksburg WV: American Association of University Women, 1970) 157; Henry Haymond, *History of Harrison County, West Virginia, from the Early Days of Northwestern Virginia to the Present* (Morgantown WV: Acme Publishing Company, 1910) 378-79. For Jackson's comment about his second wife, see George Jackson to Mary S. Jackson, 30 November 1814, John George Jackson Papers, Lilly Library, Indiana University, Bloomington.

John's childhood was influenced by events of the war into which he was born and the ever-present danger of attack by hostile Indians. These attacks made forting the normal mode of life, and some of his earliest memories centered around the days he spent at the fort erected by his grandfather Jackson at the mouth of Turkey Run.[5]

The removal of the Jackson family to Clarksburg changed their way of life very little. The Indian menace continued in most of trans-Allegheny Virginia until Anthony Wayne's victory over the Indians at Fallen Timbers in 1794. The frontier village of Clarksburg, where John grew up, was in some respects built "to answer for a Fort," with two rows of log cabins extending for about one-third of a mile across Elk Creek. The Jackson cabin was the easternmost of these dwellings. The most pretentious structure in the town, the courthouse, was a frame building, twenty-six feet by thirty-six feet, resting on stone pillars eight feet above the ground. For a time the town's only connection with older settlements was the "Pringle Packroad," a packhorse trail euphemistically known as the "State Road."

Residents of Clarksburg continued to live close to nature for several decades. Nearby woods teemed with deer, bears, turkeys, and other game, and buffalo still grazed occasionally on the natural grasses of the valleys. William Haymond, an early settler, later recalled that for a time the inhabitants lived principally on turkeys. Men undertook frequent hunting expeditions, returning with bearmeat, and also with deerskins and beaver pelts, which they marketed in Eastern towns and at Marietta. In this environment John developed a love for hunting and an expertness with a rifle that he retained throughout his life. In a speech as late as 1824, shortly before his death, this disciple of Nimrod declared to his constituents, "Year after year I go into the forest with some of you to hunt the deer and Bear, and find them abundantly within fifteen or twenty miles" of the town.[6]

---

[5]Davis, *History of Harrison County*, 156-57; Joseph Doddridge, *Notes, on the Settlement and Indian Wars, of the Western Parts of Virginia & Pennsylvania, from the Year 1763 until the year 1783 Inclusive, together with a View, of the State of Society, and Manners of the First Settlers of the Western Country* (Wellsburgh [W]V: Printed for the author, 1824) 117-19.

[6]Haymond, *History of Harrison County*, 235-36, 355, 360-61; Davis, *History of Harrison County*, 113-14. For Jackson's statement, see the Clarksburg *Intelligencer*, 15 May 1824.

Almost nothing is known of John's early formal education except that it was from a minister, "a reverend and venerable friend, from whose instructions he had learned the first rudiments of education." Circumstances suggest that this unidentified minister may have been Joseph Cheuvront, a Methodist. Cheuvront took up residence at Clarksburg about 1783 after leaving his native France and renouncing the Roman Catholic Church and his study for the priesthood. Well-educated and proficient in several languages, Cheuvront was perhaps better qualified than any other person available at the time to instruct the youth of frontier Clarksburg.[7]

In 1786 influential men in Harrison, Ohio, and Monongalia counties petitioned the General Assembly of Virginia to establish an academy west of the Alleghenies in order that "our Youths will be instructed and western Genius may possibly Reflect Honour on this rising Commonwealth." George Jackson, at the time a delegate from Harrison County, probably presented the petition. When the legislature established Randolph Academy on 31 December 1787, Jackson became one of its trustees and secured its location at Clarksburg. Although the trustees included some of the most distinguished men in the state, the frontier conditions prevailing in northwestern Virginia at the time made progress very slow, and the academy did not open its doors until August 1795. John may have attended Randolph Academy for a time. His graceful literary style, acquaintance with foreign languages, allusions to classical and historical incidents, and extensive practical knowledge were the marks of a man who had thorough and precise training in Latin, Greek, French, literature, history, geography, and mathematics, the very subjects offered by good academies of the time.[8]

The Clarksburg in which John grew to manhood aspired to become the Athens of Allegheny Virginia. Legislative leaders expected Randolph

---

[7]Jackson's statement is in the Clarksburg *Intelligencer*, 15 May 1824. For Cheuvront, see Davis, *History of Harrison County*, 564-65; Abel Stevens, *History of the Methodist Episcopal Church in the United States of America*, 3 vols. (New York: Eaton and Mains, 1864) 2:344.

[8]Monongalia County Legislative Petition, 1 December 1786, Virginia State Library, Richmond; Harrison County Legislative Petition, 16 September 1788, ibid.; Rice, *Allegheny Frontier*, 238-39; Charles H. Ambler, *A History of Education in West Virginia from Early Colonial Times to 1949* (Huntington WV: Standard Printing & Publishing Company, 1951) 5, 75.

Academy to take its place with William and Mary College and Transylvania Seminary as a part of a triad of colleges that would serve Virginia youth from the Tidewater to Kentucky. In spite of its frontier character, Clarksburg had a genteel quality lacking in most mountainous sections of Virginia. John Scripps, who lived in the town for five years beginning in 1803, deplored the presence of large numbers of "mechanics, journeymen, and employees, a reckless, drinking, swearing, gambling class who spent all their leisure and every night in the tavern," but he observed genuine refinement among the merchants and professional classes. Among the latter were George Towers, a graduate of Oxford University and principal of Randolph Academy, and Dr. William Williams, "the most literary man in the community." John read extensively from "the large and select library" of Towers and delighted in the intellectual conversation of Towers and Williams, who later became his brother-in-law.[9]

Jackson's inquiring mind, formal or informal education, and association with Clarksburg's most cultivated men inspired in him a love of knowledge. In 1793, when he accompanied his father to Richmond for the legislative session, he frequented the bookshops and read avidly. Throughout his life he added to a library that reflected the depth and catholicity of his interests. Numbering 725 volumes at the time of his death in 1825, it included 273 works on law; 90 volumes of history and biography, including writings of Edward Gibbon and David Hume, the *Annual Register*, and books on the lives of Washington, Franklin, Nelson, Kotzebue, and other prominent men; and 63 works on political matters, among them the writings of Thomas Malthus, Adam Smith, and Thomas Paine, and *The Federalist Papers*. The 66 volumes of poetry and 74 novels included most of the major British authors and numerous works in French, Latin, and Greek. Jackson never wearied of intellectual pursuits, and on one occasion in 1813 he purchased books costing a total of $220 from a Washington bookseller.[10]

---

[9]Quoted material from Scripps may be found in Haymond, *History of Harrison County*, 260; Davis, *History of Harrison County*, 283.

[10]A listing of volumes in Jackson's library may be found in Inventory of the Estate of John George Jackson, Harrison County Will Book 3, 311-26, Harrison County Courthouse, Clarksburg, West Virginia. See also Statement of Books Pur-

Aside from his intellectual interests, John also found excitement in the bustle of life in Clarksburg. His father, a leading entrepreneur in the town's business activities, operated a mill on Elk Creek, a tannery, a ferry, and other enterprises that aroused John's interest and enabled him to gain insight into the business world. Favorite occasions in the town were muster drills of the militia and court days, when cases of assault and battery, theft, defamation of character, and even murder excited the neighborhood. At such times dozens of visitors gathered at George Jackson's ordinary, where John listened to their conversations with deep interest. Court sessions also entailed a variety of social activities, and for men and boys, tests of strength and skill, such as wrestling, throwing the tomahawk, and shooting contests.[11]

John's horizons were by no means circumscribed by the hills around Clarksburg. He was entranced by his father's accounts of his experiences as a member of the Virginia House of Delegates and later of the United States Congress and the interesting people he met in Richmond and Washington. He also listened with rapt attention to recollections of life in England and Ireland and of immigration to America by his grandparents, John and Elizabeth Cummins Jackson, who made their home with his father during their declining years. Then, too, there were the visits of the venerable Methodist bishop, Francis Asbury, who lodged with the Jacksons during his visits to Clarksburg. From the eloquent and persuasive Asbury, John must have acquired some of the oratorical skill he later employed so effectively in the legislature, in the halls of Congress, and on the political stump.[12]

---

chased by John G. Jackson from Daniel Rapine, 8 July 1813, Meigs-Jackson Papers, BHPC; Schedule of Lands, Slaves, & other things the property of J. G. Jackson—Annexed to his Will, [3 December 1809], Meigs-Jackson Papers, Ohio Historical Society, Campus Martius Museum, Marietta. Dorothy Davis, *John George Jackson* (Parsons WV: McClain Printing Company, 1976) 24-25.

[11]Harrison County Legislative Petition, 19 September 1786, Virginia State Library; Clarksburg *Telegram*, 1 January 1876; Haymond, *History of Harrison County*, 197, 207.

[12]Rice, *Allegheny Frontier*, 176; Davis, *John George Jackson*, 14-16; [Francis Asbury], *The Journal of the Rev. Francis Asbury, Bishop of the Methodist Episcopal Church, from August 7, 1771, to December 7, 1815*, 3 vols. (New York: N. Bangs and T. Mason for the Methodist Episcopal Church, 1821) 2:35.

Along with his academic training and his useful apprenticeship in the school of human experience, John also studied surveying, a needed and practical skill in an area of rapidly increasing population and rampant land speculation. While in Richmond with his father in 1793, he acquired a copy of Gibson's *Surveying*, which gave him a theoretical knowledge of the subject. In assisting two uncles, Henry and Edward Jackson, both well-known surveyors, in laying off lands along the Buckhannon and West Fork rivers, he gained valuable practical experience.[13]

Four years later Jackson had an opportunity to put his surveying knowledge and skills to use. In response to a request from George Jackson, then a congressman from Virginia, Rufus Putnam, surveyor general of the United States, offered John a contract to survey a portion of the government's military lands in Ohio as soon as the Indian boundary line had been determined. Jackson went to Marietta and on 12 July 1797 signed the contract with Putnam, with his father as cosigner. John agreed to survey twenty-four townships, an area almost five miles square, on the Muskingum River, in present Licking and Muskingum counties. Setting out on 13 July 1797, with at least one helper and two experienced hunters, Jackson entered a region with "but one cabbin [*sic*] occupied by a white man who was married to an Indian woman, residing at the spot where Zanesville now stands." Fortunately, the Indians were peaceful, and within four months Jackson finished his assignment, for which he received $656.81.[14]

When Jackson had to choose a profession, he turned to law rather than surveying. Indeed, considering his familiarity with courthouse business, his recognition of the need for legal assistance in untangling the chaotic land

---

[13]Roy Bird Cook, "John George Jackson," *West Virginia Review* 12 (April 1935): 208; Davis, *John George Jackson*, 25-26.

[14]Putnam to Jackson, 10 April 1797, John George Jackson Papers; Clarence Edwin Carter, ed., *The Territorial Papers of the United States: The Territory Northwest of the River Ohio, 1787-1803*, 2 vols. (Washington DC: Government Printing Office, 1934) 2:606-607, 613-14, 616; "Original Field Notes of Township Lines, Subdivision 4, J. G. Jackson, 1797," in Office of the Auditor, Land Office, State of Ohio, State Capitol, Columbus; John G. Jackson's Receipt of Payment from Rufus Putnam, 27 November 1797, Manuscript Collection, Dawes Memorial Library, Marietta College, Marietta, Ohio; Clarksburg *Intelligencer*, 15 May 1824.

titles in western Virginia, and his strong interest in government and political thought, it would have been surprising had Jackson not been attracted to the legal profession. Moreover, his election to the Virginia House of Delegates in 1798 and his service there drew his attention to the close connection between a mastery of the law and success in politics. Finally, Clarksburg itself became a place of unusual promise for capable and ambitious lawyers during the early years of the nineteenth century.

Jackson apparently taught himself law, perhaps making extensive use of the Towers library, but he surely profited from the keen mind and varied experiences of his father. The seventeen-year-old John accompanied his father to Philadelphia in 1795 for the session of Congress and probably assisted the elder Jackson with clerical and secretarial work. John began his legal career on 15 September 1800, when the judges of the General Court of Virginia certified him as having the right "to practise [*sic*] the Law as an attorney and Council [*sic*] in the superior and inferior Courts of this Commonwealth."[15]

Although the law and politics occupied much of his attention, Jackson found ample time for the company of young women. In 1799 he courted Frances Emelia Triplett, the youngest child of Francis Triplett, a large landowner who lived near Parkersburg, on the Ohio River. Jackson may have met Frances Emelia on one of his journeys to make surveys in Ohio, or even as late as his campaign for the House of Delegates in 1798. Frances Emelia believed that Jackson had serious intentions and later claimed that he had promised to marry her. On 13 February 1800 she gave birth to his illegitimate son, who was named John Jay. During his early years, John Jay lived with his mother's family and was known as Jack Triplett.[16]

---

[15]Harrison County Court Minute Book, 1799-1801, 145, Harrison County Courthouse; Certificate of the Judges of the General Court of Virginia to John G. Jackson, 15 September 1800, John George Jackson Papers; Davis, *John George Jackson*, 34, 126-27.

[16]Davis, *John George Jackson*, 48, 53. See also Geo[rge] W. Atkinson, ed., *Bench and Bar of West Virginia* (Charleston WV: Virginian Law Book Company, 1919) 94; Thomas Condit Miller and Hu Maxwell, *West Virginia and Its People*, 3 vols. (New York: Lewis Historical Publishing Company, 1913) 2:556.

Meanwhile, almost certainly during the time that he was in Richmond for the 1798-1799 session of the legislature, Jackson had met Mary Payne, a younger sister of Dolley Madison. In March 1799 he enclosed a letter to Mary with one he addressed to James Madison. Evidently no serious correspondence between Jackson and Mary ensued immediately, and during the summer of 1799 Jackson began or renewed his courtship of Frances Emelia. Yet it was clearly his growing interest in Mary Payne that caused Jackson to break off his relationship with Frances Emelia.

Mary was one of eight children of John and Mary Coles Payne, the latter a cousin of Patrick Henry. In addition to Dolley, her sisters included Lucy—the wife of George Steptoe Washington, a nephew of George—and Anna—who married Richard Cutts, later a congressman from Massachusetts. John and Mary Coles Payne were practicing Quakers, and their daughter Mary continued to use Quaker forms of address throughout her life. In 1783, in keeping with his Quaker principles, Payne freed his slaves, sold his plantation—Scotchtown, formerly the home of Patrick Henry—and moved his family to Philadelphia. There he suffered bankruptcy and three years later died a broken man. Following his death, the family split up. Anna made her home with Dolley Madison, and Mrs. Payne took two other children, Mary and John, to live with the Washingtons at Harewood, in Jefferson County, in present-day West Virginia.

Family tradition has long held that John G. Jackson and Mary Payne were married in the first wedding performed in the White House. The tradition has no foundation in fact. On 23 September 1800 Jackson wrote Dolley Madison that "in my next Letter I may be permitted . . . to address you by the tender appellation of Sister, which next to calling Polly mine, will afford me the highest gratification," a clear indication that the wedding was not far off. Since Madison himself gave the bride away, the marriage may have taken place at Montpelier, the home of the Madisons, possibly giving rise to the idea of a White House wedding. On the other hand, the ceremony may have been at Harewood, where Mary resided.

The date of the wedding of John and Mary is also uncertain. It could have occurred as early as October 1800 or as late as January 1801. On 13 January 1801 Jackson obtained a leave of absence from the House of Delegates for the last ten days of the session. It is entirely conceivable that the leave was obtained for his marriage. Whatever the date of the wedding,

Jackson evidently returned to Clarksburg by way of Montpelier and Harewood, with Mary as his new bride.[17]

Jackson's marriage to Mary Payne led to a breach of promise suit by Frances Emelia Triplett. In 1801 her attorney, Noah Linsly of Wheeling, filed suit in the Virginia District Court at Morgantown for $2,000 damage, alleging that on 10 September 1799 John had told her that he would marry her. Instead, he had "craftily and subtly" contrived to deceive and defraud her. Witnesses were summoned, and John Williams, the clerk of the Harrison County Court, issued an order for Jackson's arrest to insure his presence at the next session of court.

The district court found in favor of the plaintiff and awarded her $400 and costs. Jackson, who apparently never denied his paternity of Frances Emelia's son, carried his case to the Virginia Court of Appeals in Richmond. He probably made that decision in the belief that the suit had been inspired by his political enemies and that his political future might be at stake rather than with any thought of proving his innocence. With William Williams of Harrison County and William G. Payne of Monongalia County as his sureties, he gave the necessary security in the amount of $800, which was accepted by the plaintiff, who was then residing in Kentucky, and her new attorney, Philip Doddridge of Wellsburg.

On 30 April 1803 the Court of Appeals rendered its decision with neither Jackson nor his attorney appearing in his defense. It upheld the verdict of the District Court at Morgantown and ordered Jackson to pay the damages awarded the plaintiff by the District Court, as well as her court costs. Jackson apparently did not comply with the court's directive, and on

---

[17]Jackson to Dolley Madison, 28 September 1800, Mary Allen Cassady Collection, Fincastle, Virginia; Jackson to James Madison, 17 July 1808, James Madison Papers, Library of Congress, Washington, D.C.; [Lucia B. Cutts, ed.], *Memoirs and Letters of Dolly Madison, Wife of James Madison, President of the United States* (Boston: Houghton, Mifflin Company, 1886) 3-5, 9-11, 16-17, 36; Allen C. Clark, *Life and Letters of Dolly Madison* (Washington DC: W. F. Roberts Company, 1914) 32. For the tradition of a White House wedding, see the statement of an unidentified writer, attributing it to assertions of her grandmother, Mary Elizabeth Payne Jackson Allen, who stated that she "had always been told that her father J. G. Jackson & her mother Mary Payne had been married in the White House," in Meigs-Jackson Papers, BHPC. See also Virginia, House of Delegates, *Journal, 1800*, 62; Cook, "John George Jackson," 210; Davis, *John George Jackson*, 48, 50-53, 55-57, 354n.

31 October 1805 the sheriff of Harrison County was ordered to attach his "goods and chattels" to satisfy the judgment against him and a ten percent per annum interest since 25 September 1802.[18]

Jackson's behavior did not stem from any attempt to avoid responsibility for his son. Perhaps out of consideration for the sensibilities of Mary Payne Jackson, he had few contacts with the child, but he evidently felt deeply troubled by his separation from him. After Mary's death and the marriage of Frances Emelia, he began to give serious thought to the lad's future. On 9 January 1810 he wrote James Madison that he had "never acquired the legal character of Guardian of my child" and that he now desired to do so.[19]

Jackson may have arranged for the youth to begin his education with Dr. David Creel of Parkersburg while he was still living with his mother's family. After the death of his first wife and his marriage to Mary Sophia Meigs, and possibly at her suggestion, he brought his son to Clarksburg and enrolled him at Randolph Academy, where he studied under the Reverend George Towers. Jackson then sent the boy, by then known as John Jay Jackson, to Washington College in Pennsylvania. On 8 February 1815 he recommended John Jay to James Monroe, secretary of war, for appointment as a cadet at the United States Military Academy at West Point. Jackson pointed out that the youth was then fourteen years old, had been "at College nearly four years," and had acquired "much reputation for his capacity, proficiency & good conduct[.]" Jackson believed that John Jay possessed "all those qualities which are necessary to enable a man to be a scientific & brave soldier" and stated that he "intended to devote him to the service of his Country." He further declared, "Peculiar circumstances not necessary to be stated, in this letter, render his appointment desirable to me."[20]

---

[18]File of Suit of *Frances Emelia Triplett* v. *John George Jackson*, Virginia District Court Records, Monongalia County Records, West Virginia Collection, West Virginia University Library; *John G. Jackson* v. *Frances Emelia Triplett*, Virginia, Supreme Court of Appeals, Order Book No. 4, 258, Virginia State Library.

[19]Jackson to Madison, 9 January 1810, James Madison Papers, Library of Congress.

[20]Jackson to Monroe, Records of the Adjutant General's Office, 1780s-1917; Application Papers to the United States Military Academy, 1815/20, Record Group No. 94, National Archives, Washington, D.C.

In his application for admission to the military academy, John Jay listed John G. Jackson as his parent or guardian. As a cadet, he earned the respect and admiration of his professors. He graduated on 24 July 1818, eleventh in his class of twenty-three. He was commissioned a second lieutenant in the United States Artillery and served under Andrew Jackson in the Seminole War. John Jay later became a distinguished West Virginian and the father of the eminent federal judge John Jay Jackson, Jr., and of the fifth governor of West Virginia, Jacob Beeson Jackson.[21]

Despite the inauspicious circumstance under which it occurred, Jackson's marriage to Mary Payne was evidently a happy one and resulted in deep and lasting friendships with the Madisons and other members of his wife's family. Jackson kept up a lifelong correspondence with Madison, based not only upon common political interests but also upon a genuine appreciation John felt for his distinguished brother-in-law. His attachment to Dolley Madison was equally strong, and they continued to exchange letters after Mary Payne Jackson's death and even after Jackson remarried. His connections with other members of the Payne family were less close, but he visited the Washingtons at Harewood frequently. On several occasions he came to the financial assistance of Richard Cutts, who married Mary's sister. Jackson's mother-in-law, Mary Coles Payne, died at his residence in Clarksburg while she was on an extended visit.

As the nineteenth century dawned, John stood on the threshold of a promising career. Although he never entirely cut loose from his moorings at Clarksburg, he had already begun to rise above its provinciality and to have more than a casual acquaintance with both the state and national capitals. The fortunes of his own family were rising, and at the same time, through his marriage, Jackson formed connections with some of the most prominent families of the Old Dominion. The affair with Frances Emelia Triplett left bitterness and regret but it also chastened him, and, in his later care for John Jay, drew from him some of the noblest actions of his life. John's star was rising, and when it set twenty-five short years later, he had added luster to the Jackson family and gained recognition as one of the most distinguished men west of the Allegheny Mountains.

---

[21]Ibid.; Letter of Stanley P. Tozeski, United States Military Academy Archives, to Stephen W. Brown, 5 March 1973; Miller and Maxwell, *West Virginia and Its People,* 2:556-57; Atkinson, ed., *Bench and Bar of West Virginia,* 94.

2 The Youthful Legislator

Speaking at a muster drill of three militia companies in Clarksburg in the spring of 1824, John G. Jackson, then a prominent federal judge, interspersed his remarks with reflections upon his political career. He told the assembled militia and others who had gathered to hear him that it had been "26 years since, in the days of my boyhood, you elected me to represent you in the House of Delegates." Jackson's use of the word "boyhood" was essentially correct, since he assumed the duties of his first elective office in December 1798 when he was scarcely six weeks past his twenty-first birthday.[1]

Jackson embarked upon his political career by boldly challenging well-entrenched politicians for one of the Harrison County seats in the House of Delegates. His opponents included the Federalist incumbents Benjamin Robinson and George Arnold and the irascible Republican John Prunty, who had earlier served three terms. Jackson and Prunty, the victors in the election, scored a triumph for the Republicans. Jackson himself won his seat with "the almost unanimous vote of his County."[2]

The new political luminary of trans-Allegheny Virginia was tall, handsome, well-read, and skilled in oratory and debate. He blended an urbanity of manner with a sense of identification with the common folk. He was closely related, through both the Jackson and Brake families, to numerous voters in the southern part of the county, and his surveying journeys in the Northwest Territory had provided opportunities for making useful ac-

---

[1]Clarksburg *Intelligencer*, 15 May 1824.

[2]Clarksburg *Bye-Stander*, 2 October 1810.

quaintances in the portions of the county along the Ohio River. Jackson also drew strength from the popularity of his father, George, who had served four terms in the House of Delegates and in 1795 had scored a political triumph by winning election to Congress.[3]

The youthful delegate quickly adapted to the routine of legislative business. Appointments to the most powerful committees of the House of Delegates went to more experienced members, but Jackson's assignments included several committees through which he might advance the interests of his constituents. He was named to a committee charged with the preparation of an amendment to a bill restricting certain officials of the federal government from holding office in the Commonwealth of Virginia, became a member of the Committee of Claims, which processed all public claims, and served on the Committee on Propositions and Grievances, which had jurisdiction over ferries, tobacco inspection stations, creation of new counties, and other public matters. His first solid success in the legislature occurred with the passage of a bill that fulfilled a campaign promise and created Wood County from the western portions of Harrison.[4]

For Jackson, the most exciting work of the legislature began on 13 December, when John Taylor of Caroline presented the famed Virginia Resolutions to the House of Delegates. The resolutions had their origins in the passage by Congress of the Alien and Sedition Acts in June and July 1798. To the extent that the laws were designed to make Federalist power secure, they were political in nature and had significant constitutional implications with respect to both federal and state governments. Both Thomas Jefferson and James Madison construed the acts as evidence that the Federalists had no intention of abiding by the Constitution. Many Republicans believed that the acts, along with the hysteria for war with France that swept the country in the spring and summer of 1798, struck at the foundations of their party and even of the nation itself.

---

[3]Dorothy Davis, *John George Jackson* (Parsons WV: McClain Printing Company, 1976) 42; Otis K. Rice, *The Allegheny Frontier: West Virginia Beginnings, 1730-1830* (Lexington: University Press of Kentucky, 1970) 352.

[4]Virginia, House of Delegates, *Journal, 1798*, 6-7, 17, 21, 26-28, 35, 37, 50-51; Samuel Shepherd, comp., *The Statutes at Large of Virginia, from October Session 1792, to December Session 1806, Inclusive*, 3 vols. (1835; reprint, New York: AMS Press, Inc., 1970) 2:170-71, 179.

On 2 and 3 July 1798 Jefferson and Madison, the principal Republican leaders, met at Montpelier and agreed that steps had to be taken to combat the detested acts. Aware that they might subject themselves to prosecution under the Sedition Act for conspiring to oppose measures of the government, they concluded that the state legislatures offered the most effective instruments of protest against the measures and, legally and constitutionally, the most defensible means of voicing disapproval. Before they ended their conference at Montpelier they had reached complete agreement on the course to be pursued.

By early October Jefferson had drafted resolves for presentation to the legislature of either North Carolina or Kentucky, and Madison had prepared resolutions for the legislature of Virginia. Very likely Madison saw the Kentucky Resolutions, as adopted on 16 November 1798, before he wrote his final draft for the Virginia legislature. In the Kentucky Resolutions Jefferson expounded the strict construction doctrine that the Constitution was a compact among the states, with certain powers delegated to the general government. He asserted that when the latter assumed undelegated powers its acts were "unauthoritative, void, and of no force." Jefferson contended that the federal government was not the exclusive or final judge of its own powers and that each state had "an equal right to judge for itself, as well of infractions as of the mode and measure of redress."[5]

The Virginia Resolutions, couched in more moderate terms, professed "a warm attachment to the union of the states." They emphasized the contractual nature of the federal government and declared that when it indulged in "a deliberate, palpable and dangerous exercise of other powers not granted" by the contract, the states "have a right, and are in duty bound, to interpose for arresting the progress of the evil, and for maintaining within their respective limits, the authorities, rights and liberties appertaining to them." As a means of protesting "the alarming infractions of the constitution" in the Alien and Sedition Acts, the General Assembly called upon other

---

[5]Ralph Ketcham, *James Madison: A Biography* (New York: The Macmillan Company, 1971) 391-95; Irving Brant, *James Madison: Father of the Constitution, 1787-1800* (Indianapolis: The Bobbs-Merrill Company, Inc., 1950) 452-61. For a copy of the Kentucky Resolutions, see *The Virginia Report of 1799-1800, Touching the Alien and Sedition Laws; Together with the Virginia Resolutions of December 21, 1798* (Richmond: J. W. Randolph, 1850) 162 (hereinafter cited as *Virginia Report*).

states to join Virginia in declaring them unconstitutional and in insuring that "proper measures will be taken by each, for co-operating with this state in maintaining unimpaired, the authorities, rights and liberties reserved to the states respectively, or to the people."[6]

The House of Delegates spent much of its time during the eight days following Taylor's presentation in debate on the resolutions. It defeated, by a vote of 96 to 68, a motion to expunge a paragraph that declared, in essence, that the policies of the general government were designed "to transform the present republican system of the United States, into an absolute, or at best, a mixed, monarchy." Jackson voted against the amendment to remove the paragraph. The House of Delegates then rejected, more decisively, a motion to emasculate the resolutions by substituting a brief statement asserting the right of the people to petition when they believed that the federal government had infringed upon their liberties. The motion to amend failed by a vote of 104 to 60. Jackson voted against it. On 21 December, after defeating efforts to weaken or change the character of the resolutions, the House of Delegates approved them by a vote of 100 to 63. The Senate followed suit on 24 December with a decisive 14 to 3 endorsement.[7]

Jackson's interest in the Virginia Resolutions extended well beyond his vote supporting them. In later years he referred to the principles involved in the resolutions as "the great cause I expoused [*sic*] in 1798 & of which I have never ceased to be the zealous advocate."[8] His views coincided with those of his father, who wrote Governor James Monroe, sincerely but ungrammatically, that "these resolutions meets with my entire approbation, and in time must do great Honor to its framers and the Legislature of that State, because its reasoning, its language, and the object of its contemplation, cannot, nor will not, be held from the great American people and the world."[9]

---

[6]*Virginia Report*, 22-23.

[7]Ibid., 155-58; Virginia, House of Delegates, *Journal, 1798*, 31-33.

[8]John G. Jackson to James Monroe, 11 March 1819, John George Jackson Papers, Lilly Library, Indiana University, Bloomington.

[9]George Jackson to Monroe, 28 March 1800, W. P. Palmer, et al., eds., *Calendar of Virginia State Papers and Other Manuscripts*, 11 vols. (Richmond: Virginia State Library, 1875-1893) 9:100.

As the divisions sharpened, Jackson and other Republicans saw an opportunity to reduce Federalist strength in western Virginia. Of the twenty-two members representing counties in present-day West Virginia in the Virginia House of Delegates in 1798, fourteen were Federalists, who opposed the Virginia Resolutions. Seven of the eight Republican members of that body resided in the trans-Allegheny counties of Brooke, Greenbrier, Harrison, Kanawha, Monongalia, and Ohio. Harrison was the only county that sent two Republicans to the House of Delegates. Prior to 1798 anti-excise men, opponents of Alexander Hamilton's whiskey tax, had provided most of the Republican leaders in western Virginia. Support of the Virginia Resolutions gave the party a new and more appealing program.[10]

The state and congressional elections of April 1799 produced gratifying results for Republicans in present West Virginia. Their candidates replaced four Federalist members of the House of Delegates who had opposed the Virginia Resolutions. In Hampshire County, which had formerly been Federalist, Republican candidates for the General Assembly won election by majorities of two to one. George Jackson defeated the incumbent Federalist congressman from northwestern Virginia, James Machir, by a margin of 204 votes. John G. Jackson elatedly declared, "Republicanism is gaining ground very fast in this District." He predicted that the time was "not far distant when the Freemen of America will see through the flimsy veil of modern Federalism & spurn the Enemies of their Liberties." With characteristic self-righteousness, he added, "I know that the truth is on our side and that truth will be omnipotent."[11]

---

[10]For the political affiliations of members of the House of Delegates, see *Virginia Report*, 159-61. For the new base of Western Republicanism, see Palmer, et al., *Calendar of Virginia State Papers*, 7:289-90, 8:306-307; Rice, *Allegheny Frontier*, 35-54; Charles Henry Ambler, *Sectionalism in Virginia from 1776 to 1861* (Chicago: University of Chicago Press, 1910) 71-72. See also James H. Broussard, "Party and Partisanship in American Legislatures: The South Atlantic States, 1800-1812," *Journal of Southern History* 63 (February 1977): 53-54.

[11]The election of 1799 in trans-Allegheny Virginia and Jackson's analysis of it are in Jackson to James Madison, 14 May 1799, James Madison Papers, Library of Congress, Washington, D.C. For a comparison of the membership in the House of Delegates in 1798 with that of 1799, see *Virginia Report*, 159-61, 233-36.

The political alignments generated by the debate on the Virginia Resolutions may have provided the basis for a close political alliance Jackson formed with William McKinley, a Republican delegate from Ohio County. McKinley, who, like Jackson, had supported the resolutions, narrowly escaped defeat in the 1799 election. He and John Morgan, the other Republican candidate, contended that when the polls at Wheeling closed at sunset on 24 April they had been elected the county's delegates to the General Assembly by a substantial margin. They charged that the sheriff had unlawfully reopened the polls the following morning, allowing sufficient persons to vote to enable their opponents, Federalists Benjamin Biggs and Ebenezer Zane, to win. On 15 January 1800 a committee of the House of Delegates recommended in favor of seating Biggs and Zane. Partly at the urging of Jackson, who represented the strongest Republican county in northwestern Virginia, the House, by a partisan vote of 82 to 48, rejected the committee report and declared McKinley and Morgan duly elected.[12]

The deep disagreements between Republicans and Federalists created by the Virginia Resolutions and by the bitterly contested elections in the spring of 1799 continued in the session of the legislature that convened on 2 December of that year, but the tide was running for the Republicans. In international affairs, French reverses in Europe brightened the hopes for peace, which Republicans expected to work to their advantage. Republican legislators were also encouraged by the presence and prestige of James Madison, who in 1799 returned to the House of Delegates as a representative from Orange County. In response to negative reactions from other states regarding the call of the Virginia General Assembly for resistance to the Alien and Sedition Acts, Madison prepared his *Report*, which stoutly defended the Virginia Resolutions. Jackson was one of the strongest supporters of Madison throughout the controversy and voted with the majority in the House of Delegates, which approved the *Report* by a vote of 100 to 60.[13]

As further evidence of his belief in the Jeffersonian principle of the limited powers of the federal government, Jackson endorsed the right of a state

---

[12]Virginia, House of Delegates, *Journal, 1800*, 86-88.

[13]*Virginia Report*, 168-77, 189-233, 236-37; Ketcham, *James Madison*, 399-403.

legislature to instruct members of the United States Senate and House of Representatives. In January 1800 he voted with the majority of the House of Delegates to give official notification to the two Virginia senators, Stephens Thompson Mason and Wilson Cary Nicholas, of its wishes on four important national issues. Two of the instructions, relating to defense, proposed to reduce the United States army to the "narrowest limits" necessary for the protection of the nation's forts and arsenals and to confine and limit the navy to levels essential to the defense of the seacoast, ports, harbors, and commerce of the United States.

Jackson also voted with the 149 delegates who urged the Virginia senators to oppose the passing of any law recognizing the principle advanced by Federalists that the common law of England was in force under the government of the United States, unless the Constitution specifically sanctioned it. Finally, he supported the majority in approving, by a vote of 102 to 49, an instruction calling upon Mason and Nicholas to procure the repeal of the Alien and Sedition laws.[14]

With a striking unity of purpose manifested in their votes on the Virginia Resolutions, Madison's *Report,* and their instructions to the United States senators, the Republicans in Virginia required only a firm party organization to weld them into a powerful political force. Indeed, Republicans throughout the country began to hope that they might be able to end Federalist control of the national government and secure Jefferson's election to the presidency. In September 1799 Charles Pinckney of South Carolina wrote "in confidence" to James Madison that there was an "absolute necessity" that the Virginia General Assembly must at its next session provide for the selection of presidential electors by the legislature rather than by popular election by districts. The legislature did not follow Pinckney's advice completely, but in December 1799 it began considering a bill to discontinue the district basis of choosing presidential electors in the hope of eliminating the possibility of giving President John Adams the electoral votes of even one or two districts of the state.[15]

---

[14]Virginia, House of Delegates, *Journal, 1799,* 79.

[15]Noble E. Cunningham, Jr., *The Jeffersonian Republicans: The Formation of Party Organization, 1789-1801* (Chapel Hill: University of North Carolina Press for the Institute of Early American History and Culture, 1957) 144-46.

In his desire to secure the election of Jefferson, Jackson retreated from his usual concern for ascertaining the will of the people. Opponents of change in the method of choosing presidential electors attempted to postpone action until the next session of the General Assembly. They contended that "the good people of this commonwealth have been accustomed to vote by districts, and viva voce, and the elections have heretofore been conducted by the sheriffs of the respective counties and no petitions have been received from the people praying, for an alteration in the mode hitherto pursued." Moreover, they declared that members of the current legislature had had no opportunity to consult with their constituents on the matter. Jackson voted against the motion to postpone action on the proposal, which failed by the slender margin of seven votes. He then voted for the main motion to change the procedure in selecting presidential electors, which the delegates approved by the even closer vote of 78 to 73.[16]

Encouraged by their victory, narrow though it was, ninety-three Republican members of the Virginia legislature, including Jackson, met at the capitol on 21 January 1800 to endorse electors pledged to vote for Republican candidates for president and vice-president of the United States. In subsequent meetings they set up a central committee at Richmond and five-member corresponding committees in each of the state's counties and boroughs for the purpose of keeping the people informed on public events and the positions of Republican candidates. Jackson was one of the members representing Harrison County.[17]

At his home in Clarksburg, John G. Jackson manifested keen interest in the campaign in the various states. During the summer and autumn of 1800 it became increasingly apparent that the New England states would give their electoral votes to President John Adams and Charles Cotesworth Pinckney and that the Southern and Western states would support Thomas Jefferson and Aaron Burr, with the assumption that they were voting for Jefferson for president. The outcome of the election, therefore, hinged to a considerable extent upon the vote of the Middle Atlantic states, particularly New York and Pennsylvania.[18]

---

[16]Virginia, House of Delegates, *Journal, 1799*, 91.

[17]Palmer, et al., eds., *Calendar of Virginia State Papers*, 9:74-87; Cunningham, *Jeffersonian Republicans: The Formation of Party Organization*, 149-52.

[18]Dumas Malone, *Jefferson and the Ordeal of Liberty* (Boston: Little, Brown and Company, 1962) 484-95; Ketcham, *James Madison*, 403-406.

A conversation with Savary de Valcoulon, a close associate of Albert Gallatin, in September gave Jackson great satisfaction. Valcoulon believed that soon after the election Governor Thomas McKean of Pennsylvania would call the legislature into session and see that necessary steps were taken to insure that "the immaculate Jefferson will be our next President." With the election of the Sage of Monticello, Jackson wrote, "will the genius of american [*sic*] Liberty be reanimated, truth & honesty long vilified and trampled under foot by the Machinists of Sedition Laws &c, &c, will resume their respective stations and shine refulgent throughout our political hemisphere." As to Virginia, Jackson characterized her politics as "decisively right."[19]

Presidential electors cast their ballots in all the states on 4 December 1800. The Virginia electors, of whom Jackson was one, met in Richmond and voted unanimously for Jefferson and Burr. Although electors in most states understood that the party intended Jefferson to be president and Burr vice-president, their tie vote in the electoral college forced the final decision into the House of Representatives.[20] On 5 February 1801, nearly a week before the House began its deliberations, Congressman George Jackson wrote that "the Fedrealists [*sic*] appear to be determined not to give up Mr. Burr, and in answer to this, those who call themselves Republicans are as desided [*sic*] not to give up Jefferson." Nevertheless, the elder Jackson concurred in a prediction made earlier by Madison that Burr "would give way." Jackson declared, with confidence, "I confess I have no Doubt if I let my reason take place, but Jefferson will take the Presidential Chair on the 4th March next."[21] Both John and his father were elated when, on 17 February 1801, on the thirty-sixth ballot, Federalists in the divided states of Vermont and Maryland abstained from voting. Their action allowed the Republican members from those states to cast their ballots for Jefferson, assuring his inauguration as president scarcely two weeks later.[22]

---

[19]Jackson's views on the approaching election were set forth in a letter to James Madison, 25 September 1800, James Madison Papers, Library of Congress.

[20]Malone, *Jefferson and the Ordeal of Liberty*, 491-505; Ketcham, *James Madison*, 404-406; Irving Brant, *James Madison: Secretary of State, 1800-1809* (Indianapolis: The Bobbs-Merrill Company, Inc., 1953) 21-29.

[21]George Jackson to James Madison, 5 February 1801, James Madison Papers, Library of Congress.

[22]Malone, *Jefferson and the Ordeal of Liberty*, 502-505.

Partisan spirit also infused local politics in northwestern Virginia. In a bitter contest for the House of Delegates in Wood County in 1800, Hugh Phelps and John C. Henderson, the Republican candidates, protested the claim of the Federalists, Abner Lord and Joseph Spencer, to victory. Phelps and Henderson charged that on 14 October 1799 Lord had granted lands to sixteen persons, who presumably lacked the necessary property qualification for the franchise, with the understanding that they would vote for him and Spencer. The Committee on Privileges and Elections of the House of Delegates, to which the matter was referred, found that at the close of the polls Lord had 57 votes, Spencer 55, Phelps 50, and Henderson 48. It struck the disqualified votes from the records, leaving Phelps with 50, Henderson 48, Lord 42, and Spencer 40.

Elated by the victory of Phelps and Henderson, Jackson moved to add a deposition of Adam Deim, who stated that at the election at Clarksburg in March, Abner Lord had asked him how he intended to vote. When Deim replied that he did not know that he was entitled to vote, Lord offered him fifty acres of land in return for his vote. The motion to incorporate Deim's deposition into the findings of the House failed by a vote of 140 to 1, with Jackson the only member favoring it. A subsequent motion to censure William Lowther, the sheriff of Wood County and a close personal and political friend of the Jacksons, for returning the names of two delegates not properly elected, was tabled, probably through Jackson's efforts.[23]

Some of the most time-consuming business of the legislative sessions in which Jackson served related to the state judicial system. Jackson became increasingly concerned over the enormous burden of work devolving upon the High Court of Chancery and the inevitable delays in obtaining justice. On 14 January 1800 the Committee of the Courts of Justice, of which Jackson was a member, recommended to the House of Delegates that Thomas Jefferson, Edmund Pendleton, George Wythe, and one other person be named to prepare, digest, and report data on the judicial system and to recommend changes to the next General Assembly. After rejecting an attempt, possibly by Jackson, to amend the report by dividing the state into five judicial districts to handle the business of the High Court of

[23]Virginia, House of Delegates, *Journal, 1800*, 20-22. For the close political connection between the Jacksons and William Lowther, see George Jackson to James Madison, 3 March 1801, James Madison Papers, Library of Congress.

Chancery, the House of Delegates approved the committee's recommendations.[24]

Although the committee appointed by the legislature reported that 2,627 suits were pending before the High Court of Chancery and that only 175 of the 489 suits instituted in 1799 had been decided, the House of Delegates procrastinated in making changes. It instructed a committee, of which Jackson was a member, to bring in a bill to change the existing system, but then postponed action until April 1801 in order that it might ascertain the sentiments of the people "on so important a subject." Jackson voted against delay, but the motion carried 89 to 78 on a roll call vote.[25]

Since a number of other northwestern Virginia Republicans, including John Prunty and William McKinley, also voted against postponement, it appears that Chancery Court reforms had become not only an issue between eastern and western Virginia but also a source of difference between Republicans and Federalists. The agitation to change the High Court of Chancery resulted in an act of 23 January 1802 that divided the state of Virginia into three districts with a Superior Court of Chancery to be held in each. The act established these courts at Staunton, Richmond, and Williamsburg and set forth in considerable detail their terms and jurisdictions.[26]

Jackson also endeavored to effect reform at the lowest judicial level. One of the sources of discontent among trans-Allegheny residents concerned the limited powers of the justices of the peace in civil suits and the resultant high costs of having relatively trivial cases appealed to the county courts. Jackson was among the supporters of a bill, passed by the House of Delegates on 8 January 1801 by a vote of 83 to 71, that extended the jurisdiction of individual justices of the peace to all cases in which the cause of action did not exceed ten dollars or four hundred pounds of tobacco.

---

[24]Virginia, House of Delegates, *Journal, 1799*, 85.

[25]Virginia, House of Delegates, *Journal, 1800*, 13, 18, 47.

[26]Ibid., 47; Shepherd, comp., *Statutes at Large of Virginia*, 2:320-24. Although Western Federalists in the Virginia legislature generally favored postponement of revision of the judicial system in Virginia, Virginia Federalists in Congress gave strong support to the federal Judiciary Act of 1801. See Ambler, *Sectionalism in Virginia*, 79-80.

Although this law eased the problem of litigation for the poorer classes of society, it did not completely satisfy their demands for change.[27]

Local and perhaps even personal interests lay behind a move by Jackson in 1799 to have the District Court of Virginia moved from Morgantown to Clarksburg. The Committee of Courts of Justice endorsed his recommendation, but the House of Delegates rejected it. The following year the House also rejected a move by Jackson to divide the judicial district into a zone including Monongalia, Harrison, and Randolph counties and another comprised of Ohio, Brooke, and Wood counties. Had such a division occurred, Jackson would very likely have argued for the moving of the court at Morgantown to Clarksburg on the ground that the latter was more centrally located.[28]

Jackson believed that although many problems and defects in state government could be corrected by legislation, others required constitutional changes. At the very outset of his service in the House of Delegates he presented a petition from the citizens of Harrison County, which he himself probably drew up, calling upon the legislature to authorize a constitutional convention to extend the franchise, reapportion representation in the General Assembly on the basis of white population, and provide for popular election of county officials. These goals, for which he fought throughout his political career, were in harmony with his Jeffersonian principles. Like Jefferson, for whom he had the utmost admiration, he was always ready to change the fundamental law when the public good seemed to require it.[29]

Attention to affairs of state and national importance never obscured Jackson's concern with matters primarily of local interest. At the outset of his legislative career, he opposed a bill to increase taxes, always unpopular in Western counties, where money was scarce. He voted for a resolution

---

[27]Virginia, House of Delegates, *Journal, 1800*, 59; Shepherd, comp., *Statutes at Large of Virginia*, 2:275. Rather than the ten-dollar ceiling set for justice-of-the-peace cases, many Western Virginians favored a fifty-dollar ceiling. Rice, *Allegheny Frontier*, 364-65.

[28]Virginia, House of Delegates, *Journal, 1799*, 4, 15-16, 22, 25, 27, 28; Virginia, House of Delegates, *Journal, 1800*, 35.

[29]Clarksburg *Intelligencer*, 15 May 1824.

that would have exempted lands, slaves, horses, and carriages. Jackson's motive may have been to ease the burden upon the wealthy, but more likely he hoped to emasculate the bill in such a manner as to insure its unacceptability. The resolution failed by a decisive vote of 55 to 93, with Jackson voting for it. On 19 January 1799 the tax measure passed the House of Delegates by a margin of 80 to 70, with both him and his colleague, Prunty, voting against it.[30] His repeated support of attempts to increase the salary of legislators or to augment their mileage allowance sprang perhaps as much from an awareness of the difficulties and sacrifices of many Western members as from any desire for personal pecuniary benefits.[31]

On 13 January 1801 Jackson was granted a leave of absence from his legislative duties for the remainder of the session, which ended on 23 January, but with the expectation that he would return when the legislature reconvened in April.[32] For more than three years, he had represented Harrison County in the House of Delegates. During that time he had been at the very center of such momentous events as the adoption of the Virginia Resolutions and Madison's *Report*, the moves of Virginia to elect Jefferson president, and various efforts at constitutional and governmental reform. Moreover, he had learned the ways of politics and the values of keeping in close touch with the will of his constituents. At twenty-four years of age, Jackson looked to his political future with confidence and high hopes.

---

[30]Virginia, House of Delegates, *Journal, 1798*, 49; Shepherd, comp., *Statutes at Large of Virginia*, 2: 144-46.

[31]Virginia, House of Delegates, *Journal, 1798*, 49; Virginia, House of Delegates, *Journal, 1799*, 41, 42-43, 52, 53, 74, 85; Virginia, House of Delegates, *Journal, 1800*, 8-9.

[32]Virginia, House of Delegates, *Journal, 1800*, 62.

3 From Log Cabin to Clapboard Mansion

For a man whose personal and public affairs gave him entrée into the elegant homes of the Washingtons at Harewood, the Madisons at Montpelier, and the great planters of eastern Virginia, John G. Jackson's periodic journeys back to Clarksburg must have seemed like a return to another world. In 1802, the year following his first period of service in the House of Delegates, Jackson attempted to remedy Clarksburg's primitive appearance by drawing up a petition, which he and fifty-six other residents signed, requesting the legislature to repeal a law requiring owners of town lots to build houses on their property within a specified time or forfeit ownership. The petitioners pointed out that there was no shortage of housing in Clarksburg and that the present law encouraged the hasty erection of buildings that were scarcely habitable. Repeal of the law, they declared, would leave the progress of the town to "natural stimulants" and "Individual exertions."[1]

Jackson had already given evidence of what "Individual exertions" might do for Clarksburg. In 1800, or very soon afterward, he replaced his log cabin, which had been built by his father and had sheltered the family from Indian attacks, with a two-story white clapboard "mansion." Graced by a wide veranda, with columns from floor to roof, the Jackson residence was the most imposing one in Clarksburg. Anything less would hardly have been

---

[1]Harrison County Legislative Petition, 23 November 1802, Virginia State Library, Richmond. For a similar memorial, drawn up by George Jackson, see Harrison County Legislative Petition, 7 December 1797.

suitable for Jackson's bride, who, as the sister of Dolley Madison and Lucy Washington, was accustomed to a considerable degree of elegance.[2]

Jackson's residence also befitted Clarksburg's most aggressive business and industrial entrepreneur and her most enterprising agriculturist. By the time Jackson reached manhood, the "ridges [were] covered with flocks graizing [*sic*], and the Valleys standing thick with corn."[3] Jackson's own farms teemed with corn, wheat, oats, rye, flax, and other products. His diversified agriculture, typical of mountain farms, also relied heavily upon the raising of livestock, particularly cattle, hogs, and sheep. Cognizant of the importance of agriculture for the economic life of the region and for his own financial security, Jackson pioneered experimental farming in the West Fork Valley.[4]

One of Jackson's major agricultural interests lay in sheep raising, a branch of husbandry well suited to the rolling land of the West Fork area. In the autumn of 1810 he advertised a desire to purchase five hundred sheep for his farms.[5] Jackson inquired of President James Madison about the "practicability of procuring a pair of Merinos, or a Ram only, & the price." As the first man in the locality, and perhaps in the entire trans-Allegheny area, to experiment with Merino sheep, Jackson did not wish to invest too heavily. Madison informed him that expected imports would reduce the price of Merino rams to about two dollars, and ewes to about one dollar. He cautioned Jackson that the "mania" or "ardor" for Merinos was confined largely to the South and suggested that he write to some friend on the James River who could purchase the animals for him at a better price.[6]

---

[2]Dorothy Davis, *History of Harrison County, West Virginia* (Clarksburg WV: American Association of University Women, 1970) 110, 282.

[3]Monongalia County Legislative Petition, 17 November 1795, Virginia State Library.

[4]John G. Jackson to James Madison, 23 June 1806, James Madison Papers, New York Public Library, New York, New York; John G. Jackson to Charles S. Morgan, 5 January 1823, Charles S. Morgan Papers, West Virginia Department of Archives and History, Charleston.

[5]Clarksburg *Bye-Stander*, 2 October 1810.

[6]Jackson to Madison, 4 December 1810, James Madison Papers, Library of Congress, Washington D.C.; Madison to Jackson, 7 March 1811, John George Jackson Papers, Lilly Library, Indiana University, Bloomington.

The following spring Jackson sent Madison a sample of a "singular fleece" from a species that he had bought in the Clarksburg area. He believed that it differed from ordinary wool and might prove useful in the manufacture of shawls and similar articles. From his brother-in-law he received the disappointing opinion that the wool from his "long fleeced Ewe" was no longer than that of several breeds and that the coarseness of its staple made it a "combing wool."[7]

In another experiment, Jackson introduced the cultivation of fuller's teasel into the West Fork Valley. The plant had a flower-covered head, with curved barbed bracts. The bracts, or modified leaves, were dried and used in producing a nap on woolen cloth.[8]

Like other residents of the West Fork region, Jackson realized that successful sheep raising depended upon the elimination of wolves, a common menace in the Allegheny Mountains. In 1809 he drew up a petition, which he and 175 other Harrison Countians signed, calling upon the Virginia legislature to reimpose a bounty on wolves sufficient to induce hunters to kill large numbers each year. The petition, written in the wake of the Embargo, declared that the majority of the region's people dressed in homespun cloth made principally of flax and wool and that, except for a very few articles, they did not rely upon foreign imports. Contending that the self-reliance of the people deserved "the patronage of the Legislature," Jackson ended the petition by expressing the hope that "at a time when patriotic organizations are formed & forming in every quarter of the Union, for promoting the growth & improvement of Sheep, Virginia would not refuse an encouragement which was given even in our colonial State by Great Britain."[9]

An equally serious threat to crops came from a caterpillar attack in 1806 that "ravaged the whole [upper Monongahela] Country" and left twenty acres of Jackson's meadow "not worth the mowing." Caterpillars did little

---

[7]Jackson to Madison, 26 April 1811, James Madison Papers, Library of Congress; Madison to Jackson, undated letter, John George Jackson Papers.

[8]Unidentified newspaper clipping, Meigs-Jackson Papers, Blennerhassett Historical Park Commission, Parkersburg, West Virginia (hereinafter cited as Meigs-Jackson Papers, BHPC).

[9]Harrison County Legislative Petition, 21 August 1809.

damage to his wheat and rye, but they almost totally destroyed his corn, flax, and oats. "In two days," Jackson wrote, "they penetrated into the centre of my Corn field cutting down to the ground every stalk & every thing green in the field." Ever ready to experiment, Jackson put fresh lime on some plants in his garden and found to his delight that it repelled the caterpillars. He threw a handful into each hill of corn and spread more in the path of the pests. "I watched their progress, the ground being almost covered with them," he declared, "& as soon as they came in contact with the lime they appeared convulsed, & enfeebled so as not to be able to crawl away." Jackson applied the lime one evening between sunset and dark and found that the next morning the caterpillars had "entirely disappeared."[10]

Agriculture appealed to Jackson not only as an economic or scientific enterprise, but as a noble way of life. He advised his wife to treat the farmers who called upon her during his absences "with your wonted civility." With thoughts worthy of Jefferson, he declared, "I shall always cultivate the friendship of the lowest yeoman of our Country & let the proud upstarts of the town pursue their own ridiculous course. The honesty of one plain farmer pleases me more than the affected friendship of all the other clans united. I know the real difference between the two classes, & I shall preserve its recollection in all my movements."[11]

Although his agricultural interests enabled him "to respire the pure air of . . . mountains seasoned with the sweets of freedom," Jackson began as early as the first decade of the nineteenth century to add industrial and commercial pursuits to his agrarian enterprises.[12] From the earliest years of his manhood he had a keen sense of the need for trans-Allegheny residents, who were cut off from Eastern sources of supply, to develop their own manufacturing establishments. When the Napoleonic Wars in Europe and the American responses to the conflict severely curtailed imports of English products into the United States, Jackson's interests expressed high

---

[10]Jackson to James Madison, 23 June 1806, James Madison Papers, New York Public Library.

[11]Jackson to Mary S. Jackson, undated fragment of a letter, Meigs-Jackson Papers, BHPC.

[12]Jackson to James Madison, 1 June 1806, James Madison Papers, Library of Congress.

patriotic duty. Moreover, his service in Congress coincided with an era in which the fostering of domestic manufactures became a matter of national priority. During the War of 1812 and the years immediately following, Jackson set up gristmills, an ironworks, tanyards, a woolen mill, and saltworks on the West Fork of the Monongahela and became the region's foremost industrial entrepreneur.[13]

Like other Western industrialists, Jackson quickly recognized the stifling effects of inadequate transportation facilities. As early as 1795 residents of the Monongahela Valley appealed to the Virginia legislature to improve roads between their settlements and the Potomac River. They pointed out that their separation from eastern Virginia by the rugged Allegheny Mountains forced them to send their goods down the Mississippi. In Spanish territory they were "treated with cruelty and Oppressions, and their monies extorted from them at the Will of a despot Governor." Moreover, they were "often delaid [*sic*] amongst a People of a Strange language . . . whose disposition [was] hostile toward them."[14]

Jackson was no less concerned with the woeful state of the roads connecting Clarksburg and neighboring areas. For several years he served as a precinct surveyor for the Harrison County Court, with responsibility for numerous roads, including the highway between Clarksburg and Morgantown.[15] At the same time, Jackson exerted political pressures at both the state and national levels for highways that would benefit the Clarksburg area. In 1810 he sought to enlist the support of John Prunty, a member of the House of Delegates from Harrison County, in obtaining authorization for a road, probably from Clarksburg to Parkersburg. Prunty bluntly told Jackson that the House would not approve the funds for the road, and on the very day that he received Jackson's request, it had displayed "violent

---

[13]Harrison County Legislative Petition, 21 August 1809; Otis K. Rice, *The Allegheny Frontier: West Virginia Beginnings, 1730-1830* (Lexington: University Press of Kentucky, 1970) 309. Jackson's industries are discussed in detail in chapter 7.

[14]Monongalia County Legislative Petition, 17 November 1795.

[15]Harrison County Court Minute Book, 1803-1805, 148-49; 1806-1807, 157; 1810-1811, 428; 1811-1812, 73; 1812-1814, 108, 286, Harrison County Courthouse, Clarksburg, West Virginia.

opposition" to a petition from Harrison and Monongalia counties for the completion of a road to the mouth of Fishing Creek on the Ohio River.[16]

Jackson fared no better in his efforts to have a road built from Washington, D.C., to Marietta at federal expense. Several years before Congress authorized construction of the National Road from Cumberland, Maryland, to Wheeling, William McKinley, Jackson's handpicked successor in the House of Representatives, offered a resolution calling for a road to be laid out under the direction of the postmaster general. The House treated McKinley's proposal with ridicule, first substituting the president of the United States for the postmaster general and then engaging in debate on whether to refer it to the Committee on Plans or a select committee. Placed in a "warm & embarased [*sic*] situation," McKinley heatedly declared that he "did not care to what committee it was refered [*sic*]" as long as he obtained his "object, which, was money."[17] Perhaps suspicious that some private advantage was involved in making Marietta—near which Jackson owned lands—the western terminus, the House finally declined to refer the proposal to any committee.[18]

Equally important to Jackson was the need for improvements in river transportation. As early as 1793 the legislature of Virginia had authorized the clearing of obstructions from the Monongahela and its tributaries to make them navigable for small crafts such as flatboats and canoes. In December 1799 the Committee on Propositions and Grievances, of which Jackson was a member, recommended that the Monongahela River and its branches become a public highway and all mill owners be required to erect slopes for their dams. The legislature enacted the recommendation into law on 20 January 1800.[19] Upon his return to the House of Delegates in 1811,

---

[16]Prunty to Jackson, 26 December 1810, John George Jackson Papers.

[17]McKinley to Jackson, 27 December 1810, Jackson Family Papers, Virginia Historical Society, Richmond.

[18]*Annals of Congress*, 11th Cong., 3d sess., 465. An example of Jackson's personal interest in the road that he proposed may be noted in John Mathews to Jackson, 21 December 1807, Jackson Family Papers.

[19]Samuel Shepherd, comp., *The Statutes at Large of Virginia, from the October Session 1792, to December Session 1806, Inclusive*, 3 vols. (1835; reprint, New York: AMS Press, 1970) 1:242-43, 2:243; Virginia, House of Delegates, *Journal, 1799*, 24.

Jackson joined with other members from the Monongahela Valley counties in seeking legislation for further aids to navigation. In 1817, as a leading exporter of farm goods and manufactures from the West Fork Valley, he was a prime mover in the organization of the Monongalia Navigation Company, a semipublic corporation charged with the construction of locks and dams in the West Fork.[20]

Jackson also sought to break the bonds of Western isolation by improvements in the mail service and the establishment of post roads. In June 1801 he sought to obtain government contracts to carry the mail between Romney and Morgantown, a distance of 90 miles, for $800 per year and from Morgantown to Marietta, a distance of 120 miles, for $1,000 a year. He expressed the belief that there would be competition "by some who cannot comply with their engagements and thus the business will be wretchedly managed as hitherto." For himself, Jackson declared, "I feel a desire to see that *establishment* particularly attended to, and am conscious I can furnish horses and Riders as cheap as any persons whatever, and give the best security in this Country." Jackson did not receive what he sought, but he was awarded a route that earned him $476 per year payable in quarterly installments.[21]

In his advocacy of internal improvements, Jackson reflected a prevailing Western attitude. His vision of land and water routes as great unifying forces between East and West was not essentially different from that of

---

[20]The name "Monongalia," as used in connection with this company, actually refers to the Monongahela River and, more particularly, its West Fork. A detailed account of the company appears in chapter 10.

[21]Jackson to Albert Gallatin, 18 June 1801, Albert Gallatin Papers, New-York Historical Society, New York, New York; Jackson to James Madison, 3 August 1801, James Madison Papers, Alderman Library, University of Virginia, Charlottesville. Jackson to James Madison, 17 June 1802, ibid.; John Payne to Jackson, 6 August 1802, John George Jackson Papers; George Jackson to John G. Jackson, 21 January 1803, ibid. For similar interests of George Jackson in the mails and post roads, see George Jackson to John G. Jackson, 24 December 1804, Meigs-Jackson Papers, BHPC; George Jackson to John G. Jackson, 14 February 1805, ibid.; George Jackson to Postmaster General [Gideon Granger], 20 December 1804, Meigs-Jackson Papers, Ohio Historical Society, Campus Martius Museum, Marietta (hereinafter cited as Meigs-Jackson Papers, OHS-CMM).

George Washington, who had made similar proposals about two decades earlier. Jackson, however, never had the political stature or popular admiration that Washington commanded, and his suggestions did not carry the weight of those of the hero of the American Revolution.

Along with his agricultural and business pursuits, Jackson had a highly successful career as a lawyer. He believed that "the Lawyer as well as the farmer must make hay while the sun shines, & it is a maxim as well understood in Law as in agriculture that unless you sow & cultivate you reap no harvest." His competence in law drew him into the very center of legal and political affairs in Harrison County. On 16 September 1799 the Harrison County Court recommended him to the governor of Virginia for the office of justice of the peace. In 1810 he became commonwealth attorney for Harrison County and served at least until he returned to the Virginia legislature the following year.[22]

As a lawyer, Jackson had a special gift for combining sound legal training and cogent argument with the practical procedures in frontier courtrooms. In 1810 he defended a sixty-year-old man charged with beating his eighteen-year-old wife. With tongue in cheek, he argued that "when January & May . . . were united, the Husband would be Jealous—the Wife would merit the imputation—& that if the fit went off by a little flagellation no one had a right to complain." He disclaimed any "bad intent" for his client and held that "from Ovid down to the present day" the falling out of lovers was a means of renewing love. He continued, "Where *blows* were added to *words* the argument was more *sound* more *impressive*, & more *lasting*, & consequently the reconciliation more sincere." Since the whipping had been severe in this case, Jackson explained, "There would be perfect harmony in [the] future for a long time." According to Jackson, the old man was pleased with the defense, and the couple made friends and left, convinced that theirs was "the condition of all mankind, where January's frosts are united with the genial warmth of May."[23]

---

[22]Jackson to James Madison, 1 June 1806, James Madison Papers, Library of Congress. See also Harrison County Court Minute Book, 1799-1801, 20, 145, 240; 1810-1811, 213.

[23]John G. Jackson to Mary S. Meigs, 21 May 1810, Meigs-Jackson Papers, BHPC.

Not all of Jackson's cases turned out so happily. Like many frontier lawyers, he occasionally engaged in contests that produced deep animosities. One such case led to a near-successful attempt on his life. On 10 December 1807 Jackson wrote James Madison of the affair with "a nerveless hand & shattered brain from the bed of sickness on which I lie prostrate." According to Jackson, "On Thursday sennight" he was "attending the prosecution of two Criminals upon a motion to commit them for trial at a tavern in Town." Rumors that the accused men would make an attempt upon Jackson's life proved well founded. About seven o'clock one evening, he was attacked as he was leaving through a door, near which his horse was being held in readiness by a servant. The leader of the "assassins," John Sommerville, struck him on the forehead with a club and knocked him "senseless to the ground." His assailants dealt him several other severe blows before they escaped.

Following the attack, friends carried Jackson back into the tavern, where he was "profusely bled in both arms." In a few minutes he showed "signs of returning animation but continual faintings succeeded during the night with the most alarming symptoms of vomiting , &c." The following morning Jackson was taken home on a litter, but he "continued alarmingly ill for three days incapable of taking any sustenance & lying in a perpetual stupor." Gradually "external applications of Brandy & opium & blistering produced a favorable change" and he began the slow road to recovery.[24]

Two weeks later Jackson wrote Madison that one of his "assassins" had fractured his skull near the right temple, making "a considerable indentation." For a time Jackson had expected that trepanning, or boring into his skull, would be necessary, but as the days passed that operation seemed more unlikely. Nonetheless, "the pressure on the brain," Jackson wrote, "produces a very troublesome swimming in the head when I go to bed unaccompanied with pain." Jackson's right arm had also been disabled, but he gradually regained strength in it.[25] The vicious attack upon Jackson filled

---

[24]Jackson to Madison, 10 December 1807, James Madison Papers, Library of Congress. The legal action of Jackson against his assailants may be traced in Harrison County Court Minute Book, 1807-1809, 48, 52-53, 120-21, 224.

[25]Jackson to Madison, 25 December 1807, James Madison Papers, Library of Congress.

his friends with great anxiety for his full recovery and "deranged" his business affairs for some time.[26]

Jackson lived in a contentious age, when men were highly sensitive to matters of personal honor. On several occasions he was a party to litigation involving charges of trespass, slander, and assault and battery. In September 1803 Benjamin Wilson, the clerk of Harrison County, accused Jackson of stating that Wilson had "filched the people [of the county] out of two hundred dollars a year by . . . false charges" and of making an entry to the detriment of Jackson. When he was cleared of the allegations, Wilson brought suit against Jackson for "false swearing & perjury."

The controversy between Jackson and Wilson, growing out of old grudges and fed by the fires of perennial personal and political differences, had widespread ramifications. Robert Bartlett, a Wilson supporter and a Federalist, called Jackson "a damned Raskle [*sic*]," and another, John Haymond, allegedly told Jackson, "You . . . have sworn false knowing it to be false; & further you . . . are not a man of truth, you . . . will tell a lie & will swear to it." The episode gave rise to several suits and countersuits, including one by Jackson against Wilson for $5,000 and another by Jackson against Bartlett for $10,000.[27]

George Jackson took steps to work out compromises with his son's enemies. The elder Jackson told Wilson that his brother, William, and Bartlett were willing to settle their cases by arbitration, since the jury had been unable to agree upon damages. Instead of healing the breach between the two prominent Clarksburg families, the offer evoked a reply from Wilson that produced more acrimony. Wilson warned that he expected justice and that "the person undertaking on the Part of Mr[.] John G. Jackson, must be Duly authorized, otherwise I shall hearken to no Questions." Angrily, George Jackson rejected Wilson's conditions. "This is two ambiguous and two much your former language with the enimies of myself & John

---

[26]James Madison to Jackson, 31 December 1807, John George Jackson Papers; Madison to Jackson, 29 January 1808, ibid.; Jackson to Edmund Randolph, 9 March 1808, ibid.; George Jackson to John G. Jackson, 4 January 1808, Meigs-Jackson Papers, BHPC.

[27]*Benjamin Wilson* v. *John G. Jackson*, Virginia District Court Records, Monongalia County Records, West Virginia Collection, West Virginia University Library, Morgantown.

G. Jackson," he wrote with his quirky spelling, "therefore in future you will be precluded from any further explanations from me except your request is in language that is fair and honorable and without threats."[28] John, meanwhile, had returned to Congress, and the arguments had an opportunity to subside.

Another conflict between Jackson and Wilson grew out of the location of the Harrison County courthouse. In 1803 Jackson presented a petition to the county court calling upon citizens to pledge money toward the construction of a new courthouse and offered to give one-fourth of an acre of land on the east side of Elk Creek from any of his lots except the one directly opposite his residence. In addition, he pledged $400 toward the costs of construction if the courthouse were built on his property.

After repeatedly postponing a decision, the county court decided on 21 May 1810 to build the edifice on a lot on West Main Street, donated by Benjamin Wilson, Jr. Jackson and other Clarksburg residents opposed the decision and in December 1810 appealed to the General Assembly to settle the dispute. The petitioners complained that two of the contractors were members of the court and noted that the site offered by Jackson was closer to the jail and also on the road to Randolph Academy. Jackson offered to increase his contribution toward the building of the courthouse to $500, or to donate his stone house and assume one-third of the costs of constructing the courthouse. Despite these inducements, on 18 January 1811 the legislature decided in favor of the site offered by Wilson.

A major reason for the rejection of Jackson's offer almost certainly lay in a charge made by Isaac Coplin, an ally of the Wilson faction and a member of the House of Delegates, that Jackson was seeking "to inhance [*sic*] the value of [his] own property." Coplin expressed doubts that Jackson intended to give the stone house to the county court and alleged that he actually expected to sell it. Moreover, he declared that Jackson had "charged the Court of Harrison with corruption in many cases" and that he had threatened Coplin "with uncles[,] cousins etc."[29]

---

[28]Wilson to George Jackson, 27 October 1804, John George Jackson Papers; George Jackson to Wilson, 1 November 1804, ibid.

[29]Davis, *History of Harrison County*, 113-15. See also James McCally to Jackson, 28 February 1811, John George Jackson Papers.

Meanwhile, Jackson visibly prospered. His legal clients included several large nonresident landholders of Harrison County and surrounding areas. In 1800 he became the agent of George Harrison, who owned 19,000 acres "on the old field fork of Elk River about 50 miles distant from the Town of Clarksburg." During the next six years he agreed to represent Benjamin P. Wright of Wilmington, Delaware, and Daniel Boardman of New York, who claimed thousands of acres.[30] Jackson also acted as an agent for persons holding military lands in Ohio, including General George Carrington of South Boston, Virginia, and Joseph W. Scott, who later acquired Carrington's lands.[31]

At the same time that he looked after the lands of his clients, Jackson substantially increased his own holdings. Perhaps the first lot he acquired was one in Clarksburg, on the north side of Main Street and west of Elk Creek. It was conveyed to him by his father in 1797 for $1,000 cash. By 1810 he had twenty-five tracts of land, consisting of 22,192 acres in Harrison County alone.[32]

Jackson also had substantial landed properties outside Harrison County, many of them undoubtedly acquired for speculative purposes. In 1803 he had a one-fourth interest in a military tract in Ohio, which he desired to sell since "the unhealthfulness of the country, & the great quantity of lands

---

[30]Jackson to George Harrison, 24 July 1800, Gratz Collection, Historical Society of Pennsylvania, Philadelphia. William P. Wright to George Jackson, 1 January 1803, John George Jackson Papers; Harrison County Deed Book 6, 86-87, Harrison County Courthouse. For other persons for whom Jackson served as agent, see Jackson to G. Bedford, 3 February 1806, Gratz Alphabetical Collection, Historical Society of Pennsylvania; Jackson to James Madison, 28 October 1805, James Madison Papers, Library of Congress.

[31]Richmond *Examiner*, 17 December 1799; Jackson to Edmund Randolph, 9 March 1808, John George Jackson Papers; Edmund Randolph to Jackson, 9 March 1808, ibid.; Edmund Randolph to Jackson, 10 March 1808, ibid.; Joseph W. Scott to Edmund Randolph, 9 April 1808, ibid. See also Jackson to James Madison, 23 October 1805, James Madison Papers, Library of Congress; Articles of Agreement between George Jackson and John G. Jackson and Elijah Mitchell, 11 February 1800, Jackson Family Papers.

[32]Harrison County Land Book, 1801-1805, 24-26; 1806-1810, 24, 26, 28, Harrison County Courthouse.

for sale in the western states have materially affected the prospects & disappointed the expectations of most persons interested in that military survey." The following year he and his mother-in-law, Mary Coles Payne, of Charles Town, Virginia, disposed of one-half of their interest in lands in Ohio, which they held jointly, to General Jonathan Dayton. In return they received 2,290 acres of military lands that Dayton owned near tracts already held by Jackson on the Licking River. Jackson expected these lands to yield extraordinarily handsome profits, but they would depend upon his ability "to interest a thoroughbred speculator, who could conduct the sales."[33]

Other properties attracted Jackson's interest. In 1810 he offered Colonel Benjamin Walker $11,600 for 10,000 acres in the Virginia Military District and 1,100 acres in the United States Military District. He agreed to pay Walker "on sight" as much as $3,000 and the balance in four equal annual payments. Jackson was so eager to acquire these lands that he did not wish to delay his offer by a single mail. He also acquired property in New Kent County and in the Georgetown section of the District of Columbia. Before he resigned from Congress Jackson leased his house and other appurtenances that he owned in Washington, except for the property that had been "occupied by Edgar Patterson for some time past as a store & counting room." The annual rent of $450 indicates the value of the property.[34]

Although Jackson acted as an agent for nonresident landholders and engaged in speculations of his own, he vigorously opposed the claims of the Indiana Company, which included most of trans-Allegheny West Virginia north of the Little Kanawha River. His father, George, had earlier led the fight against the company's claims, which dated from the Treaty of

---

[33]Jackson to Military Owners, 23 October 1803, Jackson Family Papers; Jackson to Mary [Coles] Payne, 26 February 1804, ibid.; Jackson to Dayton, 30 June 1805, Meigs-Jackson Papers, OHS-CMM.

[34]Jackson to Benjamin Walker, 2 April 1810, Gratz Collection. Other land interests of Jackson in Ohio are noted in Samuel Coates to Jackson, 20 July 1805, Jackson Family Papers. See also Thomas M. Randolph to Jackson, 30 May 1807, John George Jackson Papers; John Payne to Jackson, 14 June 1805, ibid.; Articles of Agreement between John G. Jackson and Barbara Suter, 19 April 1810, Jackson Family Papers.

Fort Stanwix in 1768. In 1803 opponents of the company circulated petitions throughout the western counties calling upon the government of Virginia to defend their rights and protect their titles in suits the company had lodged against a number of them. The elder Jackson argued that the settlers had paid large sums in taxes annually, while the company had never paid anything. Nor had it "expended one farthing in defense against Indian hostility, which never entirely ceased until the year 1795," and which "compelled every man who resided within the aforesaid boundaries, for almost thirty years, to be, not only the provider for his family, but . . . to become an active and viglent [*sic*] soldier."[35] Although the General Assembly refused to undertake the defense of western Virginians against the Indiana Company, it reaffirmed its rejection of the company claims and thereby partially allayed the fears of the people.[36]

John G. Jackson assailed the Indiana claims in Congress. He declared that "a tract of country . . . possessing the most salubrious climate in the United States, a most fertile soil, and temperature second to none in the Union; situated, too, upon large navigable rivers; scarcely contains thirty thousand inhabitants." Moreover, he added, "our most valued citizens are abandoning their homes, which are sold for much less than their value, and removing to a country where no such dispute can annoy them." Jackson concluded that had the people of northwestern Virginia accepted a company offer to compromise, they might have suffered "much less than the injury we have so sensibly felt."[37]

Success crowned most of Jackson's endeavors. Not only did he witness extinction of the Indiana Company claims, but he also saw his own landholdings increase vastly in extent and value. His agricultural and industrial enterprises proved highly productive. His legal clients included nonresidents of West Virginia as well as local citizens and institutions. In 1807 Jackson informed his friend, Caesar A. Rodney of Delaware, that he could

---

[35]Harrison County Legislative Petitions, 7 February 1803, 4 December 1804. For a full discussion of the Indiana Company claims as they affected northern West Virginia, see Rice, *Allegheny Frontier*, 63, 69, 118-29, 133-34.

[36]George Jackson to John G. Jackson, 12 November 1804, John George Jackson Papers.

[37]*Annals of Congress*, 8th Cong., 2d sess., 1079.

not undertake certain commissions requested by Rodney at a time when the superior and quarterly courts of Harrison County were in session because he could not "make a charge which would indemnify me for what is a sufficient indemnity to a Lawyer having a most extensive & valuable practise." Many of his cases derived from the chaotic Virginia land system that produced confusion in titles, which Jackson believed contributed to immigrants' finding western parts of the state unattractive and to arrested economic development.[38]

One acquisition symbolized the deep personal tragedies that accompanied Jackson's successes during the first decade of the nineteenth century. On 25 March 1808 he received a deed from his father for a cemetery plot at the "Orchard Place" about one-half mile from John's house. The elder Jackson stipulated that his son should get a "Legislative sanction" if possible and that the ground should be "consecrated."[39] By the time he obtained the deed, sorrow had already taken a heavy toll in losses in John's family.

Jackson's personal misfortunes began in the summer of 1806, when a fever epidemic took the lives of two of his young children, sparing only an infant daughter, Mary. "The distresses of my family and the loss of our dear Children," he wrote James Madison, "have almost deprived me of my senses." Jackson told Madison that his daughter Mary had "been snatched from the brink of the Grave" and that he felt confident "that her restoration to health alone has saved her Mother—to have lost all her Children at one blow would have given a shock too severe to be borne by her."[40]

Later that summer several other members of the Jackson family fell victim to the same fever. Jackson wrote Madison in late September that "at

---

[38]See, for example, Certificate of Appointment of J. G. Jackson as Attorney for the Bank of Zanesville, 2 March 1812, Meigs-Jackson Papers, BHPC; Jackson to Rodney, 24 May 1807, Gratz Collection. Jackson's concerns about confused land titles are set forth in an undated draft of a petition to the Virginia legislature sometime after 1820, Meigs-Jackson Papers, BHPC.

[39]Harrison County Deed Book 7, 247-48.

[40]Jackson to Madison, 25 August 1806, James Madison Papers, Library of Congress. See also Dolley Madison to Mrs. John Payne, 4 August 1806, in *Memoirs and Letters of Dolly Madison, Wife of James Madison, President of the United States*, ed. Lucia B. Cutts (Boston: Houghton, Mifflin and Company, 1886) 63; Thomas M. Randolph to Jackson, 15 November 1806, John George Jackson Papers.

this moment my Father[,] Mother & two Sisters all lie in one house in a most dangerous and alarming situation." With his recent losses deeply etched in his thoughts, Jackson expressed the fear "that unless a favorable crisis occurs immediately . . . they will all follow our dear Children ere two weeks more have elapsed."[41] Fortunately, his parents and sisters recovered from their afflictions.

The greatest source of sorrow and anxiety to Jackson was the steadily declining health of his wife, Mary, who suffered from tuberculosis. In the summer of 1807 her illness, at which Jackson was "exceedingly alarmed," prevented him from making a planned visit to Ohio. In early October Mary had an attack of "violent chills, agues & fevers, & a most alarming Pleurisy which continued for two weeks under all the most alarming Symptoms." Although she slowly began to recover from the attack, she was, Jackson declared, "reduced to a Skeleton & cannot walk across her Chamber."[42] Despite an eagerness to visit family and friends, Jackson had no illusions that they would be able to travel during the coming winter.

Compounding Jackson's troubles and adding to his grief was the death, on 21 October 1807, of his mother-in-law, Mary Coles Payne, who had resided with the Jacksons for several months. Her illness came on suddenly and resulted from a "violent stroke of the dead palsy," which paralyzed her left side. External applications, bleeding, blistering, and rubbing proved futile, and within an hour she lapsed into a coma. Her death had a severely detrimental effect upon Jackson's wife, who during the following week suffered such chills and fever and such a disordered stomach "as to baffle all the medical skill" that the Clarksburg area afforded.[43]

Mary Jackson continued to decline. Jackson wrote Madison that the only thing keeping her alive was the hope of seeing her sisters again; but, he admitted, "All things considered I shall consider the undertaking as arduous & difficult as passage of the Alps was to Hannibal & his army." Two

---

[41]Jackson to Madison, 29 September 1806, James Madison Papers, New York Public Library.

[42]Jackson to James Madison, 21 June 1807, James Madison Papers, Library of Congress; Jackson to James Madison, 11 October 1807, ibid.

[43]Jackson to James Madison, 18 October 1807, ibid.; Jackson to James Madison, 25 October 1807, ibid.

months later Jackson described his wife's illness as "an affection of the breast & throat with a hard dry cough which sometimes changes & she spits freely, once or twice mixed with blood." At that time he anticipated that the month of March would bring "a decisive crisis" if no favorable change had occurred before then.[44]

On 13 February 1808, Mary died. Jackson wrote Madison that "my miseries are past endurance; without speaking of the incalculable & unparrallelled [*sic*] misfortunes. You knew my Mary well, yes, you gave her to me at the altar, you witnessed our union, & our happiness[,] you saw the little prattlers that she gave me. In the short period of seven fleeting years all these things took place & all but one—& she too dearest of all has been torn from me in the same period."[45]

During the autumn of 1808 Jackson became exceedingly apprehensive about the health of Mary, the only remaining child left of those born to him and Mary Payne Jackson. Soon after his wife's funeral, he left Clarksburg for Harewood, where he placed Mary under the care of her aunt, Lucy Washington. The child's frequent illnesses excited Jackson's fears that she, too, might be taken from him. He wrote Madison that "more I cannot bear."[46] Fortunately, his daughter survived the illnesses and diseases of childhood and lived until 1881, when she died at the age of seventy-six.

The deep personal tragedies that Jackson suffered might have crushed the spirit of a less determined man. John, however, immersed himself in his agricultural pursuits, nascent industrial enterprises, land transactions, legal work, and public affairs. In this way he was able to transcend sorrow and disappointment and, like the phoenix, rise anew to life and its challenges.

---

[44]Jackson to James Madison, 19 November 1807, ibid.; Jackson to James Madison, 15 January 1808, ibid.

[45]Jackson to James Madison, 17 July 1808, ibid. See also Davis, *History of Harrison County*, 419.

[46]Jackson to James Madison, 4 September 1808, James Madison Papers, Library of Congress. See also Jackson to D[olley] P. Madison, 8 October 1808, ibid.

4 Jeffersonian Congressman

One of the political legends relating to the Jackson family concerns the circumstances under which John succeeded his father as congressman from the First District of Virginia. The tradition holds that a speech of the able but uneducated George Jackson produced such derisive amusement among some of his colleagues that Jackson, in a moment of irritation, declared that he would go home and send his son, John, to Congress and that they would not laugh at him.[1] The story may not be true, but in 1803 the brilliant, well-educated, and ambitious John took the seat that his father had held from 1795 to 1797 and again from 1799 to 1803.

Jackson and his wife found Washington a small capital. The government employed less than three hundred persons, including members of Congress. The city consisted of two sections connected by Pennsylvania Avenue, a thoroughfare either dusty or muddy, depending upon the season, and often nearly impassable after dark. One community, made up chiefly of employees of the Executive Department, clustered near the White House. The other, near the Capitol, consisted mostly of boardinghouses, where members of Congress had lodgings. Nearby Georgetown provided the business and commercial center, where congressmen and their wives did much of their shopping.[2]

---

[1]Henry Haymond, *History of Harrison County, West Virginia, from the Early Days of Northwestern Virginia to the Present* (Morgantown WV: Acme Publishing Company, 1910) 378-79.

[2]James Sterling Young, *The Washington Community: Eighteen Hundred–Eighteen Twenty-Eight* (New York: Columbia University Press, 1966) 25-30.

Upon arriving in Washington, John and Mary went to the Madison residence at 1333-1335 F Street, N.W. The Jacksons were not lonely in their new home, for Mary's two sisters resided in Washington, and both enjoyed political and social entrée into national capital society. Dolley Madison, the older one, served as hostess for the widowed President Jefferson, and the youngest sister, Anna, who made her home with the Madisons, married Richard Cutts, a congressman from Massachusetts, within the year. The Jacksons took rooms at a boardinghouse on the northeast corner of Fifteenth and F streets, a short distance from the Madison residence. Jackson made the establishment, run successively by J. M. Simmes, a Mr. Rhodes, and Mrs. Barbara Suter, his Washington home during his first seven years in Congress, and in 1810 he bought the building himself. From his lodgings, he customarily walked to the Capitol for the sessions of the House of Representatives.[3]

The Jacksons at once entered the surprisingly sophisticated social life of the capital city. Undoubtedly, they attended the Jockey Club races, for which both the House and the Senate adjourned almost as soon as they had organized. They attended the numerous parties and drawing rooms of the Madisons, to which came "every distinguished newcomer and countless friends, drawn by their host's wisdom and fund of amusing anecdotes and by Dolly's [*sic*] warmth." John and Mary were also invited to the dinners of President Jefferson, served at four o'clock in the afternoon and lasting until evening.[4] For business and social occasions the Jacksons required elegant attire. On the very day Congress convened John had a Georgetown tailor outfit him with new clothes, including black velvet pantaloons, a black coat, a silk waistcoat, a cravat, and other apparel.[5]

---

[3]Dorothy Davis, *John George Jackson* (Parsons WV: McClain Printing Company, 1976) 77-78.

[4]Ibid., 77, 80-82, 85. For entertainment and other expenses of the Jacksons, see, for example, Statement of J. M. Simmes to John G. Jackson, 6 January-7 February 1807, Meigs-Jackson Papers, Blennerhassett Historical Park Commission, Parkersburg, West Virginia (hereinafter cited as Meigs-Jackson Papers, BHPC).

[5]Statement of Edward Fennell to John G. Jackson, 17 October 1803-20 March 1804, Meigs-Jackson Papers, BHPC. See also Statement of Edgar Patterson to Mrs.

When the twenty-six-year-old Jackson entered the House of Representatives on 17 October 1803, the most momentous questions confronting Congress related to the Louisiana Purchase. The two immediate issues, which dealt with the constitutionality of the acquisition and the ratification of the treaty of purchase, were quickly resolved. On 25 October 1803 the House approved overwhelmingly, 90 to 25, the treaty and conventions relating to Louisiana, which the United States had signed on 30 April 1802. Jackson, reflecting the enthusiastic approbation with which the Western country viewed the transaction, voted with the majority.[6]

The most divisive and heated debates concerning the Louisiana Purchase grew out of proposals for the administration of the territory. On 27 October 1803 the House of Representatives resolved itself into a committee of the whole to consider a Senate bill that gave the president "all the military, civil, and judicial power" in the territory until Congress established a provisional government. The Federalists generally branded the powers conferred upon the president by the bill as unconstitutional. Republican Congressman Caesar A. Rodney of Delaware, a close friend of Jackson, countered with the argument that the limitations set upon the powers of Congress by the Constitution applied only to its relations with the states and not with the territories.[7]

In his first significant remarks as a congressman, Jackson spoke to the constitutional issues relating to the Louisiana question, evincing an acute knowledge of the Constitution. Like most of his colleagues, he had no misgivings about taking possession of Louisiana immediately. He rejected the position of Joseph B. Varnum of Massachusetts that the United States did

---

John G. Jackson, 29 January 1806, ibid.; Statement of Baker Riggs to John G. Jackson, 23 May 1809, ibid.; Statement of Edward Fennell to John G. Jackson, 25 May, 22 June 1809, ibid.; Statement of John Cox and H. Miller to John G. Jackson, 24 April 1810, ibid.

[6]*Annals of Congress*, 8th Cong., 1st sess., 369, 488. See also Henry Adams, *History of the United States of America*, 9 vols. (New York: Charles Scribner's Sons, 1909-1911) 2:94-130; Edward Channing, *The Jeffersonian System, 1801-1809*, vol. 12 of *The American Nation: A History*, ed. A. B. Hart, 28 vols. (New York: Harper & Brothers, 1904-1918) 73, 80; Dumas Malone, *Jefferson the President: First Term, 1801-1805* (Boston: Little, Brown and Company, 1970) 311-12.

[7]*Annals of Congress*, 8th Cong., 1st sess., 491-98.

not acquire full sovereignty until the expiration of twelve years. "If we do not possess the exclusive sovereignty," Jackson declared, "it would be impossible to legislate, as the act of legislation is the highest attribute of sovereignty."

Constitutional concerns caused Jackson to oppose the majority of his own party, which favored conferring upon the president sweeping powers over the government of Louisiana. He declared during the debate on the interim government of the province that he would "prefer an interregnum to doing anything which should militate against the Constitution, or principles that have long been respected." He further asserted that he did not wish "to adopt the principle of the right of this House to delegate such extensive powers for even one day; for if they possess the right of delegating them for one day, they possess the co-extensive right of delegating them forever." Jackson disclaimed any fear of abuse of power by President Jefferson, but he stated that he had reason to believe that the president himself was "inimical to the expression of Executive power" as envisioned in the bill.[8]

On 28 October the bill empowering the president to take possession of Louisiana and establish a government for it passed the House by the decisive margin of 89 to 23. Jackson abstained from voting. After his remarks, he could not vote for the bill; party loyalties and devotion to Jefferson probably prevented him from voting against it. The following day the House passed a measure to put the Louisiana Purchase treaty into effect. In an almost unanimous vote of 85 to 7, Jackson again stood with the majority of his party.[9]

Later debates on the government of Louisiana revealed Jackson's great devotion to popular sovereignty and the Bill of Rights. On 29 February 1804 he spoke forcefully against a section of a bill that would have vested legislative powers in Louisiana in a governor and a legislative council of thirteen members appointed annually by the president. Jackson contended that the United States Constitution and the constitutions of all the states had rejected such "aristocratical and monarchical" features. He scoffed at the suggestion that the tears shed by the French residents of Louisiana at the

---

[8]Ibid., 510-11.

[9]Ibid., 546, 548-49.

lowering of the French flag and the hoisting of the American flag were an indication that they were not ready for self-government. He even advanced the dubious idea that the tears were of joy.[10]

Jackson also opposed giving the French residents liberty "by degrees." Instead, he wanted them to have full rights at once, lest the United States be accused of concealing "the principle of despotism under the garb of Republicanism" and of being insincere in its professions that all men were created equal. Quite aside from constitutional mandates and concepts of the rights of man, however, he held that the treaty with France required that French residents of Louisiana be "maintained and protected in the free enjoyment of their liberty, property, and the religion which they profess."[11]

Perhaps with some inconsistency, Jackson offered a proposal of his own whereby the power of the president to appoint the legislative council would expire at the end of one year. During that year the territory would be laid off into counties, and thereafter the legislators would be elected by these units by vote of all free white males twenty-one years old or over. On 17 March 1804 his substitute section carried by 74 to 23. He opposed the final bill, which extended the provisions to two years instead of one, but it passed by the decisive margin of 66 to 21. The Senate refused to accede to the House substitute. The House enacted a compromise bill whereby members of the legislative council were elected at large, but Jackson, who believed that the multiplicity of languages spoken by the people made balloting by counties essential, refused to vote.[12]

Partly because of preoccupation with Louisiana matters, the House of Representatives deferred consideration of the Twelfth Amendment to the Constitution of the United States. With a presidential election approaching and the experience of 1800 still etched in their minds, Republicans in the House wished to avoid the possibility of another tie for the presidency. In the very first session of Congress after the election of 1800, an amendment to separate the offices of president and vice-president in electoral voting passed the House of Representatives by more than the two-thirds

[10]Ibid., 1069-70.

[11]Ibid., 1071-72.

[12]Ibid., 1191-93, 1198-99, 1206, 1229-30.

majority required, but it failed in the Senate by a single vote. The two succeeding sessions postponed action on the proposed amendment.[13]

For about seven weeks in the autumn of 1803, the House again considered the proposed Twelfth Amendment. On 8 December Jackson spoke in favor of it. With an intemperance that on numerous occasions ruffled the feathers of his colleagues, he lashed out at Federalist Congressman Samuel D. Purviance of North Carolina, who opposed the amendment. Purviance voiced the fears of small states that the dictates of politics would always assure large states the two chief offices and lead to "fraud, intrigue, venality, and corruption." He declared that the Constitution was "inviolable and intangible" and that small states would not have entered the Union if they had contemplated changes in it. Jackson, with great asperity, answered that Purviance had not "paid a proper attention" to the amendment and that the results he professed to fear would ensue if it were not passed. As Jackson perhaps anticipated, the amendment passed the House 83 to 42, won Senate approval, and was ratified in time for the 1804 elections.[14]

Their harsh exchanges nearly involved Jackson and Purviance in a duel, which neither desired. They resolved their differences, but only after considerable correspondence and declarations that they intended no personal affronts. Jackson, always easily aroused, was only temporarily restrained by the experience, and six years later he actually fought a duel with another North Carolina congressman.[15]

Republicans, who had evinced some intraparty dissension during the debates on the Twelfth Amendment, closed ranks when they perceived an effort by the Federalists to confer sweeping powers upon the federal judiciary. Federalist domination of the judicial branch of the government had long irritated Republicans, who particularly resented the "midnight" appointments of President John Adams and his appointment of John Marshall as Chief Justice of the Supreme Court. Republicans in the Seventh Con-

---

[13]Malone, *Jefferson the President: First Term*, 393-94.

[14]*Annals of Congress*, 8th Cong., 1st sess., 758-61, 775; Malone, *Jefferson the President: First Term*, 394.

[15]For the resolution of the misunderstanding between Jackson and Purviance, see four undated written exchanges and one dated 12 December [1803], in Meigs-Jackson Papers, BHPC.

gress forced the repeal of the Judiciary Act of 1801, thereby abolishing circuit court judgeships to which Federalists had been appointed, but they were not able to eliminate Federalist control of the judiciary. In February 1803 Marshall further fanned the flames of partisanship. Speaking for the Supreme Court in the case of *Marbury* v. *Madison,* he pronounced the doctrine of judicial review and found for the first time in American history an act of Congress unconstitutional, a decision not to be rendered again for more than half a century.

The indignation of the Republicans reached new heights in May 1803 when Associate Justice Samuel Chase, in a charge to a Baltimore grand jury, denounced Republicans in both federal and state governments. At the suggestion of John Randolph, the House of Representatives at its next session named a committee to inquire into Chase's conduct. The committee extended its investigation to include the conduct of Chase in an earlier treason trial of John Fries in Philadelphia and the libel trial of James Thomson Callender in Richmond.[16]

Jackson thoroughly approved of the inquiry into Chase's actions. "Like a grand jury," he declared in the House of Representatives on 6 January 1804, "we ought, in my opinion, at the instance of any member, to send for all persons possessed of information calculated to throw light upon the conduct of any individual inculpated." But he warned that "though it may be the duty of this House to impeach an officer, it is necessary that facts, warranting such an impeachment, should first be presented." Jackson voted for the inquiry, which the House approved by a vote of 81 to 40.[17]

In December 1804 the House considered eight articles of impeachment against Chase and voted on each separately. All except three carried by margins of more than two to one. Jackson voted with his party on six

---

[16]Adams, *History of the United States,* 2: 147-58, 218-44; Noble E. Cunningham, Jr., *The Jeffersonian Republicans in Power: Party Operations, 1801-1809* (Chapel Hill: University of North Carolina Press for the Institute of Early American History and Culture, 1963) 79-80; Marshall Smelser, *The Democratic Republic, 1801-1815,* in *The New American Nation,* ed. Henry Steele Commager and Richard B. Morris, 33 vols. to date (New York: Harper & Row, Publishers, 1954-) 64-69. For the Callender case, see Richard R. Beeman, *The Old Dominion and the New Nation, 1788-1801* (Lexington: University Press of Kentucky, 1972) 224-27.

[17]*Annals of Congress,* 8th Cong., 1st sess., 833-34, 875.

of the articles, but in opposing two of them he gave evidence that partisan spirit could not be allowed to overcome his regard for legalities. He questioned the fifth article, which charged Chase with illegally entering a capias, rather than a summons, against James Callender, and maintained that under Virginia law Chase had discretionary power to decide which was applicable. He did not vote on the sixth article, which charged Chase with violating a Virginia law by trying Callender at the same term of court at which his case was presented to the grand jury, even though he considered Chase's action "a high-handed arbitrary proceeding.[18] Jackson, like Randolph and other staunch Republicans, was deeply disappointed when the Senate acquitted Chase of the charges against him.

Although Jackson usually chose to base his arguments on legal and constitutional grounds, he took the path of compromise in the famous Yazoo land question. Widely regarded as the spokesman for Secretary of State James Madison, his brother-in-law, Jackson became deeply enmeshed in the controversy in the House of Representatives over the Yazoo claims. In the course of the debate, he crossed verbal swords with the vituperative John Randolph, differed with most of the Virginia delegation in the House, and became the target of an attack by William Duane, the often scurrilous editor of the Philadelphia *Aurora*.[19]

The Yazoo question originated in a series of land grants made by the Georgia legislature between 1789 and 1795. In a "setting of land giveaways and casual corruption," some of the most powerful speculators in the coun-

---

[18]Ibid., 8th Cong., 2d sess., 747-61. The articles against Chase charged that he had (1) restricted counsel in the trial of Samuel Fries and debared the prisoner from addressing the jury; (2) displayed a similar spirit of persecution in the trial of James Callender; (3) refused to admit evidence in Callender's trial and showed intent to oppress and convict him; (4) displayed conduct marked by "injustice, partiality, and intemperance" throughout Callender's trial; (5) entered a capias, which was limited to capital offenses, rather than a summons as Virginia law provided; (6) violated a Virginia law requiring that Callender be tried at the same term of court at which he was presented; (7) "descend[ed] from the dignity of a judge" at a trial in Delaware; and (8) criticized the United States and the state of Delaware. Ibid., 728-30.

[19]See, for example, C. Peter Magrath, *Yazoo: Law and Politics in the New Republic; The Case of Fletcher v. Peck* (New York: W. W. Norton & Company, 1966) 44.

try "made their bid for Georgia's rich western holdings." Four influential companies alone received thirty-five million acres west of the Chattahoochee River in what has been called "the greatest real estate deal in history." They acquired their empires by methods so patently fraudulent that Governor George Mathews vetoed the legislation. Eventually the people of Georgia raised such an outcry that in 1796 a new legislature felt obliged to declare the actions of its predecessor null and void.[20]

Disappointed speculators turned to the Federalist-controlled national government. In the heated political atmosphere of the late 1790s the Federalists branded the repeal of the Yazoo grants by the Georgia legislature as interference with vested property rights. They contended that only the courts, and not a subsequent legislature, could invalidate an act once passed and that federal power could overrule Georgia's anti-Yazoo policy.

The Jefferson administration favored a compromise that would facilitate the cession of the Georgia lands to the United States. In 1801 Jefferson appointed Secretary of State Madison, Secretary of the Treasury Albert Gallatin, and Attorney General Levi Lincoln as commissioners to represent the federal government on a joint United States-Georgia commission to investigate the claims of settlers and others within the proposed cession. The federal commissioners reported to Congress that the title of the Yazoo claimants generally had no sound basis but that the best interests of the United States and the tranquility of future inhabitants of the Yazoo lands rendered it "expedient to enter into a compromise on reasonable terms." Madison and the other commissioners recommended that Congress set aside five million acres in the Mississippi Territory for the satisfaction of legitimate claims.[21]

The recommendation of the commissioners led to a full-scale debate in the House of Representatives, with John G. Jackson and John Randolph, almost equally fiery protagonists, leading the opposing sides. The eccentric Randolph was an implacable enemy of Madison, whose position in the Jefferson administration and influence in the House of Representatives contrasted sharply with Randolph's own declining power. Randolph had already declared, "This is one of the cases which . . . I can never desert

[20]Ibid., 1-19.

[21]Ibid., 29-36.

or relinquish, till I shall have experienced every energy of mind, and faculty of body I possess, in refuting so nefarious a project." At a Washington dinner party he attacked one of the defenders of the Yazoo speculators in language so violent that the ladies left the room. The one-hundred-pound Randolph then "smashed a wine glass on his opponent's head and threw the bottle at him."[22]

In a "sharp but well-reasoned speech" on 31 January 1805, Jackson responded to arguments set forth earlier by Randolph. He stated that in view of "a general denunciation of every man who dares, to favor the [committee] report," he wished to make clear the reasons for the vote he would cast in favor of it. He angrily rejected Randolph's contention that the desire of a majority of the House to admit the claims of the land companies and effect a prompt settlement provided evidence that "unprincipled men have ascendancy" in the government.[23]

Jackson had less success in refuting Randolph's charge that grantees of lands from the Georgia legislature in 1795 were guilty of fraud and that later claimants were "a set of hypocrites," pretending to be "innocent purchasers without notice of fraud." He attempted to demonstrate through historical and documentary evidence the validity of the Yazoo claims and the propriety of settling them by compromise. However, his conclusion that the speculators had shown moderation and might have been awarded fifty million rather than five million acres if the courts had settled their case had obvious weaknesses.[24]

A charge by Randolph that supporters of the compromise were united by "the spirit of Federalism" struck a sensitive chord with Jackson, who had always opposed Federalism with vehemence. Jackson answered Randolph that if Federalism "consists in complying with prudent advice and honest engagements . . . I will cherish it, and hug it to my bosom with the affection of a father for a long lost son returning to the paths of virtue." He re-

---

[22]*Annals of Congress*, 8th Cong., 1st sess., 1104; Magrath, *Yazoo*, 39-49. For similar expressions, see Thomas M. Randolph to Jackson, 15 November 1806, John George Jackson Papers, Lilly Library, Indiana University, Bloomington; Thomas M. Randolph to Jackson, 30 May 1807, ibid.

[23]*Annals of Congress*, 8th Cong., 2d sess., 1064-65; Magrath, *Yazoo*, 44.

[24]*Annals of Congress*, 8th Cong., 2d sess., 1065-67, 1078-79.

minded Randolph that the previous year, in speaking of the speculators, Randolph had asserted, "let them get a decree of the courts in their favor, let them take possession of the property, and I will expend the last dollar in the Treasury, and sacrifice the last life in the nation to fight them out of the country." Randolph interrupted with the declaration that he still said so.[25]

Both Jackson and Randolph soon returned to more cogent arguments. Jackson insisted that the Yazoo claimants, though denounced as "swindlers, liars, hypocrites, and accessaries [*sic*] to a stupendous robbery," must be accorded the right of petition. Randolph, insofar as "his extreme indisposition and excessive hoarseness" permitted, argued that no contract existed between Georgia and the grantees in 1795 because a contract could not legally be concluded on the basis of fraud.[26]

During the later stages of the debate Jackson attacked an amendment requiring congressional confirmation of the decisions of the commissioners. Ignoring the fact that the crux of the problem rested with a few large speculators, he declared that the House of Representatives was "totally incompetent" to pass judgment on 1,500 claims. The amendment mustered only 6 votes, but the House approved, by a vote of 68 to 58, a resolution authorizing the federal commissioners to meet with representatives of Georgia and settle the Yazoo claims. Jackson voted with the majority.[27] He and John Dawson were the only Virginia congressmen who voted for the compromise. The other 17 representatives, including John Randolph and even Jefferson's sons-in-law, Thomas Mann Randolph and John W. Eppes, opposed it. William B. Giles, a former congressman from Virginia, told John Quincy Adams that the Yazoo scheme had produced such indignation in the Old Dominion that anyone from that state who voted for the compromise would certainly lose his seat. Adams understood Giles to mean that Jackson would fail of reelection.[28]

---

[25]Ibid., 1074-75.

[26]Ibid., 1079-1100.

[27]Ibid., 1173.

[28]Ibid.; Norman K. Risjord, *The Old Republicans: Southern Conservatives in the Age of Jefferson* (New York: Columbia University Press, 1965) 41; Charles Francis Adams, ed., *Memoirs of John Quincy Adams, Comprising Portions of His Diary from 1795 to 1848*, 12 vols. (New York: J. B. Lippincott & Co., 1874-1877) 1:343.

Concerned for his political future, Jackson felt obliged to address a circular letter to his constituents. In it he declared that the Constitution had always been his "polar star" and that he had "always voted on questions of *policy* and *private rights* according to the known rules of equity, and the dictates of an honest conscience." In doing so in the Yazoo question, however, he had been denounced in Congress and in the Philadelphia *Aurora* as acting in a spirit of Federalism. Jackson admitted that he had sometimes voted with the Federalists, but he denied that he had ever "in the smallest degree been guilty of a dereliction of republican principles."[29]

Jackson's reference to the *Aurora* drew a stinging response from William Duane, its editor. In a move clearly designed to unseat Jackson at the next election, Duane sent a letter to the editors of the Federalist Morgantown *Monongalia Gazette*, who issued it as a political broadside. Duane declared that in the *Aurora* article to which Jackson alluded, "*The name of J. G. Jackson never was at any time, nor in any one instance thought of sufficient consequence to be deemed worthy of notice.*" He accused Jackson of questionable speculations in lands sold for the direct tax and declared that he had purchased two or three thousand acres for less than twenty dollars, a charge branded by Jackson as entirely untrue. Duane excoriated Jackson as "perhaps one of the least respected men who hold seats in Congress," who had cooperated with Federalists and "a set of worthless speculators." He had "travelled over all parts of the continent, and employed every artifice of fraud [,] corruption and intimidation, to carry into effect the plunder of a district of country twice as large as the state of Virginia."[30]

The Federalists circulated Duane's broadside extensively in Jackson's congressional district in the days immediately prior to the elections. Jackson wrote Madison that he had preferred not to run for reelection, but fear that a Federalist might be elected from his district had induced him to enter the race. During the month of April 1805 he appeared at the elections in five of the six counties in his district, which was larger than the state of New Hampshire.[31]

---

[29][William Duane], "To the Editors of the Monongalia Gazette," 27 March 1805, Broadside, James Madison Papers, Library of Congress, Washington, D.C.

[30]Ibid.

[31]Jackson to Madison, 29 April 1805, James Madison Papers, Library of Congress.

In a circular addressed to the electorate of Brooke County, which he was unable to visit during his campaign, Jackson stated that his character had undergone the "severest scrutiny & criticism from quarters expected, and unexpected." He denounced the attacks of the *Aurora* as in reality assaults upon majority rule and accused Duane of exercising a tyranny of the press, which was "as odious as those of Dionysius, and Nero." In an attempt to divert attention from the Yazoo compromise, he reminded his constituents of his efforts to promote a national road to strike the Ohio River at Marietta and declared that he had always favored two roads, with one built to Wheeling having preference. He also adverted to his vigorous support of the Louisiana Purchase and his role as a "western man" in upholding the interests peculiar to that section.[32]

The election results proved highly gratifying to Jackson. His opponent, Thomas Wilson, carried only his home county of Monongalia. Although Wilson polled 409 votes to Jackson's 141 in that county, Jackson won heavily enough in Harrison, Wood, Ohio, and Randolph counties to amass 1,031 votes to Wilson's 771. Jackson thus held a 260-vote lead, even without Brooke County, for which results are not available. On the basis of his 34-vote majority there in the previous election, he confidently expected to win by a more substantial margin than he had achieved in his initial race.[33]

Compared with the acrimony produced by the Yazoo question, the debates on a resolution for retrocession of the District of Columbia to Maryland and Virginia appeared almost serene. When the resolution came before the House on 31 December 1804, Jackson offered an unsuccessful motion to postpone consideration until that date a year later. On 8 January 1805 he declared that at first he had felt strongly in favor of retrocession, but he asserted that "after the maturest deliberations I have changed the opinion I had partially formed." Although he had found nothing in the Constitution specifically to prevent it, he believed that retrocession would violate the spirit of the document, "since in adopting the Constitution, the people had consented that a partial transfer of territory should be made to

---

[32]Jackson, "To the Freeholders of Brooke County," 24 April 1805, draft in Meigs-Jackson Papers, BHPC.

[33]Jackson to Madison, 29 April 1805, James Madison Papers, Library of Congress.

Congress for specified purposes and they did not authorize Congress to dispose of it."

From the standpoint of policy, Jackson believed that there was even less reason for retrocession. He admitted that residents of the District of Columbia were denied the right to vote, but they were only a minute fraction of the population of Virginia or Maryland and could not hope to exercise much political influence in either of those states. The solution to their situation, Jackson declared, was "a local legislature, a free representation, a government given by the generous feelings and liberality of the States and of Congress; and if it be necessary, I have no doubt they will, by an amendment to the Constitution, permit them to realize these expectations." He therefore voted against the resolution to retrocede the District of Columbia to Maryland and Virginia, which lost in the House of Representatives with only 28 members in favor and 50 in opposition.[34]

The District of Columbia also became the focal point for a review of the slavery question. In January 1805 Congressman James Sloan of New Jersey introduced a bill into the House of Representatives calling for the eventual emancipation of slaves born in the District of Columbia after 4 July 1805. His motion failed by a vote of 47 to 65. Jackson, who had begun to acquire slaves of his own, did not vote on the question.[35]

Congress showed more concern over proposals to either prohibit the importation of slaves into the United States or place a tax on those imported. The Constitution provided that Congress should have no power to prohibit slave importations before the year 1808. The states, however, might do so, and several had enacted restrictive legislation. As slavery became more profitable and the demand for Negroes increased, South Carolina in 1803 repealed her law forbidding the importation of slaves. In response to her action, Congressman David Bard of Pennsylvania, which

---

[34]*Annals of Congress*, 8th Cong., 2d sess., 920-22, 981.

[35]Ibid., 995. For Jackson's slaves, see, for example, Harrison County Minute Book, 1803-1805, 165-67, Harrison County Courthouse, Clarksburg, West Virginia; Jacob Means to Jackson, 7 November 1804, Meigs-Jackson Papers, BHPC. Jackson steadily increased the number of his slaves, which in 1819 numbered thirty-seven, with twenty-five over sixteen years old. Harrison County Tithable List, Book 2, 236, Harrison County Courthouse; Meigs-Jackson Papers, BHPC.

was at that time the center of the antislavery movement in the United States, proposed a tax of ten dollars on each slave brought into the country.

Amid widespread sentiment to postpone action on Bard's resolution, Jackson, on 17 February 1804, spoke in favor of immediate reconsideration. He charged that those desiring postponement hoped to defeat the purpose of the bill and gain time for the importation of sufficient slaves to fill the market before Congress acted. "If, therefore, it is our intention to legislate at all on the subject," declared Jackson, "let us take time by the forelock, and act now or never." Despite his efforts, the House of Representatives voted 56 to 50 to defer action. A year later, Jackson offered and then withdrew an amendment to a bill before Congress for the purpose of clarifying the act of the previous session, which seemingly allowed slaves to be brought into Louisiana. Upon reflection, he concluded that the entire bill should be rejected or recommitted, since the Constitution authorized the slave trade.[36]

Reasons for Jackson's opposition to a grant of land in Indiana to George Rapp and his followers are more obscure. His reasons appear to have had overtones of nativism and perhaps involved an effort by Jackson to curry favor with his constituents. In 1806 the Rappites, immigrants from Württemburg who had established the Harmony Society in western Pennsylvania, sought lands in the Territory of Indiana. They asked Congress to sell them a tract for two dollars an acre, with one-fourth of the purchase price payable at the end of six years and the remainder in six annual installments, with no interest. Originally Lutherans, the Rappites had become millennialists and formed a socialistic society that practiced celibacy and religious customs somewhat similar to those of the Shakers.

Jackson vigorously opposed any special concessions to the Rappites, who, it was asserted, expected to live largely as "cultivators of the vine." He declared, "If disposed to grant favors, let us grant to those who have the greatest claims. There are many old soldiers of the Revolution who would rejoice to purchase land on these terms." He objected to giving the petitioners their choice of the best lands and to charging them no interest. According to Jackson, many men were willing to pay six dollars an acre for

---

[36]*Annals of Congress*, 8th Cong., 1st sess., 820, 1020, 1031-32, 1035-36; *Annals of Congress*, 9th Cong., 1st sess., 442-44. See also Channing, *Jeffersonian System*, 100-105.

much of the land under discussion. Congressman Jeremiah Morrow of Ohio believed that Jackson was misinformed and made the obliquely accusatory statement that "I never seek for information in the lobby, nor the gallery, nor Pennsylvania avenue." Jackson, in characteristic vein, hotly retorted that he had his information on authority as respectable as any that Morrow might provide. He thereupon moved to postpone consideration of the bill indefinitely, but his motion lost by six votes.

The following day Jackson seconded a motion by Congressman Christopher H. Clark of Virginia to recommit the bill in behalf of the Rappites to the Committee on Public Lands. Jackson raised the point that the lands they sought had formerly belonged to Virginia, which had ceded them "for the common benefit of the Union," and that to use them for "the benefit of individual foreigners" was a violation of a trust. Moreover, he declared, the production of wine would reduce a tariff revenue that had been obtained largely from the rich.

Congressman John Smilie of Pennsylvania denounced Jackson's sensitivity to the rights of Virginia, which seemed always, in the inferences of Jackson, to be trampled upon. Smilie pointed out that honest men might differ on what constituted "the common benefit of the Union." The vote on the bill to provide lands to the Harmony Society resulted in a tie, 46 to 46. The speaker defeated the bill by voting against it.[37]

For most of Jackson's constituents, moves to reduce the duty on salt assumed greater importance than the debates over providing Indiana lands to a relatively obscure religious group. In 1804 John Mills, a member of the Virginia House of Delegates from Ohio County, wrote Jackson that a reduction of the salt duty would be most welcome in Ohio County, if it could be effected with "propriety." He stated that salt sold at $5.50 per bushel there and that he expected it to increase in price. Congressional maneuver, however, tied reduction in the tariff on salt to maintenance of the fund to protect American commerce in the Mediterranean, and Jackson failed in his endeavors to have it reduced.[38]

---

[37]*Annals of Congress*, 9th Cong., 1st sess., 463-69, 477. See also Alice F. Tyler, *Freedom's Ferment: Phases of American Social History from the Colonial Period to the Outbreak of the Civil War* (Minneapolis: University of Minnesota Press) 121-25.

[38]Mills to Jackson, 17 December [1804?], Meigs-Jackson Papers, BHPC; *Annals of Congress*, 9th Cong., 2d sess., 299, 319-20, 627-28, 635, 641-44, 653-55, 688, 1278.

Jackson was scarcely any more successful in his efforts to obtain a road from the Potomac River to the Ohio. On 28 November 1803 he moved that five percent of the proceeds from the sale of public lands in Ohio be used for the construction of a road from the Atlantic Ocean to the Ohio River. John Randolph noted that Congress had already set aside three percent for the exclusive use of the state of Ohio. Jackson countered Randolph's objection with the declaration that he was asking for five percent more. At that point Joseph B. Varnum of Massachusetts moved to substitute two percent, rather than the five percent preferred by Jackson. His motion carried without dissent.[39] On 22 March 1806, during the House debate on a Senate bill for the laying out of a turnpike from Cumberland, Maryland, to the Ohio, Jackson noted that a compact between the federal government and the state of Ohio had provided for a "turnpike or other roads." Because of other important measures, he agreed to postpone consideration, but he proposed an amendment to the Senate bill that would allow "a discretion to lay out the road at any point between Steubenville and Grave creek on the Ohio." His proposal failed of passage.[40]

No incident during Jackson's second term in Congress aroused more popular excitement than the Aaron Burr conspiracy. After his rejection by the Republican Party in 1804 and his loss of control over the party in New York, Burr knew that his political future was at best uncertain. When he mortally wounded Alexander Hamilton in a duel at Weehawken, New Jersey, on 11 July 1804, his career abruptly drew to an end. Nevertheless, Burr retained considerable popularity in the West, and there he hoped to rebuild his political fortunes. He took advantage of a restiveness among the Creoles of Louisiana, a vagueness in the boundary between Louisiana and Spanish territory, and the ambitions of unscrupulous or credulous Western leaders to lay plans for the Southwest that bordered on treason.

Jackson found himself almost unwittingly involved in the Burr episode. In November 1805 Burr visited Jackson at Clarksburg during a homeward journey from Cincinnati. If Burr mentioned his schemes at all, he probably gave Jackson a distorted view, as he did other Western leaders. Jackson must also have known and perhaps visited Harman Blennerhassett, the

---

[39]*Annals of Congress*, 8th Cong., 1st sess., 553, 556, 631-32, 636.

[40]*Annals of Congress*, 9th Cong., 1st sess., 835-40.

proprietor of a handsome estate on an island in the Ohio River near Parkersburg. Indeed, Blennerhassett Island, in Jackson's own congressional district, became the scene of the overt act of treason alleged in the Burr conspiracy. From there the conspirators dispatched boats and supplies, which they had assembled, down the Ohio for Burr's use.[41]

The Burr conspiracy struck even closer home to Jackson. On the night of 3 and 4 January 1806, Burr and several associates appeared at the United States military post at Chickasaw Bluffs, at present-day Memphis, Tennessee, and inquired whether they could have quarters for the night. The only officer present was Second Lieutenant Jacob Jackson, a younger brother of John. Burr told young Jackson that he had faced attempts in Kentucky to prosecute him on charges that he was planning to invade Spanish dominions. He assured Jackson that he was acting in accord with high officials of the federal government, who had approved an unofficial war against Spanish possessions. Burr stated that the subjects of Spain were in a "very distressed situation" and that his expedition would relieve them from the tyranny of their government.

Burr played heavily upon the credulity of his host. He asked whether Jacob knew the opinion of John G. Jackson regarding his plans. When Jacob replied that he did not, Burr inquired about Jacob's own views. The young Jackson said that if the plan had the approval of the government he was willing to participate. He consented to take service with Burr and received a promise of a captain's commission. He declined, however, to provide Burr with small arms, soldiers to accompany him, or even a soldier to carry a letter to Colonel John McKee in the Chickasaw country. He did allow some of his men to repair muskets and run lead balls for Burr.

Jacob became alarmed when Burr continued to press him, finally asking that he and the soldiers under his command accompany Burr southward. Jacob stated that he could not "seduce the soldiery from their duty while [he] held a commission." He observed that his family was respectable and that he would not do anything to injure them or his own repu-

---

[41]Burr to Jackson, 27 October 1805, John George Jackson Papers. The best account of Burr's activities in the West is Thomas Perkins Abernethy, *The Burr Conspiracy* (New York: Oxford University Press, 1954). See pages 69 and 107-109 for information on the rendezvous at Blennerhassett Island.

tation as an officer. Jackson then bluntly told Burr that he did not want to hear any more about the schemes unless they were completely honorable.

In spite of his suspicions, Jacob fell increasingly under Burr's spell. He consented to offer his resignation from the army and join Burr as soon as he had an acceptance, provided he found Burr "patronized by the United States." Burr reminded Jackson that he knew his father and expressed the hope that the young officer would join him as soon as possible. Fortunately for Jacob, Burr's plans were exposed before his involvement became any deeper. Federal authorities arrested Burr and his close associates and held them for trial in Richmond, Virginia.[42]

Unaware of Burr's attempt to enlist the support of his younger brother, Jackson, along with 108 other members of the House of Representatives, voted for a resolution, introduced by John Randolph, to request the president to lay before Congress all essential information concerning the conspiracy.[43] About a month later Jackson declared in a letter to a worried Jonathan Dayton, who had allegedly agreed to furnish Burr with provisions, that Burr's activities had "opened a wide field of conjecture, & suspicion—as to the aids in money requisite to carry on his extensive project of aggrandizement, which have been furnished, & the sources from whence such streams of wealth could flow into his *treasury*." He told Dayton, with whom he had at various times engaged in land transactions, that although Burr's supporters included office seekers and "flaming patriots of ephemeral existence," he believed that the former vice-president had implicated very honorable men who had never actually participated in his activities.[44]

Whether Jackson by then knew of Jacob's connections with Burr remains unknown. None of his surviving correspondence includes any reference to his brother. At any rate, he wrote James Madison that in the trans-Allegheny region "public expectation stands on tiptoe, gaping at every rumor afloat thro the Country." He cited as an example a report by a Chil-

---

[42]Evidence of Lieutenant Jacob Jackson . . . [19 October 1807], *Annals of Congress*, 10th Cong., 1st sess., 683-85.

[43]*Annals of Congress*, 9th Cong., 2d sess., 336, 355-57.

[44]Jackson to Dayton, 9 February 1807, Gratz Alphabetical Collection, Historical Society of Pennsylvania, Philadelphia.

licothe, Ohio, newspaper that Burr had assassinated General James Wilkinson, an accomplice who had betrayed him.[45]

Never doubting the loyalty of the Jacksons, Madison designated Jackson to take depositions from witnesses "from all points on the Ohio River & in the adjacent Country South of Cincinnati." For that purpose Jackson sent his cousin, young George Jackson, Jr., to gather information, subpoena witnesses, and particularly to "procure proof of the arrival by Blenarhassett [*sic*] or of other persons with boats &c at the mouth of the Cumberland or elsewhere." He instructed George to learn as much as possible concerning "the rendezvous at such place of persons who were on the Island near the little Kanhawa [*sic*] about the period of Blenarhassetts [*sic*] escape." He further informed George that "the primary & indeed almost entire" object of his investigation was to determine whether Blennerhassett and others at the island had acted upon the direction of Burr. Jackson requested George to make the depositions he had obtained available for Burr's trial in Richmond.[46]

His part in gathering evidence in the Burr case caused Jackson "much trouble & vexation." He took deep umbrage at charges of improprieties in procuring letters and in taking affidavits of witnesses. Existing materials provide no clues as to the nature of the alleged improprieties, but it is possible that they were connected with the activities of his brother Jacob. John bitterly resented the fact that Chief Justice John Marshall, who presided at Burr's trial, allowed attacks upon his procedures to be heard in court, for they "excited a suspicion if not of their justice at least of their serious nature." Nor was Jackson satisfied that the grand jury allowed the charges to be dropped without an investigation, which he believed would have exonerated him of any wrongdoing. Acquiescence in Marshall's "partiality of the accused," he maintained, "will disgrace the Government & its Friends"

---

[45]Jackson to Madison, 26 March 1807, James Madison Papers, Alderman Library, University of Virginia, Charlottesville.

[46]John G. Jackson to George Jackson, Jr., 18 April 1807, VFM #14, Manuscripts Department, Ohio Historical Society, Columbus. Jackson provided his cousin with "one of the best horses in the Country and one hundred & fifty dollars" in order to expedite his work. Jackson to Caesar A. Rodney, 19 April 1807, Gratz Alphabetical Collection. A copy of the letter is in VFM #14, Manuscripts Department, Ohio Historical Society.

and produce "a military despotism, where another Buonaparte or a Burr will give Law to the Republic."[47]

Jackson revealed a grasp of the significance of the political enmity between Jefferson and Marshall and of the seriousness of the charge of treason against a high public official. His sympathies were entirely with Jefferson, and he resented efforts to defend Burr by attacking the president. Because Burr was "a great offender & a quondam great man," he declared, the court was willing "to bend every principle of criminal law to the purposes of his acquittal."[48]

Except for the circumstances surrounding the purchase of Louisiana and the international implications of the Burr conspiracy, most of the work of Congress during Jackson's first four years in the House of Representatives revolved around domestic issues. During those years Jackson often spoke for or reflected the views of the administration. On occasion he differed with his own party. Whether combating the Federalists or the "Quids" in the Republican ranks, he spoke with vigor and assurance, and not infrequently with an acerbity that left deep political and personal scars. His wide and sometimes profound learning, cogent reasoning, and solid connections with the executive branch of the government made him a formidable adversary. They also stamped him as one of the most promising young congressmen to arrive in Washington in the wake of the Jeffersonian victory of 1800.

---

[47]James Madison to Jackson, 30 May 1807, John George Jackson Papers; Jackson to James Madison, 5 July 1807, James Madison Papers, Library of Congress.

[48]Jackson to James Madison, 21 June 1807, James Madison Papers, Library of Congress.

5 DEFENDER OF AMERICAN RIGHTS

In the spring of 1807 John G. Jackson entered the race for congressman from the First District of Virginia for the third time. He defeated his opponent, Noah Linsly, a Wheeling Federalist, apparently by a substantial margin. In Brooke and Randolph counties he received 230 votes to 137 for Linsly. The Federalists usually held a commanding majority in Monongalia County, but Jackson "invaded their strong hold" and won a majority of 43 over Linsly. In Wheeling itself he trailed Linsly by only 19 votes, garnering 84 to his opponent's 103.[1]

Jackson returned to a Washington preoccupied with foreign affairs, which would demand much of the attention of Congress during his next two terms. He himself had long watched the events in Europe with keen interest and insight and had formed firm ideas regarding policies of the new American nation. A staunch advocate of the freedom of the seas, Jackson had expressed the hope in 1801, while he was a member of the Virginia legislature, that Napoleon would join the Armed Neutrality of the North to force Great Britain to respect the "immutable rights of nations" on the high seas. Such an association, he believed, should "interdict all Commercial Intercourse" with Great Britain, and the United States should aid it with all its power.[2]

---

[1]Washington *National Intelligencer*, 28 April 1807; John G. Jackson to Caesar A. Rodney, 19 April 1807, Gratz Collection, Historical Society of Pennsylvania, Philadelphia; Wheeling *Repository*, 9 April 1807.

[2]John G. Jackson to James Madison, 3 August 1801, James Madison Papers, Alderman Library, University of Virginia, Charlottesville.

Anti-monarchical views and a belief in a special mission for the United States in world affairs lent a distinct coloring to Jackson's analysis of foreign affairs. The failure of the coalition of powers against France and preliminary discussions leading to the Peace of Amiens in 1802 appeared to him to be "another striking proof of the advantages of a republic over monarchy." Americans, he declared, should thank "the genius who presides over the destinies of the U. S. (viz. the *vox populi*) that we were not drawn into the destructive vortex altho menaced by the wrath of God by Mr. Adams." The mistaken policy of England, he concluded, must show that the United States should "be justly considered as an asylum for the virtuous oppressed of all nations."[3]

Although Jackson had earlier opposed large peacetime military forces, he regarded the protection of American seamen as the quintessence of the maintenance of neutral rights. He took great satisfaction in the unanimous approval by the House of Representatives on 17 November 1803 of a resolution that "free ships make free goods."[4] When on 23 January 1806 the House took up the question of appropriating a sum not to exceed $150,000 for the defense of American ports and harbors, Jackson declared, "It is high time that the representatives of the nation should deliberate on the subject." He held that the United States should "not only repel the aggressions, but . . . [should] chastise those who offer them." The nation should "expend the last cent before we submit to degradations offered to us." With consistency, Jackson supported bills that came before the House in April 1806 to provide the president with $300,000 to build two frigates and to create a "Naval Peace Establishment."[5]

During the winter of 1806 Jackson pressed for retaliatory measures against Great Britain. On 29 January, after waiting two months for the Ways and Means Committee to act, the House moved to bypass the committee and consider America's relation to England. Brushing aside a proposal by John Smilie of Pennsylvania to delay discussion because a similar resolution was also in a special committee, Jackson declared, "[I]n the name of

---

[3]John G. Jackson to James Madison, 19 December 1801, James Madison Papers, New York Public Library, New York, New York.

[4]*Annals of Congress*, 8th Cong., 1st sess., 563-64.

[5]*Annals of Congress*, 9th Cong., 1st sess., 377, 382, 1076, 1078.

heaven, if we are not disposed to do anything, let us tell the people so." Jackson undoubtedly sympathized with a resolution offered by John Gregg of Pennsylvania to ban importation of products grown or manufactured in Great Britain. Conversely, he must have abhorred an alternative resolution, offered by Congressman John Clay of Pennsylvania, that in effect would have bowed to the *Essex* decision and reimposed the "rule of 1756," which held that trade closed to a nation in time of peace remained so in time of war.

Recognizing the dangers of a split between Republicans who favored the Gregg Resolution and conservative members of the party who supported Clay, the Jefferson administration offered a compromise resolution. Introduced by Joseph Nicholson of Pennsylvania, it excluded from nonimportation goods that Americans could not produce themselves or obtain from other countries. Endeavoring to force Great Britain to terms without injury to Americans, Nicholson presented a list of articles that could be restricted without any damage to the American economy.[6]

Ever loyal to Jefferson and to Madison, the secretary of state, Jackson spoke at length on 11 March in favor of the Nicholson Resolution. Again he found himself in verbal combat with John Randolph, who had alleged "backstairs" influence upon the administration and charged that the measure jeopardized the interests of the entire nation for the benefit of a few merchants. Jackson held that the Nicholson Resolution was beneficial to farmers as well as merchants. He disagreed with those who urged patience with Great Britain on the ground that she was standing alone in the face of "universal despotism." He argued that Great Britain herself was more dependent upon materials from abroad than was the United States and that cutting off her trade was as serious as a French army invading Ireland. Unless the United States took some coercive steps, he maintained, Great Britain would never negotiate. Jackson rejected the contention that the nation would lose more by going to war than by enduring suffering and losses. He declared that he would as soon go to war to protect the freedom of the seas as "the right of highway on terra firma."[7]

---

[6]Norman K. Risjord, *The Old Republicans: Southern Conservatism in the Age of Jefferson* (New York: Columbia University Press, 1965) 54. For Jackson's response to Smilie, see *Annals of Congress*, 9th Cong., 1st sess., 411.

[7]*Annals of Congress*, 9th Cong., 1st sess., 724, 726-29, 737.

Jackson undoubtedly helped forge a strong Republican phalanx in support of the administration. Galling as were the British interferences with American trade, he declared, they were "as but a drop in the ocean" compared with the impressment of three thousand American seamen. "It is far better to die contending for our rights, than tamely to sit down and crouch under injustice," he insisted. Fortunately for Jackson and other administration supporters, John Randolph alienated numerous members of the House with a "severe philippic" attacking the president, the secretary of state, and Congress itself, furthering the decline of his own influence in the House. The administration scored a victory on 17 March when the Nicholson Resolution passed the House 87 to 35, with only 9 Republicans joining the Federalist minority.[8]

Excitement over British interferences with American trade subsided during the summer of 1806. Jackson believed that Madison's policies were partially responsible and expressed the belief that "if Great Britain is not madly determined on a war of extermination with all nations, she will not be deaf to the remonstrances of ours."[9] In the changed atmosphere, a proposal of Randolph to suspend the Non-Importation Act, which had not yet gone into effect, received a favorable response in the House of Representatives. Convinced that the mere threat of nonimportation had produced a beneficial effect in Anglo-American relations, the House voted to suspend the act until 1 July 1807. Jackson voted with the majority.[10]

Meanwhile, Randolph and conservative Republicans raised objections to moves to acquire Florida. As early as 1804 James Monroe, the American minister to France, had tried in vain to negotiate a Spanish recognition of American claims to West Florida. His successor in Paris, John Armstrong, wrote Madison in December 1804 that France intended to profit financially from any American understanding with Spain. Randolph opposed a request of Jefferson for two million dollars for the acquisition on the ground that the money would end up in the coffers of France. Despite Randolph's opposition, on 11 January 1806 the House appropriated the money re-

---

[8]Ibid., 732-33, 738; Risjord, *Old Republicans*, 57-58, 60-61, 70-78.

[9]John G. Jackson to James Madison, 23 June 1806, James Madison Papers, New York Public Library.

[10]*Annals of Congress*, 9th Cong., 2d sess., 114, 127, 382.

quested by a vote of 77 to 58. Although he deplored the secrecy surrounding the administration's request and a dissembling attitude by Randolph, Jackson believed that the nation must have the Floridas. He staunchly supported moves to acquire the territory.[11]

As the second session of the Eighth Congress drew to a close in 1807, Mary Jackson's declining health diverted Jackson's attention from national problems. By the time Congress adjourned on 3 March, Mary was so ill that her mother decided to accompany the Jacksons to Clarksburg. Mary was then in the last stages of tuberculosis, and in addition, she may have been pregnant, since she bore Jackson a son some time in 1807.[12]

In June 1807 while Jackson was in Clarksburg, news arrived that the British man-of-war *Leopard* had attacked the *Chesapeake*, an American frigate, in Chesapeake Bay. The commander of the *Leopard* forcibly removed alleged British deserters. During the boarding his men killed three and wounded eighteen of the crew of the *Chesapeake*. Angered by the insult, Jefferson ordered all British warships out of American waters and made the complete cessation of impressment a sine qua non for the restoration of amicable relations between the United States and Great Britain.[13]

Jackson reacted to the *Chesapeake* incident with an indignation that was extreme even for him. He took the lead in organizing a mass meeting of Harrison Countians, who were as outraged as he, and personally drew up resolutions they adopted in condemnation of the British attack. To the assemblage, which included Federalists as well as Republicans, Jackson made an address of "some length, recapitulating the British attacks upon our rights, our commerce[,] our seamen & our sovereignty & such a flame was kindled by it, that it was difficult to suppress an avowal of the opinion that the day

---

[11]James Madison to John G. Jackson, 4 March 1825, John George Jackson Papers, Lilly Library, Indiana University, Bloomington; James Madison to John G. Jackson, 1 April 1805, ibid.; *Annals of Congress*, 9th Cong., 1st sess., 749, 953, 995, 1028. See also Risjord, *Old Republicans*, 44-48.

[12]Lucy Washington to Mary Coles Payne, 15 February 1807, Mary Allen Cassady Collection, Fincastle, Virginia. See also Dorothy Davis, *John George Jackson* (Parsons WV: McClain Printing Company, 1976) 122-24.

[13]Samuel Flagg Bemis, *A Diplomatic History of the United States*, 5th ed. (New York: Holt, Rinehart and Winston, Inc., 1965) 145-46.

of negociation [*sic*] has passed by."[14] Jackson believed that "never did there occur, & there never (in my opinion) can occur any event which will so effectually unite the nation & swallow up all the political schismatics that have disgraced us too long."[15]

Because of the crisis, Congress convened on 26 October 1807, nearly a month before the customary time. Jackson, however, could not be present for the opening. Throughout the summer and autumn his wife slowly wasted away. The death of her mother at Clarksburg in mid-October had such an adverse effect upon her that Jackson abandoned plans for returning to Washington for the beginning of the session.[16] Other troubles also descended upon him. In October he fell victim to influenza during an epidemic that swept the Western country. Then, in late December, irate litigants in a criminal case he was prosecuting in Clarksburg waylaid him and inflicted injuries that endangered his own life.[17]

Although he could not be present when Congress assembled, Jackson watched the events with all the attention his personal circumstances would allow. He wrote Madison that he considered it "almost cowardice to be absent from our posts" at such a critical time. He particularly regretted his inability to participate in choosing the Speaker of the House and selecting the committees, because he believed that the decisions made would have an important effect on the course of future events.[18]

The continuing attacks of Randolph and his followers on the Jefferson administration struck Jackson as nothing short of treason. Randolph's rid-

---

[14]John G. Jackson to James Madison, 2 August 1807, James Madison Papers, Library of Congress, Washington, D.C.

[15]John G. Jackson to James Madison, 8 November 1807, James Madison Papers, Alderman Library. See also Jackson to Madison, 2 August 1807, James Madison Papers, Library of Congress.

[16]John G. Jackson to James Madison, 18 October 1807, James Madison Papers, Library of Congress; John G. Jackson to James Madison, 25 October 1807, ibid.

[17]John G. Jackson to James Madison, 11 October 1807, ibid.; John G. Jackson to James Madison, 10 December 1807, ibid.; John G. Jackson to James Madison, 25 December 1807, ibid.

[18]John G. Jackson to James Madison, 11 October 1807, ibid.

icule of Jefferson's call for improved coastal fortifications and the construction of gunboats led Jackson to declare that even at this juncture a few "ci-devant Republicans" would oppose "the wisest measures of resistance." He told Madison that he yearned to return to the House to help make sound judgments and to cover "with confusion & disgrace the machinations of that Junto who riot upon the anticipated ruin of their Country."[19]

Meanwhile, Mary Jackson continued to decline. Although she lingered on until 13 February 1808, Jackson knew that the Christmas of 1807 would be her last. In an attempt to cheer her, he purchased Pinnickinnick, a tract near their house. Its lofty hill covered with fruit trees and "its beautiful rivulet meandering through the meadow" presented a scene suited to Mary's "excellent taste" and one "which she so delighted in." Jackson later confessed, "It [also] . . . had charms for me, but [since Mary's death] they have fled from my grasp."[20]

On 25 February 1808, less than two weeks after Mary's death, Jackson resumed his responsibilities in Congress. During his absence divisions had deepened, not only between Federalists and Republicans but also within Republican ranks, over responses of the administration to the British Orders in Council and to the Berlin and Milan decrees of Napoleon.[21] On 22 December 1807 Congress passed the Embargo, which banned the departure of all vessels lying in American harbors and bound for foreign ports. Madison informed Jackson on 31 December that "the Embargo is now in operation, and if no symptoms of flinching appear as I hope will be the

---

[19]John G. Jackson to James Madison, 27 November 1807, ibid.

[20]John G. Jackson to James Madison, 20 November 1807, ibid. Jackson's statement regarding Pinnickinnick appears in his will, dated 1 January 1809, reproduced in an undated newspaper clipping, probably from the Clarksburg *Telegram*, Meigs-Jackson Papers, Blennerhassett Historical Park Commission, Parkersburg, West Virginia (hereinafter cited as Meigs-Jackson Papers, BHPC). See also Davis, *John George Jackson*, 134; John G. Jackson to Mary S. Meigs, 17 May [1810?], Meigs-Jackson Papers, BHPC.

[21]*Annals of Congress*, 10th Cong., 1st sess., 1683. For the effects of the British and French policies, see Risjord, *Old Republicans*, 79-86; Bemis, *Diplomatic History of the United States*, 147-51.

case, cannot fail to do good in many ways." Jackson staunchly supported the Embargo and the various acts supplemental to it.[22]

The failure of the Embargo to force the two great European belligerents to respect the rights of the United States as a neutral nation deeply disappointed Jackson. He attributed the continued embarrassments suffered by the United States to the "perfidy of our own Countrymen" and declared that "they have impressed England with a belief that the people do not cooperate with the govt. & hence their perseverance in the ruinous measures resorted to by them." He particularly lashed out at the "mercantile cupidity & the disaffection of Massachusetts." In a *volte-face* from his public position in the debate on the Nicholson Resolution, he declared that the mercantile interest would "ride triumphant upon the necks of the agricultural & manufacturing interest" and "on that of the govt too."[23]

Although the outcries against the Embargo became louder, Jackson remained one of its strongest defenders. On 2 December 1808 he spoke on American relations with Great Britain. He traced the effects of both British and French policies upon American commerce and declared that he had no sympathy for either of the belligerents. Nevertheless, he concluded that British actions had proved more harmful to American interests than the French and that the Embargo was a means of forcing recognition of American rights by the warring powers. The time had come, Jackson declared, when "if we do not submit, it is war; if we do submit, it is tribute." He hoped that our motto might again be "*Millions for defence, and not a cent for tribute.*"

Convinced that the United States must not retire from the ocean, Jackson supported measures to increase the strength of the navy. He defended the president, who had been charged by his enemies with lack of candor and a desire to excite a war. He himself found the "principle of Executive confidence repugnant to the Constitution," but he believed that in the existing situation Jefferson must be guarded in his statements. Jackson noted that the Constitution vested the powers of war and peace, raising armies

---

[22]James Madison to John G. Jackson, 31 December 1807, John George Jackson Papers; *Annals of Congress*, 10th Cong., 1st sess., 1712-13.

[23]John G. Jackson to James Madison, 17 July 1808, James Madison Papers, Library of Congress.

and navies, and levying taxes in Congress and that the president could not conduct a maritime war without the support of Congress.[24]

Meanwhile, Federalists in Harrison County held a public meeting in Clarksburg to protest administration policies with respect to Great Britain. Jackson's political adversary, Benjamin Wilson, Jr., served as chairman. The participants endorsed resolutions charging the administration with partiality toward France and calling for repeal of the Embargo. Recognizing the political character of the meeting, Jackson addressed a public letter to James Pindall, who had served as secretary. He denied the allegation that the government had given any advantage to France and suggested that in view of the magnitude of the crimes that Great Britain had committed, such as had occurred in the *Chesapeake* affair, men of all parties should stand together. He justified the Embargo by providing a catalog of violations of American coastal waters by the belligerents, which made the most stringent measures necessary.[25]

Undeterred by the report from Harrison County, Jackson on 10 January 1809 struck again at critics of the administration. He bitterly denounced a charge by Congressman Josiah Quincy of Massachusetts that the original purpose of the Embargo was to preserve American seamen and vessels, frighten George Rose, the British minister to the United States, compel Great Britain to yield to the coalition of European powers, and bring about American entry into that coalition. Only the first of Quincy's contentions, Jackson said, was correct. To Jackson, Quincy and other Federalists were no better than Nero, "to whom the melody of music produced by the bow which he drew across the strings of his fine toned instrument, was not half so harmonious . . . as the crackling fires of Rome, the crash of falling towers, the cries of its women and children, and the universal ruin of his country." It was time, he declared, that they cease their attacks upon the president and desist from their "treasonable activities." With mounting impatience, he warned that he would "not suffer the mantle of charity longer to cover such men."[26]

---

[24]*Annals of Congress*, 10th Cong., 2d sess., 550, 634-60, 1050.

[25]Morgantown *Monongalia Gazette*, 20 January 1809.

[26]*Annals of Congress*, 10th Cong., 2d sess., 1122, 1132.

Although he urged congressmen not be influenced by newspapers or a few popular meetings, Jackson knew that the Embargo could not remain in effect indefinitely. He therefore supported a resolution offered by Wilson Cary Nicholas of Virginia for setting a termination date for the Embargo, with the stipulation that if England and France still had their objectionable decrees in effect at that time the United States would issue letters of marque and reprisal against them. Any other course following removal of the Embargo, Jackson believed, would amount to submission. He favored continuing the act in effect until at least 1 June 1809, which he believed was consistent with "the honor and dignity of the nation." He asserted that this date would give the European powers time to decide whether they would have war or render justice to the United States, but he may have desired to place termination beyond the retirement of Jefferson, for whom the unpopular measure had become almost a point of honor.[27]

Jackson especially resented allegations that the president and Secretary of State Madison had pressed the Embargo upon Congress in opposition to other cabinet members. In a letter not entirely devoid of political overtones, he wrote to Jefferson concerning a speech reportedly made by former Secretary of the Navy and Attorney General Robert Smith at Martinsburg, (West) Virginia, in which Smith had made such charges. Jackson attributed Smith's "venom & Gall" to the possibility that Madison, rather than Smith, would soon be presiding over the national affairs. Jefferson affirmed his confidence in Smith and dismissed the statements allegedly made by him as efforts of the Federalists to sow discord among members of the administration.[28]

Even after the Embargo proved unworkable, Jackson favored persevering in it for the sake of the honor of the nation. He declared that "he was not yet prepared for burning the law of nations, and substituting force for law." On 23 February 1809 Jackson proposed an amendment to the Non-Intercourse Bill then before the House. Strikingly similar to Macon's Bill Number 2, it authorized the president to remove the Embargo at the end of fifty days against the belligerent repealing its objectionable decrees and

[27]Ibid., 1232, 1254-56.

[28]Jackson to Jefferson, 9 October 1808, John George Jackson Papers. See also Jackson to D[olley] P. Madison, 8 October 1808, James Madison Papers, Library of Congress; Jefferson to Jackson, 13 October 1808, John George Jackson Papers.

to issue letters of marque and reprisal. Jackson's amendment failed of passage.[29]

On 25 February Jackson proposed another amendment, which could not be considered as an offer to either power that the United States would take sides against the other. This amendment authorized and required the president, if Britain refused to repeal her decrees, to use militia and regular troops "to take possession of the territories of His Britannic Majesty, bordering on the United States and to hold the same." The motion required the president to instruct commanders of public armed vessels of the United States to "subdue, seize, and take any armed or unarmed British vessels on the high seas or elsewhere" and to grant commissions to privateers. The same provisions relating to the sea applied to France if she did not repeal her decrees. John W. Eppes declared that Jackson's amendment embodied "a proposition which he hoped might unite all parties in the House." Barent Gardenier of New York, however, maintained that Jackson's amendment was unconstitutional in that the power to declare war belonged to Congress and could not be delegated. Jackson's second amendment was also defeated.[30]

Although Jackson moved to postpone action, the Non-Intercourse Bill passed the House on 27 February 1809, by a vote of 81 to 40. Perhaps many of the members by then shared the view of James Sloan of New Jersey, who declared that "the people, as well as himself, were so heartily tired of the embargo that they would be glad to get anything else in its place." Sloan noted that the bill contained a limitation on the time that the Embargo would remain in force and stated his hope that "it would [then] be *dead, dead, dead.*" Jackson apparently could not bring himself to vote in favor of the final bill, and, as he frequently did on such occasions, he abstained from voting. He is listed as among the eleven members of the House "in the city, but not present at the vote, being absent from illness or other causes."[31]

Jackson clearly hoped to make the handling of foreign affairs the major issue in the presidential election of 1808 in western Virginia and in his own race for reelection to Congress the following year. On 10 September 1808

---

[29]*Annals of Congress*, 10th Cong., 2d sess., 1507-10.

[30]Ibid., 1523, 1524, 1526.

[31]Ibid., 1527, 1541.

a number of Ohio County Republicans, probably at Jackson's suggestion, met to consider the merits of "the several gentlemen in nomination for President and Vice-President" of the United States. They named a committee of seven members, chaired by William McKinley, Jackson's close political ally. The committee drew up a resolution affirming that the federal government had "adopted the most wise and prudent measures in their power, to prevent the calamities of war, and to support the dignity of the nation." The committee further stated that "we can in no way more clearly evince our approbation of the measures of the present administration than by electing James Madison President, and George Clinton Vice-President" in the coming elections. Although the congressional elections were nearly a year away, the Ohio County gathering also resolved that "the past services of our present Representative in Congress, John G. Jackson, meet our approbation, and, together with his firm adherence to republican principles, merit a continuation of our support at the next congressional election."

Before adjourning, the Ohio County gathering set up a Committee of Vigilance of thirteen members to call meetings of neighboring groups as often as might be necessary. In addition, it established a standing committee of five members who were directed to correspond with the Committee of Vigilance and, if necessary, summon meetings of citizens. With an organization reminiscent of that set up in Virginia in 1800 to promote the election of Jefferson as president, the Ohio Countians resolved to "use every justifiable means in their power, to promote the republican Electoral ticket for the state of Virginia, and also the election of John G. Jackson for Congress."[32]

Elated at the victory of Madison in 1808, Jackson faced his own contest for reelection with considerable confidence. The day after Madison's inauguration, Jackson left Washington for Clarksburg and the waging of his campaign. He told Madison on the eve of the elections in the six counties that made up his congressional district that the parties had "taken their stand . . . decisively, the one for base submission [and] the other for resistance in all its forms."[33] Jackson declared that "never were the exertions

[32]Wheeling *Repository*, 17 September 1808.

[33]Jackson to Madison, 24 March 1809, James Madison Papers, Library of Congress; Davis, *John George Jackson*, 150.

of my friends & those of Mr. [Noah] Lindsley [*sic*] my opponent half so great."[34]

On 6 March 1809 Joseph Tomlinson, Thomas Evans, and William McKinley disseminated a handbill entitled "Address to the Freeholders of Ohio County, Virginia." In it they extolled Jackson's record in Congress, his zeal in protecting the rights of the United States, and his concern for the local interests of his constituents. They declared that he was "a leading and influential member of the republican party in Congress" and that he was "acquainted with, and in the confidence of the president and heads of the executive departments of our government, which added to his eminent talents, and acquaintance with public business, qualified him in a peculiar manner, for the high station, of representative of the people."[35]

In an address entitled "To the Citizens of Ohio County," the Federalists took sharp issue with the charges of the Republicans that the New England states had engaged in treasonable activities, that Noah Linsly had given support to Aaron Burr, and that Linsly would have less influence in Congress than Jackson. Oddly enough, they did not publish their address until April, "lest it should be considered an electioneering production." On 12 August, long after the elections, William McKinley, in another handbill addressed to the Federalists, declared, "It is not my destruction alone that you aim at; but your deep-rooted hatred is at J. G. Jackson, esq. and to accomplish his ruin it is necessary that all his friends should be first put down."[36]

Despite the bitterness engendered during the campaign, Jackson was reelected to Congress in the spring of 1809 by a vote of 1,326 to 872. He carried every county with the exception of Ohio, Linsly's home county, and he lost that by only two votes. He told Madison that if the Erskine

---

[34]Jackson to James Madison, 8 April 1809, James Madison Papers, Library of Congress.

[35]For a copy of this handbill, see Daniel P. Jordan, ed., "Congressional Electioneering in Early West Virginia: A Mini-War in Broadsides, 1809," *West Virginia History* 33 (October 1971): 65-68.

[36]Ibid., 68-78.

Agreement with Great Britain had been known to the people before the election his majority would have been even greater.[37]

Although it had produced a soothing effect upon the people, Jackson believed that the Erskine Agreement of April 1809, by which Great Britain promised to withdraw her Orders in Council and the United States promised to remove nonintercourse restrictions upon her, offered little hope for an enduring improvement in relations between the two countries. His contention that "Great Britain has in fact promised nothing" proved to be remarkably accurate. He opposed a bill, introduced by Randolph on 24 May 1809 in the wake of the Erskine Agreement, calling for the immediate abandonment of the additional military forces created by the act of 12 April 1808 and for the application of the unexpended balance appropriated for gunboats toward equipping the militia. He pointed out that Madison, in his presidential message, had stated that "It will rest with the judgment of Congress to decide how far the change in our external prospects may authorize any modifications of the laws relating to the Army and Navy establishments" and that the House had already set up committees for that purpose. Despite Jackson's objections, Randolph's bill passed without the necessity of a roll call vote.[38]

Two days later Jackson took issue with Randolph again. He spoke against a resolution introduced by Randolph approving the "promptitude and frankness" with which Madison had met the overtures of the British government toward the restoration of harmony and free commercial intercourse with the United States. Aware of the dubious compliment intended, Jackson declared that the House should not single out specific administration policies for endorsement or censure. He maintained that it had "nobler duties to perform than passing abstract resolutions out of which no legislative act is contemplated; merely for the purpose of pouring the oil of adulation upon the head of the Chief Magistrate." Moreover, he believed that the people were "enlightened and intelligent" and did not need

---

[37]Washington *National Intelligencer*, 8 May 1809; John G. Jackson to James Madison, 17 April 1809, James Madison Papers, Library of Congress; John G. Jackson to James Madison, 1 May 1809, ibid. See also Daniel Porter Jordan, Jr., "Virginia Congressmen, 1801-1825" (Ph.D. dissertation, University of Virginia, 1970) 378.

[38]*Annals of Congress*, 11th Cong., 1st sess., 63-64, 67, 71, 440.

to "wait for this House to spirit them to an examination and decision of great national questions." The House, on motion by Jackson, tabled Randolph's resolution.[39]

On 30 May Jackson was appointed chairman of a select committee of the House of Representatives to consider the parts of President Madison's message pertaining to foreign relations. Jackson vigorously denied that he was "the oracular organ" of the administration and declared that he was "unwilling to have [his] rights invaded by an insinuation of this kind." In keeping with his declaration of independence of view, he continued to favor the United States's strong stand to protect her rights as a neutral. During subsequent debates regarding revisions of the Non-Intercourse Act, he held to his view that the United States had suffered far more acutely from British restrictions than from the French decrees. He contended in June 1809 that the United States should not allow its waters to be a place of refuge for armed vessels of either belligerent while the nation was at peace. If, as a result of these policies, "we have war and are attacked," he declared, "I would be armed at all points; I would fight the shark at sea and the tiger on land."[40]

Even Jackson was unprepared for the news that George Canning, the British Foreign Secretary, had repudiated the Erskine Agreement on the ground that the minister to the United States had exceeded his instructions.[41] Madison was forced to reimpose nonintercourse against Great Britain, a decision Jackson assured him he had authority to make under provisions of the Non-Intercourse Act.[42] Jackson continued to hope that Erskine would make some "eclaircissement" that might "find its way to the public." Inevitably, he believed, the people would express "in language alike, audible & unequivocal, their honest indignation at this flagitious out-

---

[39]Ibid., 109, 114, 219.

[40]Ibid., 152, 225-28.

[41]For the reaction of the government and the American people to the repudiation of the Erskine Agreement, see, for instance, Thomas A. Bailey, *A Diplomatic History of the American People*, 8th ed. (New York: Appleton-Century-Crofts, 1969) 132.

[42]Jackson to Madison, 28 July 1809, James Madison Papers, Library of Congress.

rage, & their firm determination to rally round their public functionaries in support of their insulted honor & independance [*sic*]." For himself, he declared, "My blood boils at the recital of Mr[.] Canning's intolerable insults."[43]

The Non-Intercourse Act soon proved as much a failure as the Embargo. In the spring of 1810 debate in the House of Representatives revolved around Macon's Bill Number 2, which provided for the restoration of nonintercourse against Great Britain if France should repeal her decrees or against France if Britain should repeal hers. Jackson took very little part in the debates, but he spoke against giving the president authority to protect American commerce with the "public armed vessels." American naval strength was scarcely sufficient, he declared, to protect the coasts from pirates, and to employ it against Great Britain was "using pigmy means for gigantic purposes."[44]

Jackson's defense of the administration sometimes led to personal exchanges with his colleagues. The most serious of these encounters occurred during a House investigation into the activities of General Francisco Miranda, the South American revolutionary. In his endeavor to obtain support for winning the independence of his native Venezuela from Spain, Miranda sought first to obtain funds from Great Britain. Partly in order to learn more of British intentions, James Madison, then secretary of state, made known through an intermediary that he would receive Miranda during the latter's visit to the United States. Miranda attended a cabinet meeting and sat next to President Jefferson at dinner, both unwise arrangements that gave rise to reports that he had obtained at least semiofficial support for his plans.

Miranda made the most of his opportunities while he was in the United States. He organized a private filibustering expedition, with vessels supplied by Samuel G. Ogden and manned by young Americans, and gained support from Colonel William Stephens Smith, surveyor of the port of New York and the son-in-law of former President John Adams. Venezuelan authorities, however, foiled his plans, seizing his American vessel, the *Leander*, and lodging the American participants in the attempted coup in a Cartagena prison. The incident produced a loud outcry in the United States.

---

[43]Jackson to Madison, 17 August 1809, John George Jackson Papers.

[44]*Annals of Congress*, 11th Cong., 2d sess., 2022-23.

Federalists, supported by Aaron Burr, tried to implicate the administration, particularly Jefferson and Madison, in the Miranda affair, although neither official had acted improperly. Madison had, in fact, made it clear to Miranda at the outset that the United States would not sanction an armed expedition against Spain. Nor would she engage in illicit or nefarious activities in behalf of Miranda. The most reprehensible action was that of Federalist Rufus King, the American minister to London, who arranged for Miranda to be received by Madison in the first place and knowingly allowed some of his associates to become involved in Miranda's activities under the illusion that they had official sanction. When Madison realized that he and Jefferson would be pictured as accomplices of Miranda, he took steps, with Jefferson's approval, to prosecute criminally Ogden, Smith, and others responsible for sending out vessels. The trial jury, dominated by Federalists, acquitted Smith and Ogden, and the administration, chastened for its indiscretion, was ready to end the matter.[45]

On 13 June 1809, nearly four years later, the House of Representatives considered the petition of thirty-six American citizens who had participated in Miranda's expedition and were then "confined in the vaults of Cartagena, South America." During the debates a resolution was introduced to empower the president to take steps to liberate the prisoners if it were clear that "they were involuntarily drawn into the unlawful enterprise." Congressman Joseph Pearson, a North Carolina Federalist, was among those who held that participants in the Miranda expedition did not know its purpose or destination and discovered too late "the deception that had been practiced upon them." Pearson revived the allegation that some of the "principal officers of this Government" had connived in the preparation for the expedition. Specifically, he charged that the trial of Ogden and Smith had adduced evidence that the expedition had been "begun, prepared, and set on foot, with the knowledge and approbation of the President of the United States and the Secretary of State." Therefore, Pearson urged an appropriation of money for the release of the prisoners.[46]

---

[45]Stephen W. Brown, "Satisfaction at Bladensburg: The Pearson-Jackson Duel of 1809," *North Carolina Historical Review* 58 (January 1981): 29-31. For a detailed account of Miranda's activities in the United States, see Irving Brant, *James Madison: Secretary of State, 1801-1809* (Indianapolis: The Bobbs-Merrill Company, Inc., 1953) 323-39.

[46]*Annals of Congress*, 11th Cong., 1st sess., 269, 277-79.

Pearson, who had been a member of the House for less than three weeks, either through malice or indiscretion, opened an old wound. Jackson, always quick to rise to the defense of the administration, declared that he opposed "squandering money on these persons, whilst the old soldiers of the Revolution were yet unprovided for and in distress." He professed to agree that if the government of the United States had connived with or encouraged the participants in the expedition, it should indemnify them and conduct a full investigation. He then vented his anger on Pearson personally, declaring, "I do not know the method of doing it, but I believe if there was any manner of bringing the gentleman to the bar to exhibit and substantiate his charge, it ought to be done." He asked whether "any new testimony is forthcoming in addition to that on which the House at the last session, made a solemn decision?"[47]

Nathaniel Macon of North Carolina, the Speaker of the House, expressed disapproval of Jackson's antagonistic manner and regretted that "his colleague had used such words." Jackson responded that he had not reprehended Pearson's remarks but merely wished to say that if they were correct he would take a different view than that which he held. Macon reminded Jackson that it was not the practice "to call to the bar of the House any member for what he should say in debate."[48]

The following day Pearson himself responded to Jackson, who, he said, had been as "agitated, quickened, and roused, as if some *demon*, some evil spirit had rushed through these walls, and threatened us with destruction." Although Jackson had demanded that Pearson be called "to the bar of the House" to explain his charges, the North Carolinian declared that he did not "conceive the language and the propositions of the gentleman [Jackson] as *directly insulting*."

Pearson might have stopped at that point, but, like Jackson, he declared his belief that from the manner of Jackson's remarks "more was intended than expressed" and that the statements were "well calculated to produce unpleasant sensations, if not a wound to [his] feelings." Pearson added that he had not stated facts, but only inferences deducible from circumstances, and that it was not his fault if Jackson could not see the dif-

---

[47]Ibid., 281.

[48]Ibid., 282.

ferences. He then declared, with Jackson before him, that "not only the call of my country shall be obeyed, but also any *private* call which it may be honorable to meet." Pearson's vehemence excited Jackson even more. The Virginian professed himself at a loss to understand "how gentlemen, when they say that they feel themselves offended, should lay themselves open again." Throwing off the cloak of congressional immunity, he thundered back, "I hold myself responsible anywhere for anything which I have said."[49]

Numerous reports and abusive editorials in rabidly partisan newspapers in the following weeks exacerbated the wounds of Jackson and Pearson, real or imagined, and goaded them into positions in which each felt compelled to protect his honor. The most vituperative of the articles appeared in the Baltimore *Federal Republican and Commercial Gazette* about two weeks after Congress adjourned. The writer declared that in Congress "no man makes more bluster or a greater parade of courage than a certain valorous knight from a Western District of Virginia, sometimes called . . . the knight of the order of Triplet [*sic*]." This crude reference to Jackson's personal misstep with Frances Emelia Triplett was coupled with the assertion that "he is a mere puff of wind, which would evaporate at the first appearance of danger."

In an exceedingly sarcastic and contemptuous tone, the writer of the article attempted to convey the impression that Jackson would do everything possible to avoid a duel. He stated that Jackson had failed previously to respond to an invitation by Congressman John Rowan of Kentucky to repeat remarks made in the House of Representatives outside that chamber; that in defending his uncle in a trial, Jackson had taken "improper liberties" with a witness and apologized when the witness demanded it outside the Harrison County courthouse; and that he had made frantic efforts through a mysteriously arranged conference to avoid a duel with William G. Payne, a Monongalia County lawyer, in 1804. Finally, he charged Jackson with cheating at cards in Richmond and failing to demand satis-

---

[49]Ibid., 305. For details of the exchanges between Jackson and Pearson in the House of Representatives, see also Brown, "Satisfaction at Bladensburg: The Pearson-Jackson Duel of 1809," 32-33.

faction of John Evans, an expert marksman from Monongalia County, who circulated the story.[50]

Nine days after the article in the Baltimore newspaper appeared, the *National Intelligencer* carried a report of Jackson's remarks concerning Pearson. The report was generally accurate, but there were some questions about Jackson's phraseology. Pearson, under pressure to challenge Jackson, inquired of the latter on 7 August whether the *Intelligencer* statement was incorrect. If so, Pearson believed that Jackson should correct it; if not, he regretted that he had been deceived by Jackson. He asked Jackson for an immediate reply in order that he might determine his course of action.[51]

Jackson, then at home in Clarksburg, made his reply on 25 August, the day after he received Pearson's letter. He told Pearson that he had not used certain words attributed to him but was not able to recall his precise words. At his request, his friend, Congressman John W. Eppes of Virginia, had reduced them to writing. When Jackson heard nothing further from Pearson he either destroyed the copy or left it in Washington. Jackson told Pearson that he was unable to make any real distinction between the version of his remark that the "groundless & slanderous charge [of Pearson against the Jefferson administration] should be made openly & not covertly avowed" and Pearson's own acknowledgement that he and his friends understood that Jackson "would always oppose (or repel) any unfounded, declamatory or unworthy charge" made against it. Jackson declared that he found the North Carolinian's manner offensive and that if he "had ever disposition to terminate this affair to [Pearson's] satisfaction, [he] could not ask correction by the editor."[52]

Nearly two months passed without further communication between Jackson and Pearson. Jackson occasionally heard rumors that Pearson intended to seek satisfaction. He took the precaution of retaining a copy of the letter he sent to Pearson in August and had it signed by his close friend, James Pindall, an eminent Clarksburg attorney and staunch Federalist.[53] On

---

[50]Baltimore *Federal Republican and Commercial Gazette*, 15 July 1809.

[51]Washington *National Intelligencer*, 24 July 1809; Pearson to Jackson, 7 August 1809, John George Jackson Papers.

[52]Jackson to Pearson, 25 August 1809, Meigs-Jackson Papers, BHPC.

[53]Davis, *John George Jackson*, 163.

21 October Pearson arrived unexpectedly in Clarksburg with his friend, Major James Stephenson of Berkeley County. The next day Pearson informed Jackson that he had received his letter of 28 August (actually 25 August) on 17 September. He had found it unsatisfactory and had authorized Stephenson to arrange a duel.[54]

Jackson accepted Pearson's challenge, and Pindall agreed to serve as Jackson's second. Stephenson then sent Pindall a note asking that the duel be fought in Pennsylvania, about fifty miles away, in order to avoid prosecution under Virginia law. Pindall assured Stephenson that there was no more risk in having the duel in Virginia than in Pennsylvania, and they agreed that it should take place a few miles out of Clarksburg, on the road to Philippi. Pindall proposed that it should take place either immediately or on the evening of 22 October. Stephenson replied that Pearson's pistols were in disorder and asked that it be deferred until the morning of 23 October. Pindall agreed, and early on the appointed day he and Stephenson met to establish the precise rules of the rencontre.

In setting the rules, Pindall and Stephenson agreed that "The parties shall not reserve fire, but fire immediately on receiving the word." At that point Pindall discovered that Pearson intended to use pistols with sights. He objected on the ground that sighted pistols were not used in affairs of honor between gentlemen and pointed out that Jackson had procured pistols without sights. When Pearson refused to remove the sights from his pistols, Pindall advised against pushing Jackson too far, since, under the code duello, he was allowed the choice of weapons and might select a "rifle gun," with which he and "all classes of people are so expert in this part of the country." At that point, Stephenson evidently proposed that they postpone the duel until Congress reconvened in the late fall, by which time they might determine the propriety of the use of sighted weapons. Pindall stated that he could not be in Washington at that time and again reminded Stephenson and Pearson that if Jackson were not allowed the customary

---

[54]Pearson to Jackson, 22 October 1809, John George Jackson Papers. James Stephenson of Berkeley County, West Virginia, served as a Federalist congressman from 1803 to 1825. William Thomas Doherty, *Berkeley County, U.S.A.: A Bicentennial History of a Virginia and West Virginia County, 1772-1972* (Parsons WV: McClain Printing Company, 1972) 78.

choice of weapons, he might consider himself "discharged from all other obligation or responsibility to Mr. Pearson for what he had said."[55]

Both Jackson and Pearson were aware of the possible tragic consequences of the duel. Pearson brought his personal physician with him, and Jackson probably engaged the services of his brother-in-law, Dr. William Williams of Clarksburg. Jackson also compiled a list of all his property, including books and silverware. He penned a brief note to Dolley Madison on the day of the duel, but it is not clear whether he wrote it before or after negotiations with Pearson had broken down. In it he urged Dolley not to "allow alarms of danger and duels" to distress her.[56]

After Congress reconvened on 27 November, Pearson renewed his challenge to Jackson. They agreed that the duel should take place at the Bladensburg, Maryland, dueling ground under rules that do not make clear how the question of sighted pistols was resolved. Stephenson continued as Pearson's second, and Republican Congressman Benjamin Howard of Kentucky consented to act as Jackson's second. On 3 December Jackson sent a farewell note to Dolley Madison and asked her to "say good bye for me to my beloved friend Madison." In admiration of Madison, he declared that "if he does not guide the helm [of this nation] successfully, the requisite qualifications for that station cannot be found on earth."[57]

Details concerning the duel itself are scanty. The antagonists evidently exchanged two shots. On the second Jackson received a hip wound that left him lame for the remainder of his life. There were reports that his injuries were likely to be mortal. Before Pearson, who escaped unscathed, left the dueling ground, he expressed a desire to shake hands and effect a reconciliation with the perhaps dying man. Jackson is said to have granted

---

[55]Statement of James Pindall, 28 October 1809, Meigs-Jackson Papers, BHPC.

[56]John G. Jackson to Dolley Madison, 23 October 1809, James Madison Papers, Alderman Library. Jackson's list of property appears in "Schedule of Lands, Slaves, & other things the property of J. G. Jackson—Annexed to his Will [1809]," Meigs-Jackson Papers, Ohio Historical Society, Campus Martius Museum, Marietta (hereinafter cited as Meigs-Jackson Papers, OHS-CMM). The document is reproduced in Davis, *John George Jackson*, 329-40.

[57]John G. Jackson to Dolley Madison, 3 December 1809, James Madison Papers, Alderman Library.

Pearson's request and assured him that "if he died, he freely forgave Mr. Pearson."[58]

Three days after the duel Ezekiel Bacon of Massachusetts reminded the House of Representatives of resolutions it had passed in 1796 providing for the expulsion of any member engaging in a duel while Congress was in session. Bacon moved that the infraction of the rules by Jackson and Pearson be referred to the Rules Committee, but the House tabled his motion.[59]

Jackson considered himself fortunate to have survived the duel. On 16 December Pearson, who had resumed his seat in the House, wrote John Steele, whose daughter Ann had married Pearson's brother Jesse, that Jackson was "in a fair way to recovery & that he may is my ardent wish."[60] By 28 December Jackson had, in fact, improved sufficiently that he was moved from Maryland to Washington. He regained strength slowly, but he was not able to take his seat in the House until 12 April 1810, less than two weeks before Congress adjourned. His return was cheered by his friends' professions that they had missed him and that "things would have gone on better" had he been present. Even Pearson came to Jackson hat in hand, and Jackson extended his own hand. Although neither man spoke, Jackson stated that Pearson "looked such a look as would melt a savage heart and disarmed me of anger."[61]

Beneath Jackson's civility lay a deep and lasting hostility toward Pearson. The only delight he had in a carriage ride with a young woman of

---

[58]Raleigh (N.C.) *Minerva*, 14 December 1809. For other primary accounts of the duel, see also Raleigh (N.C.) *Register*, 14 December 1809; Raleigh (N.C.) *Star*, 14 December 1809. Secondary accounts of special value are in Clarksburg *Telegram*, 8 December 1875; Brown, "Satisfaction at Bladensburg: The Pearson-Jackson Duel of 1809," 38-39; Davis, *John George Jackson*, 164-65; Roy Bird Cook, "John George Jackson," *West Virginia Review* 12 (April 1935): 209. A copy of the rules for the duel at Bladensburg is in the John George Jackson Papers.

[59]*Annals of Congress*, 11th Cong., 2d sess., 702-703.

[60]Pearson to John Steele, 16 December 1809, in H. M. Wagstaff, ed., *The Papers of John Steele*, 2 vols. (Raleigh NC: North Carolina Historical Commission, 1924) 1:617-18; Jackson to Return Jonathan Meigs, Jr., 3 May 1810, Meigs-Jackson Papers, BHPC.

[61]Jackson to Mary S. Meigs, 14 April 1810, Meigs-Jackson Papers, BHPC.

Washington in April 1810 came from the knowledge that it would "mortify Pearson," who had an interest in her.[62] In 1813, when he met Pearson and his wife at President Madison's drawing room, he spoke to Mrs. Pearson but passed the congressman without greeting him.[63] Ironically, Pearson's seat in the House was only three seats from Jackson's. Yet, declared Jackson, "We never speak. My blood boils whenever I see him, to think of his conduct towards me & the perpetual injury I received at his hands."[64]

Jackson's continued bitterness toward Pearson undoubtedly derived partly from the fact that his injuries deprived him of any major role in the second session of the Eleventh Congress and ultimately forced him to give up his seat in the House of Representatives. In the late summer of 1810, the lameness resulting from wounds sustained in the duel may have caused Jackson an "unfortunate fall" that left him unable to travel to Washington for the third session of the Eleventh Congress, scheduled to convene on 3 December 1810. On 13 September Jackson informed Madison that he had decided to resign his seat in Congress. To the president he confessed, "I will frankly declare that nothing but imperious necessity could induce me *now* to forego the pleasure of giving my feable [*sic*] cooperation to those whose talents, virtues, & patriotism command the homage of every real friend to his country." Jackson wrote Governor James Monroe that a relapse of an old illness prevented his return to Congress, but, in an open letter to his constituents, he attributed his resignation to injuries caused by the duel with Pearson.[65]

In November 1810 an election, described by Jackson as the "warmest contest" he had ever witnessed, was held to determine Jackson's successor. Federalism remained strong in the First Congressional District, and many believed that Jackson was the only Republican who could win. Fearful that

---

[62]Jackson to Mary S. Meigs, 17 April 1810, ibid.

[63]Jackson to Mary S. Jackson, 27 May 1813, ibid.

[64]Jackson to Mary S. Jackson, 6 June 1813, ibid.

[65]Jackson to Madison, 13 September 1810, James Madison Papers, Library of Congress; Jackson to Monroe, 28 September 1810, in W. P. Palmer et al., eds., *Calendar of Virginia State Papers and Other Manuscripts*, 11 vols. (Richmond: Virginia State Library, 1875-1893) 10:90-91; Stanley Griswold to Jackson, 30 November 1810, John George Jackson Papers; Clarksburg *Bye-Stander*, 2 October 1810.

the Republicans might lose the congressional seat, Jackson pressed a reluctant William McKinley into the race against Federalist Thomas Wilson, whom Jackson had defeated three times. The Federalists spread rumors that McKinley, who had participated in the Whiskey Rebellion in 1794, had never received a pardon from President Washington. Jackson countered the allegation by procuring a copy of the official proclamation of pardon. After two days of voting in Monongalia County Wilson had a 160-vote lead over McKinley, but Jackson's exertions in Harrison County gave McKinley 404 votes to 249 for Wilson at the end of four days of balloting. On the basis of McKinley's 40-ballot margin in Wood County, Jackson correctly predicted that he would win by 80 to 100 votes.[66] However, much to Jackson's dismay, McKinley, his handpicked successor, proved an unhappy and ineffective congressman. The day after he took his seat he wrote Jackson that he would be glad to step down if Jackson should decide to run again in 1811. Five days later he told Jackson, "I can do nothing here, you or some other person will have to come forward in the spring."[67]

As a congressman, Jackson proved an ardent spokesman for the administration and a steadfast advocate of measures designed to promote the honor and independence of the new nation. In some respects, his views anticipated those of the War Hawks, who became a conspicuous element of the new Congress in 1810. His speeches were delivered with both polish and gusto, but his impetuosity and hot temper sometimes antagonized his colleagues and undermined some of his effectiveness. Although the characterization of Jackson by a later writer as "the most remarkable man west of the [Allegheny] mountains"[68] is clearly too extravagant, he nevertheless proved to be a vigorous man at a time when the nation needed vigorous men.

---

[66]Jackson to Madison, 17 November 1810, James Madison Papers, Library of Congress.

[67]McKinley to Jackson, 9 February 1811, Meigs-Jackson Papers, OHS-CMM; McKinley to Jackson, 13 February 1811, ibid.

[68]Henry Haymond, *History of Harrison County, West Virginia, from the Early Days of Northwestern Virginia to the Present* (Morgantown WV: Acme Publishing Company, 1910) 387.

6 An Era of Transition

As he watched from afar the continuing debate in Congress over foreign affairs and the clamor for action against England raised by young War Hawks such as Henry Clay, John C. Calhoun, and Felix Grundy, John G. Jackson must have yearned to be in Washington. He nevertheless resisted entreaties by William McKinley to seek his old seat. For the next three years he devoted his attention to his business affairs, served one term in the Virginia House of Delegates, and engaged in a brief but unsatisfying military campaign in the War of 1812. Amidst it all, he found time for courtship and taking a new wife.

Only thirty years old when Mary Payne Jackson died, Jackson was not inclined to remain too long a bachelor. His closest friends, including Dolley Madison, encouraged him to remarry.[1] At one time Washington rumors linked him with a daughter of Vice-President George Clinton and even with the widowed Lucy Washington, the sister of his first wife and Dolley Madison.[2]

---

[1]Jackson to Mary S. Meigs, 18 March 1810, Meigs-Jackson Papers, Blennerhassett Historical Park Commission, Parkersburg, West Virginia (hereinafter cited as Meigs-Jackson Papers, BHPC); Jackson to Mary S. Meigs, 4 April 1810, ibid.; Jackson to Mary S. Meigs, 3 May 1810, ibid.

[2]Senator Philip Read of Maryland told Jackson that it was "credibly reported" that Jackson would marry Clinton's daughter. Jackson to Mary S. Meigs, 17 April 1810, ibid. The rumor that Jackson would marry Lucy Washington had no foundation, although he declared that "she loves me like a brother, & has had possession of my child a long time; & altho ours is not an ordinary attachment I assure you there never was any thing of matrimony in it." Jackson to Mary S. Meigs, 14 April 1810, ibid.

Jackson's most serious intentions were directed toward a young woman identified only as "D. H." Their courtship took place in Washington, but circumstances suggest that she and her family resided in Richmond. Jackson was ready to leave Clarksburg to marry her when Joseph Pearson arrived and challenged him to the duel. After the duel, Jackson began to suffer doubts about his feelings for "D. H.," and in January 1810 he ceased to write to her. He burned her letters, and when she wrote to him in February, he refused to reply. Insisting that he had never "designed any thing wrong," he later offered the rather lame explanation that the whole problem sprang from a "misapprehension of my real feelings, & some little management of the Sister of Miss H."[3] Many of Jackson's friends had expected him to marry "D. H.," and his decision to break off their relationship caused considerable embarrassment. Jackson declared that "D. H." deserved "a heart devoted to her," but that "I had none to give altho the world pronounced her in every sense worthy of mine; and it was right that I should act as I have."[4]

Jackson's decision to terminate the affair with "D. H." evidently resulted from his simultaneous attraction to Mary Sophia Meigs, the only child of Return Jonathan Meigs, Jr. Jackson met Mary, then only fifteen years old, in June 1808, when he stopped in Marietta, Ohio, to congratulate Meigs on his appointment to the United States Senate to succeed John Smith, who had resigned because of his unsavory connection with the Burr conspiracy. Jackson's visit with the Meigs family again in October convinced him that "such a being [as Mary] could fill up the chasm in my happiness," but Mary rebuffed his attentions.[5]

Much to Jackson's "chagrin & mortification," Mary repeatedly refused him permission to call upon her. When she finally consented on the day before he was to fight the duel with Pearson, Jackson's "joy [was] surrounded with sorrow." Fearing that her letter might cause her embarrassment should he be killed, he "consigned the paper to the flames." Jackson

---

[3]Jackson to Mary S. Meigs, undated fragment of a letter, [1810], ibid.; Jackson to Mary S. Meigs, 7 April 1810, ibid.

[4]Jackson to Mary S. Meigs, 7 April 1810, ibid.; Jackson to Mary S. Meigs, 21 April [1810], ibid.

[5]Jackson to Mary S. Meigs, 29 December 1809, ibid.

had another reason for concern. "I am not insensible," he wrote Mary on 29 December 1809, "of the disparity between 17 & 30 years [actually Jackson was then 32] & although I am still young my youth depends upon my health[,] my strength & activity." He promised her even then that if his hopes were realized he wanted "to live again—To have a Mary whom I shall be proud to honor, & happy to love."[6]

Following the duel new doubts assailed Jackson. Weeks passed without a letter from Mary, and Mrs. Meigs expressed some reservations about whether Jackson could "inspire . . . reciprocal feelings" in her daughter. Jackson's health gave additional reason for anxiety. He stated following the duel, "I was borne down by the most severe & alarming illness of my life; it has left me a skeleton." Nevertheless, he promised Mary that "If I am a cripple my presumption shall not extend so far as to importune you—the prospect is favorable on that point but this summer will decide it." Jackson told Mary that during his illness her father had been "incessant in his attentions & watched over me day & night; when I wished for death his kindness dispelled my despair & called me back to life." He implored her to let him know her feelings and to "put an end to my pursuit at once."[7]

In spite of Mary's reluctance, Jackson continued to ply her with professions of his esteem. On 18 March he wrote to her, "My attachment to you is the result of deliberate judgment formed after a thorough acquaintance with the world. Here I have mixed much with the great world & vanity aside have ranked amongst them[;] my fortune, connections &c have given me all that éclat which often captivates the fair, when more substantial merit fails." Jackson assured her that "after a full view, I have seen none here to whom I paid attention, or for whom I felt the regard you have inspired."[8]

Mary's father and mother evidently considered the young widower a suitable husband for their daughter and encouraged the marriage. Meigs even discussed the future with Jackson, assuming that he and Mary would be married. Jackson stated that he had considered "a seat opposite Marietta where I can retain slaves," a preferred site, or a place near Zanesville, but if all ended well "my Muskingum Mary shall decide." To Mary he con-

---

[6]Ibid.

[7]Jackson to Mary S. Meigs, 3 March 1810, ibid.

[8]Jackson to Mary S. Meigs, 18 March 1810, ibid.

fessed, "Ours . . . is a novel Courtship[;] it reminds me in some degree of those of Royalty where the parties are engaged & I had almost said married without seeing each other."[9]

Spring brought Jackson increasing strength, giving rise to an unrealistic hope that he might leave for Clarksburg on 20 April and go from there directly to Marietta.[10] There he would try to overcome Mary's indecision, which he attributed to either an inferiority complex or the doubts of a very young girl faced with the prospect of being thrust into the midst of a sophisticated Washington society. He wrote Mary, who had attended a girl's school in Philadelphia, "If you were indeed so destitute of accomplishment as you pretend to be, there would be no ground for your fears of my disappointment."[11] She was a "most *be witching* girl," he told her, and the fact that she was not "a *City girl* went very far in fixing [his] attachment" to her. He was certain that his friends would find her "lovely, charming & sensible." Besides, he declared, "A City girl would not well suit a rustic like me."[12]

In his efforts to reassure Mary, Jackson drew her attention to his own shortcomings. "I am 31 years old [actually he was nearing 33]—am a cripple & the fates have decreed me to be bald for all the hair is coming out, off the top of my head from excessive fevers last winter," but rather than being "cadaverously pale & emaciated," he was "as fat as an Italian singer."[13] Although he had suffered acutely from an inflammation in his leg, he fully expected to recover. He reminded Mary that he would not press his suit unless he was "perfectly restored," but he did not believe that she would reject him merely because of lameness.[14]

---

[9]Ibid.

[10]Jackson to Mary S. Meigs, 31 March 1810, ibid.

[11]Jackson to Mary S. Meigs, 20 April 1810, ibid. See also Andrew Menade to Return J. Meigs, Jr., 26 June 1802, ibid.; Andrew Menade to Return J. Meigs, Jr., 25 May 1803, ibid.

[12]Jackson to Mary S. Meigs, 4 April 1810, ibid.

[13]Jackson to Mary S. Meigs, 20 April 1810, ibid.

[14]Jackson to Mary S. Meigs, 28 April 1810, ibid. See also Jackson to Mary S. Meigs, 21 May 1810, ibid.; Jackson to Mary S. Meigs, undated fragment of a letter, ibid.

Perhaps because of his uncertainty, Jackson said nothing to his Washington friends of his courtship of Mary Sophia Meigs. He was, therefore, taken by surprise on 4 April 1810 when Dolley Madison, who had invited him to a carriage ride, asked about a rumor that he planned to marry a girl from his own country. Jackson assured Dolley that "it was the first time I had heard of it" and "changed the subject." He wrote Mary that he had "ever since doubted whether I did right for she is my confidant[e] in all things," but, he added, "it *seems* too *romantic a love affair* to build such *hopes on* as would justify my telling even her."[15]

On 2 May Jackson told Dolley Madison of his love for Mary, who had during previous weeks become more receptive to his professions. The gracious First Lady insisted that Jackson must bring Mary to Washington. Jackson wrote Mary, however, that "I must improve greatly before I dare presume to ask you at the altar, for an interchange of vows." Realizing that he had deeply wounded "D. H." and her family and caused them much embarrassment, Jackson confessed to Mary that "what I fear much more[,] I must suffer a wound which I have inflicted to be cicatrixed [*sic*] by time, before you are mine in truth." He told Mary that "Sister M[adison] says next fall will be time enough, so I hope, but she will write me in the meantime concerning the affair I refer to; it is the same I formerly mentioned in my letter to you; & which but for the Duel would have sealed our Destiny."[16]

Jackson's letter evidently caused Mary, who must have had serious questions about the "D. H." affair all along, further misgivings. Soon afterward she wrote Jackson that it might have been better had they never met. Her statement so "*sorely distressed*" Jackson that on 6 June, despite her desire that he delay his journey until 20 June, he left Clarksburg for Marietta.[17] Meanwhile, he wrote her poems, which he hoped would convey his sentiments to her.[18]

---

[15]Jackson to Mary S. Meigs, 4 April 1810, ibid.

[16]Jackson to Mary S. Meigs, 3 May 1810, ibid.

[17]Jackson to Mary S. Meigs, 21 May 1810, ibid. See also Jackson to Mary S. Meigs, 3 and 5 June 1810, ibid.

[18]Jackson to Mary S. Meigs, 20 June 1810, ibid.

Persistence brought Jackson success. Soon after his arrival in Marietta, Mary consented to marry him. Since he had told Dolley Madison that he would not wed Mary until the fall, he immediately asked her what she thought of "a speedy union in reference to its influence upon the affair of D. H." He declared to her that he would "sacrifice much to the feelings of that honorable and respectable family, but not so much as I foolishly intended when I saw you at Montpelier in July." He assured Dolley that his "mind will no longer indulge its vagaries. Indeed it is this dear Girl that unhinged it in the case of D. H. and therefore there cannot be a loop on which to hang a doubt."[19] At last on 19 July 1810, Jackson married Mary in Marietta, with the Reverend Stephen Lindley performing the ceremony.[20]

For Mary Meigs Jackson the most pleasant prospect following her marriage was that of becoming the mistress of Monte Alto, as Jackson now called his Clarksburg estate.[21] Soon after her arrival in Clarksburg, the Jacksons sent to Harewood for Jackson's daughter Mary, who at once became devoted to her stepmother. Apparently Mary Meigs Jackson had already become acquainted with Jack Triplett, Jackson's illegitimate son, who lived not far from Marietta. Imbued by a deep sense of right, she insisted that Jackson bring the bright ten-year-old lad to Clarksburg and give him his name. Ill at ease and caring nothing for the glitter of Washington society, Mary devoted herself to providing Jackson with a warm and happy home.[22] Her success may have weighed as heavily as his physical disabil-

---

[19]Jackson to Dolley Madison, undated fragment of a letter, Mary Allen Cassady Collection, Fincastle, Virginia.

[20]Washington County Probate Court Records, Marriage Records, 1:66, Washington County Courthouse, Marietta, Ohio. See also Jackson to James Madison, 13 September 1810, James Madison Papers, Library of Congress, Washington, D.C.; Stanley Griswold to Jackson, 30 November 1810, John George Jackson Papers, Lilly Library, Indiana University, Bloomington.

[21]For the designation of the estate as Monte Alto, see Jackson to Madison, 12 October 1809, James Madison Papers, Library of Congress.

[22]Dorothy Davis, *John George Jackson* (Parsons WV: McClain Printing Company, 1976) 182-83. For Mary's refusal to accompany Jackson to Washington, see, for example, Jackson to Mary S. Jackson, 29 January 1814, Meigs-Jackson Papers, BHPC; Jackson to Mary S. Jackson, 30 January 1814, ibid.

ities in Jackson's decision to resign his seat in the House of Representatives.

Few of Jackson's friends expected him to remain politically inactive. Stanley Griswold, the judge of the Illinois Territory, reported a rumor in Detroit that Jackson would be appointed governor of the Michigan Territory upon the expiration of the term of William Hull on 1 March 1811. Griswold did not believe that Jackson's health would prevent his acceptance of the post, which he described as "a snug, handsome, and pleasant retreat."[23]

Jackson's idea of a "pleasant retreat" in 1810 centered around a Virginia circuit judgeship, which would allow him to remain in Clarksburg. In early January Hugh Nelson, the judge of the Eleventh Judicial Circuit of Virginia, wrote Jackson that the House of Delegates was considering the addition of a new chancellor west of the Allegheny Mountains in Jackson's own area and that Nelson supported the move. Jackson received similar reports from Dabney Lee, who favored Jackson as chancellor of the new court, and John Prunty, a Harrison County delegate in the Virginia legislature.[24] Jackson's hopes soared when Nelson resigned his own judgeship on 28 March 1811 and both he and Prunty recommended Jackson to Governor James Monroe as Nelson's successor.[25]

Unwilling to trust his case entirely to his friends, Jackson addressed a formal letter of application to Monroe on 5 April. He drew attention to his extensive legal experience, his popularity in his district, and his lifelong residence west of the Alleghenies. The state of his health, which had forced him to give up his seat in Congress, would in no way, he assured the governor, interfere with the performance of any judicial duties. On the same day that he wrote Monroe, Jackson asked Madison to intercede in his behalf if he could do so in good conscience and with "perfect propriety." He

---

[23]Griswold to Jackson, 30 November 1810, John George Jackson Papers.

[24]Nelson to Jackson, 7 January 1810, ibid.; Lee to Jackson, 9 June 1810, Meigs-Jackson Papers, BHPC; Prunty to Jackson, 26 December 1810, John George Jackson Papers.

[25]Nelson to Jackson, 29 March 1811, John George Jackson Papers; Prunty to Monroe, 5 April 1811, Virginia, Executive Papers, Virginia State Library, Richmond.

told the president that the appointment should go to someone living within the circuit rather than "incur the risque of offending by sending a stranger to us."[26]

Jackson, however, failed to receive the appointment. On 12 April Madison informed him that Nelson's successor had been named a week or two previously. "Your name," he told Jackson, "had been brought into view and in high auspices, but it does not appear that your willingness to accept the office (or the sufficiency perhaps of your health) was counted on." John Tyler also informed Jackson that his request for assistance had arrived too late. Nelson himself stated that when the question of the appointment was presented to the governor's council, one member asserted that Jackson was "considered a resident of the State of Ohio."[27]

Unable to conceal his bitter disappointment, Jackson would not "even conjecture who is sent from the land of Talents & illumination to enlighten us miserable backwoodsmen, who cannot furnish one man to fill a local office amongst us." He vowed "to break the chains of servitude riveted by the wise men of the East" and to do battle "while my tongue & pen can urge any thing in the cause of our poor despised country." Sending a judge from the East to deal with Western litigation, he declared, was equivalent to sending "a mere land lawyer to plead admirality [*sic*] causes in the maritime districts."[28]

The vacancy in the circuit judgeship occurred in the midst of the April elections in which William McKinley sought to retain his seat in Congress. McKinley attended elections in Ohio, Monongalia, and Harrison counties and asked Jackson to send some person to either Randolph or Wood County prior to the election.[29] Troubled by serious doubts about McKinley's chances of success, Jackson apparently did not campaign with the vigor

---

[26]Jackson to Monroe, 5 April 1811, Virginia, Executive Papers; Jackson to Madison, 5 April 1811, James Madison Papers, Library of Congress.

[27]Madison to Jackson, 12 April 1811, John George Jackson Papers; Tyler to Jackson, 23 May 1811, ibid.; Nelson to Jackson, 31 May 1811, ibid.

[28]Jackson to Madison, 19 April 1811, James Madison Papers, Library of Congress.

[29]McKinley to Jackson, 13 February 1811, Meigs-Jackson Papers, Ohio Historical Society, Campus Martius Museum, Marietta, Ohio.

that he had displayed in 1810. McKinley carried Ohio County by 233 votes to 101, but Thomas Wilson, his Federalist opponent, amassed majorities in most other counties and won the election by 102 votes. Jackson declared that McKinley "never was here before & his coming ruined our hopes as his manners &c are unpopular, & here the People vote for men more than principles."[30]

Jackson's own popularity remained undiminished. On the day of the election he was "taken up for the [Virginia] assembly & voted in," which, he told Madison, "I truly regret as my old friend Prunty was dropped." Jackson declared that he could "scarcely tell how it happened[,]" but in "yielding to the wishes of the People[,] I forgot my condition & every thing that forbade my going to the assembly."[31] Jackson, still bitter over his failure to obtain the circuit judgeship, may have in fact inspired the popular move, for he vowed that once he was in the legislature he would oppose confirmation of anyone it considered.

In mid-November Jackson, with a servant, set out for Richmond. Still unable to ride a horse and dependent upon a cane for walking, he traveled in a gig. He went by way of Washington, where he attempted to sell the "immense" boardinghouse run by Mrs. Suter, which he had purchased the previous year. He failed to dispose of it, as few could buy and make the required payment and those who could afford it made no offers.[32]

While in Washington Jackson called on the Madisons, who invited him to stay with them during his visit. He delighted in conversations with Dolley, Anna Cutts, and Lucy Washington. Lucy introduced him to Madame Betsy Patterson Bonaparte, who was "blazing with diamonds." The former wife of Jerome Bonaparte, whose marriage was disapproved by Napoleon and annulled by the French Council of State, Betsy remembered Jackson and invited him to visit her. Jackson attended the sale of the furniture of

---

[30]Jackson to James Madison, 19 April 1811, James Madison Papers, Library of Congress. See also Daniel Porter Jordan, Jr., "Virginia Congressmen, 1801-1825" (Ph.D. dissertation, University of Virginia, 1970) 402.

[31]Jackson to Madison, 19 April 1811, James Madison Papers, Library of Congress.

[32]Jackson to Mary S. Jackson, 4 December 1811, Meigs-Jackson Papers, BHPC.; Davis, *John George Jackson*, 188-89.

the Russian minister and bid $560 for a pair of "looking glasses and marble stands," but they went to another for a few dollars more.[33]

In Richmond, Jackson wrote to Mary to keep up her fortitude. He told her that his was a "necessary absence upon which so much depends," probably a reference to his decision to fight for the circuit judgeship. Much to his satisfaction, Jackson found that the "D. H." affair was "passing fast into oblivion." On his way from his lodgings to the capitol each day he passed the house where "D. H." lived with "Mrs. R.," evidently a close relative. When he met the latter, Jackson bowed, without speaking, but he did not know for certain whether she had looked at him. He believed that "D. H." was not in town, and he did not expect to see her.[34]

When Jackson took up his work in the legislature, he was already an experienced statesman. He served as chairman of the Committee on Privileges and Elections and as a member of the Committee for Courts of Justice, a position he undoubtedly much desired. Other important assignments included membership on a joint House-Senate committee to examine the condition of the Bank of Virginia and committees charged with adopting a preamble and resolutions concerning the foreign affairs of the United States, the study of land taxes, and congressional redistricting in Virginia.[35]

In the very midst of the legislative session, Richmond suffered one of its greatest disasters. On the night of 26 December 1811, between 700 and 800 persons gathered in the Richmond Theater for a performance of *The Father; or, Family Feuds*, a play by Denis Diderot. Jackson, who attended in the company of a friend, sat near the stage. The play itself, which lasted until ten o'clock, was followed by a pantomime entitled *Raymond and Agnes; or, the Bleeding Nun*. This "after piece," according to Jackson, "consisted of a dumb shew" for which "a lamp was suspended from the ceiling which was incautiously drawn up without putting it out." About half past eleven the lamp set fire to the scenery and sparks "fell in flakes upon the stage."

---

[33]Jackson to Mary S. Jackson, 4 December 1811, Meigs-Jackson Papers, BHPC.

[34]Ibid.

[35]Virginia, House of Delegates, *Journal, 1811*, 5, 17, 40, 47, 50.

When the fire was discovered, the crowd fell into a panic, and some of them became hysterical. Within moments the entire ceiling of the theater burst into flames, and the stricken crowds pushed into the entrance. Jackson tried to get out through a window, but he could get no closer than two feet to it. By then the cries and screams of the people were horrible, and smoke filled the entrances, causing many people to suffocate. Jackson held his breath until it was nearly gone. As his life passed before him, he suddenly felt "a vacuum" under his feet and dropped to a lower floor on a level with the orchestra pit. There a strong current of air rushing through an outer door revived him. All around him he now saw dead bodies and piles of injured and dying. He rose to his feet, and, unable to obtain his cane, made his way toward the outer door. One woman, a Mrs. Douthat, clung to him and begged him to save her. Although Jackson thought of his own life, he carried her with him to safety in an act of genuine heroism.[36]

Jackson wrote James Madison that he had once again "escaped from the jaws of death."[37] Among the victims of the conflagration were Governor George William Smith, A. B. Venable, and other prominent Virginians. In accordance with a resolution introduced by Jackson, the House of Delegates called upon members to wear crape on their left arms for one month, but it agreed to adjourn only two days, instead of one month, as he proposed, in a memorial to the governor and others who perished.[38]

Upon resuming its work, the legislature quickly chose James Barbour, the Speaker of the House of Delegates, to fill the vacancy created by the death of Governor Smith. Barbour's election required the House to choose a new Speaker. On 4 January 1812 Jackson nominated James Robertson of Amelia County. John Tyler, the son of the federal judge and himself a future governor of Virginia and president of the United States, nominated Andrew Stevenson, a delegate from Richmond. Stevenson was elected.[39]

---

[36]Jackson to Mary S. Jackson, 27 December 1811, Meigs-Jackson Papers, BHPC. For a reproduction of the program relating to the performance at the Richmond Theater, see Davis, *John George Jackson*, 192.

[37]Jackson to Madison, 27 December 1811, James Madison Papers, Library of Congress.

[38]Virginia, House of Delegates, *Journal, 1811*, 50.

[39]Ibid., 63.

The House turned again to routine matters. On 8 January 1812 it took up resolutions introduced by James Robertson on 17 December expressing approval of American policy with respect to British and French encroachments on the nation's neutral rights. The first of the measures, recommended by a select committee, of which Jackson was a member, "viewed with approbation the uniform zeal with which just remonstrances have been made by the general government, for the purpose of obtaining from Great Britain, by honorable negotiation, a redress of the many wrongs inflicted upon us by her Orders in Council, and other measures equally hostile to the interests of the United States."[40]

Charles F. Mercer of Loudoun County offered a substitute clearly intended to defeat the purpose of Robertson's resolutions. His motion declared that "this assembly will never be found wanting, in the discharge of that duty [of supporting the federal government] when a proper occasion calls for its performance." Yet, it continued, "[T]his Assembly deem all attempts by any State Legislature, to influence or controul [*sic*], to accelerate, retard, or defeat, the constitutional measures of the general government, to be not only highly impolitic, but, if not prohibited by the letter, most obviously, at war with the spirit of the federal constitution." The substitute resolution mustered only 28 votes. Jackson was one of 128 members who opposed it. He then voted for the original resolution, which carried by a vote of 142 to 31.[41]

Jackson gave strong support to Robertson's second and third resolutions. The second, passed 131 to 32, stated that "however highly we value the blessings of peace, and however we may deprecate the evils of war, the period has now arrived when peace, *as we now have it*, is disgraceful, and war is honorable." The third resolution, adopted with only one dissenting vote, pledged the support of the General Assembly to the federal government "in all constitutional and legitimate measures . . . adopted, in vindication of the rights and interests of the United States and in support of the character and dignity of the government thereof; and for these purposes we pledge 'our lives, our fortunes and our sacred honor.' "[42]

---

[40]Ibid., 35, 40.

[41]Ibid., 70-71.

[42]Ibid., 73, 75-76.

Jackson believed he rendered his greatest service to his constituents in the passage of legislation that established a high chancery court at Clarksburg, made favorable adjustments in the land taxes, and authorized the construction of roads beneficial to Harrison County.[43] His first success in his fight for judicial reform came on 14 December 1811 when the House, as a committee of the whole, agreed to consider a bill proposed by the Committee of Propositions and Grievances, to which various petitions "complaining of the present organization of the Superior Courts of Chancery" were referred.[44]

Perhaps in connection with the proposed bill, Jackson took the unusual step of seeking an opinion on proposed legislation from John Tyler, a former governor of Virginia, who in 1811 became the federal judge for the district of Virginia. Since his letter to Tyler is no longer extant, there is no way of knowing precisely what Jackson asked, but Tyler made it clear that he considered the questions improper. "The principal [*sic*] layed [*sic*] down in our most excellent constitution in the plainest & broadest language that the executive[,] judicial[,] & legislative functions should be kept seperate [*sic*] and distinct from each other," Tyler wrote, "would in spirit appeare [*sic*] to me to be violated whensoever any two of these departments should cooperate to produce the passage of any law." He refused to answer them "in a quasi extrajudicial manner," declaring that for him to decide upon a law before its passage would be "stepping out of the line of prudence."[45]

Creed Taylor, a judge of the Superior Court of Chancery, to whom Jackson also addressed questions, was more cooperative and supportive. He declared that he had always been opposed to the idea that the legislature had "the legitimate power to amalgamate the courts of law and equity as now organised [*sic*]." If, however, the General Assembly should add one or more courts to his district, Taylor would hold them "with promptitude." He expressed the view that a chancellor might hold courts at two different places, but he opposed a circuit of courts on the ground that, for

[43]Jackson to Mary S. Jackson, 28 January 1812, Meigs-Jackson Papers, BHPC.

[44]Virginia, House of Delegates, *Journal, 1811*, 32.

[45]Tyler to Jackson, 23 December 1811, John George Jackson Papers.

purposes of justice, suitors should attend the chancellor, not he attend them.[46]

On 3 January 1812, on motion of Jackson, the House ordered that a special committee draw up a bill for the extension of the jurisdiction of the Superior Court of Common Law. When the special committee, of which Jackson was a member, reported its bill on 16 January, opponents forced through an amendment that would have emasculated it. Jacob Beeson of Wood County, one of Jackson's political allies, won a tactical victory in securing suspension of the thirty-eighth rule of the House of Delegates and referral of the bill and its amendments to a select committee, of which Jackson was chairman. Much to Jackson's satisfaction, on 21 January the House adopted, by a vote of 112 to 51, the bill proposed by the committee.[47]

The bill, which also passed the Senate, increased the number of chancery court districts in Virginia from three to nine. The new Fourth District Court would sit in Clarksburg on 18 May and 18 October each year and serve the counties of Brooke, Ohio, Wood, Harrison, Monongalia, and Randolph. The law required the judge, who also presided over the Third District Court at Winchester, to be a resident of either Clarksburg or Winchester.[48] In 1812 Dabney Carr became the first chancellor of the Fourth District Court. With respect to the selection, Jackson said, "I am satisfied as I was ineligible to the place[,] it being created whilst I was a member of the assembly."[49] His successes in obtaining a High Court of Chancery for Clarksburg and in enlarging the terms of the superior courts of law for Harrison County undoubtedly enabled him to accept with a better feeling the election of Daniel Smith as the successor to Hugh Nelson as judge of the Eleventh Judicial Circuit of Virginia, the post to which he himself had aspired.[50]

---

[46]Taylor to Jackson, 7 January 1812, Jackson Family Papers, Virginia Historical Society, Richmond.

[47]Virginia, House of Delegates, *Journal, 1811*, 63, 84, 90.

[48]Virginia, General Assembly, *Acts, 1811*, 19-21.

[49]Jackson to Mary S. Jackson, 2 February 1811, Meigs-Jackson Papers, BHPC.

[50]Virginia, House of Delegates, *Journal, 1811*, 18, 92.

Land tax reform became, for Jackson, another crusade. As chairman of a committee to consider changes, he reported a bill to the House of Delegates that posed a potential threat to the inadequately taxed lands claimed by nonresidents of the western counties. The measure, as passed, required commissioners to assemble lists of taxable property within their jurisdiction no later than 5 August 1812. Under the law, nonresident owners had to provide the commissioners with descriptions of their lands and redeem, by 1 November 1812, any property on which taxes had become delinquent. Otherwise, county sheriffs should sell them and apply the monies collected to the newly established Literary Fund for the education of poor children.[51]

Jackson took special pride in securing appropriations for roads for the benefit of Harrison Countians. He obtained $1,000 for the Parkersburg-Point Pleasant road, $1,000 for a highway from Clarksburg to Marietta, and $750 for a road through the southern portion of Harrison County.[52] Keenly aware of the need for additional banking facilities in western Virginia, Jackson supported a bill to increase the banking capital of the state, but he voted with the minority against establishment of a new bank at Richmond, with a branch only at Lynchburg, and abstained from voting for creation of an independent bank at Norfolk.[53]

As a member of the legislature, Jackson renewed efforts he and other officers of the 11th, 113th, and 119th regiments of the Virginia militia had made in 1810 to form a new brigade made up of militia of Harrison, Randolph, and Wood counties. Largely through Jackson's efforts, the legislature in 1812 established the 20th Brigade of Virginia militia. William Marteney nominated Colonel Isaac Booth of Randolph County, and Jacob Beeson placed Jackson's name in nomination for brigadier general of the organization. On 9 January, by joint ballot, the House and Senate, by a

---

[51]Ibid., 13; Jackson to Mary S. Jackson, 28 January 1812, Meigs-Jackson Papers, BHPC; Virginia, General Assembly, *Acts, 1811*, 26-30.

[52]Jackson to Mary S. Jackson, 28 January 1812, Meigs-Jackson Papers, BHPC; Virginia, House of Delegates, *Journal, 1811*, 18, 36, 65, 85, 89-90; Virginia, General Assembly, *Acts, 1811*, 95.

[53]Virginia, House of Delegates, *Journal, 1811*, 88, 96-97.

vote of 112 to 70, chose Jackson.[54] Jubilant at his selection, Jackson later wrote to his wife, "I am now victorious—my enemies are foiled & I am reinstated in the estimation of the world in all I have lost by the machinations of enemies."[55]

Jackson was not without military experience. He had held a captaincy in the Harrison County militia of the 119th Regiment since 28 September 1808, and, on recommendation of the Harrison County Court, on 23 May 1809, Governor John Tyler had officially appointed him colonel commandant of the regiment.[56] Jackson, who was elated that the Federalist county court had chosen him, a "hot democrat," over the majors of the regiment, with but five dissenting votes, took his oath of office on 23 August.[57]

Reflecting Jackson's concern for American rights, the 119th Regiment, at his instigation, adopted resolutions on 29 October 1809 offering its services to President James Madison. Although he saw no immediate need for the regiment, the president commended the patriotic spirit of the resolutions and pronounced the zeal and support of the people as "the only foundation on which, next to the favor of Heaven, we ought to rest the security of every thing dear to a free and independent Nation."[58]

---

[54]Ibid., 13, 24, 71. Previous efforts to obtain a new brigade had failed. See Harrison County Legislative Petition, 24 October 1810, Virginia State Library, Richmond; John Prunty to Jackson, 26 December 1810, John George Jackson Papers.

[55]Jackson to Mary S. Jackson, 10 January 1812, Meigs-Jackson Papers, BHPC. Jackson's official commission, dated 9 January 1812, is in the John George Jackson Papers.

[56]Harrison County Court Minute Book, 1807-1809, 226-27, 290; 1809-1810, 41, 146, Harrison County Courthouse, Clarksburg, West Virginia; undated affidavit of Benjamin Wilson, Clerk of the Harrison County Court, Virginia, Executive Papers, Militia, Harrison County, 1784-1829, Virginia State Library; John Tyler to John G. Jackson, 23 May 1809, John George Jackson Papers.

[57]Jackson to John Tyler, 16 May 1809, Virginia, Executive Papers, Militia, Harrison County, 1784-1829; Harrison County Court Minute Book, 1809-1810, 146.

[58]Madison to Jackson, 3 December 1809, John George Jackson Papers.

As the newly appointed general of the 20th Brigade, Jackson left Richmond on 28 January 1812 for Washington. Upon his arrival he expressed to his friend Congressman Thomas Gholson, Jr., of Virginia, a desire to enter the regular army. Gholson agreed to draw the matter to the attention of Virginia's congressional delegation, which, under the system then in use, would make a recommendation to President Madison. Jackson believed that his chances of an appointment to a full colonel were good, but he recognized that his connections with the president might be a disadvantage.[59]

Almost immediately upon his return to Clarksburg Jackson found himself beset with problems not uncommon among frontier militia. He lodged a protest with Governor James Barbour over the "irregular" action of the Harrison County Court in January 1812 in recommending John Sommerville over Major Isaac Coplin to be his successor as lieutenant-colonel of the 119th Regiment.[60]

James Pindall, Jackson's old friend, also proved vexatious. Acting upon a call for men by Governor Barbour on 5 May, Jackson instructed the lieutenant-colonels of the 11th and 119th regiments to call their troops together and direct the majors of their battalions to furnish the needed men. At the battalion muster, Pindall, a major in the 119th Regiment, refused to carry out Jackson's order on the ground that "the militia he commanded were not French Conscripts & he could not conceive any reason why they should be called out when no war existed." Pindall then arrested Captain George I. Davisson, his brother-in-law, for criticizing his conduct and requested Jackson to arrange a court-martial for him. Jackson questioned the authority of a major to arrest and informed the governor that, as Pindall's superior officer, he desired to set aside the latter's request.[61]

Jackson attributed his difficulties with his brigade to political enmity and resentment among other officers that his appointment had not been in accordance with the principle of advancement by grades. Wearying of the dissension, he wrote Governor Barbour that "in the present state of my feelings, Virginia has nothing to bestow that I could ask or would willingly

---

[59]Jackson to Mary S. Jackson, 2 February 1812, Meigs-Jackson Papers, BHPC.

[60]Jackson to Barbour, 21 February 1812, Virginia, Executive Papers.

[61]Jackson to Barbour, 5 May 1812, ibid.; Jackson to Barbour, 1 July 1812, ibid.; James Pindall to Jackson, 1 June 1812, John George Jackson Papers.

accept[.] I was reluctantly dragged into the shambles last winter, & the butchery I then suffered shall never be repeated."[62]

Meanwhile, much to Jackson's gratification, the war spirit was rising in western Virginia. He assured Madison, "My voice is for war—& I would willingly add my arm too if we engage in it vigorously."[63] Upon hearing of the American declaration of war against Great Britain on 18 June 1812, Jackson wrote the president that he had "always intended if we engage[d] in war with Great Britain to enter the army." Trying to avoid the appearance of writing a letter of application, he stated that his recovery from his physical disability had been so substantial that he was ready to render his services "in any station however subordinate when fighting is a part of the duty, & I am entitled to ride." He declared that he was willing "after approving the war to wage it."[64]

Jackson received little encouragement in his desire for immediate military action. On 9 July Governor Barbour ordered him to Xenia, Ohio, to join other members of a commission of the United States Government charged with a duty "highly important to a meritorious class of Citizens." The assignment actually called for nothing more than the surveying of the line between the Virginia military district in the Old Northwest and lands ceded by the state to the federal government. The disappointed Jackson wrote Madison that because of important business in the Harrison County Court, he could not accept the post unless the survey were postponed three weeks, perhaps his means of avoiding an unexciting responsibility.[65]

Despite the advice of Return Jonathan Meigs, Jr., his father-in-law, that if the war were a short one "you have no occasion to go in the army—if a long one there will be Chances enough,"[66] Jackson grew restless at his in-

---

[62]Jackson to Barbour, 15 May 1812, Virginia, Executive Papers.

[63]Jackson to Madison, 30 March 1812, James Madison Papers, Library of Congress.

[64]Jackson to Madison, 26 June 1812, ibid.

[65]Barbour to Jackson, 9 July 1812, John George Jackson Papers; Jackson to Madison, 24 July 1812, James Madison Papers, Library of Congress.

[66]Meigs to Children, 19 July 1812, Meigs-Jackson Papers, BHPC.

activity. General William Hull's slow advance to Detroit, his failure to cut British supply lines to Fort Malden, and the British capture of the *Cuyahoga* with a valuable cargo and papers filled Jackson with disgust. While "the utmost confusion prevails in the state of Ohio," he wrote Governor Barbour, "we in their vicinity remain idle." His men constantly asked when they would march, and he himself would go "in any capacity," even as a private.[67]

When the old and inept Hull surrendered to the British, Jackson wrote Madison that "my solicitude [for the frontiers] is so great that if I possessed any discretionary power as a militia officer I would order out all the efficient men of my Brigade to march immediately." He stated that he had forty officers of his brigade at Clarksburg, all willing to engage as privates. Professing such a restoration of health "that I can endure any service," he ended his letter by declaring, "I hope & pray we may be called on, there will be no contest for rank, & I am willing to set the example of descending from the highest grade to the lowest."[68]

In September Jackson presided over a meeting of the officers of the 20th Brigade and other citizens at the Harrison County courthouse. He reported the capture of Hull's army and read letters received from "a source entitled to respect," actually his father, George Jackson, asking for immediate aid from Virginians. Under Jackson's close direction, the gathering adopted resolutions declaring that "we deem it criminal to stand by, while the storm of war rages" and calling for a military force "to chastise & drive him [the enemy] out of our Country." The men pledged themselves to take the field as soon as they were provided with arms and requested the president to enlist their services immediately. Jackson sent a copy of their resolutions to Governor Barbour with an explanation that the dangerous situation in Ohio made it necessary to depart from normal channels of

---

[67]Jackson to Barbour, 28 August 1812, John George Jackson Papers. For accounts of Hull's activities, see, for instance, Reginald Horsman, *The War of 1812* (New York: Alfred A. Knopf, 1969) 34-38; John K. Mahon, *The War of 1812* (Gainesville: University of Florida Press, 1972) 44-51.

[68]Jackson to Madison, 31 August 1812, U.S. War Department, Letters Received, Registered Series, National Archives, Washington, D.C.

communication.[69] He also advised Madison that "so great is the anxiety here that many will go even if not called on by the constituted authorities."[70]

On 3 September, prior to receiving the brigade's resolutions, Governor Barbour ordered Jackson's 20th Brigade to march to Point Pleasant, filling the ranks in each regiment with volunteers, if necessary, and taking arms not in working order to Point Pleasant for repair. When some of the men who had no rifles "positively refused" to comply with an order of Benjamin Wilson that they take muskets, Wilson threatened to arrest their captain. Realizing that "if that step had been taken we should not have marched a man from this Country," Jackson prevailed upon the men to carry the muskets to Point Pleasant, but even then they vowed that they would not go into battle with them.[71]

Jackson was not happy with Barbour's orders to march his men to Point Pleasant. He professed a desire to serve in a subordinate capacity and to see action before assuming command over men who had been in battle. Claiming that "no man is my superior as a marksman," he told the governor, "I want to be associated with a corps of mounted riflemen."[72] In mid-October Jackson and a small party of friends from Clarksburg arrived in Franklinton (now Columbus), Ohio, to join the Detroit-bound army of General William Henry Harrison "and cooperate with them as a corps of mounted Riflemen."[73]

A problem immediately arose when Jackson informed Harrison that he and his men "expected to be furnished with forage & rations on the public account." Harrison told Jackson that he would employ the Clarksburg men

---

[69]Resolutions Adopted by Officers of the 20th Brigade and Other Citizens at Clarksburg, 2 September 1812, Virginia, Executive Papers; Jackson to Barbour, 3 September 1812, ibid.

[70]Jackson to Madison, 4 September 1812, U.S. War Department, Letters Received, Registered Series.

[71]Jackson to Barbour, 11 September 1812, Virginia, Executive Papers. See also George I. Davisson to Barbour, 14 September 1812, ibid.; Jackson to Barbour, 16 September 1812, ibid.

[72]Jackson to Barbour, 11 September 1812, ibid.

[73]Jackson to James Madison, 21 October 1812, James Madison Papers, Library of Congress.

even though the laws made no provision for such cases, but that he had no authority "to engage any compensation to the party." Jackson promised personally to "obviate any difficulty on that score by assuming upon [himself] the responsibility of paying them." At the same time he asked Harrison what indemnity for the expense he might expect, since his limited resources might require him to discharge some of his men. Jackson declared that "for myself I neither wish or will accept any compensation whatever."[74]

Despite the somewhat tenuous nature of his position, Jackson did not hesitate to provide Madison with gratuitous information on the strengths and weaknesses of Harrison's army. He reported that supplies and equipment of all kinds were "unquestionably ample, including a fine train of artillery," but he believed that there were no trained artillerists and urged that an adequate number be sent without delay in order that they might join the army before it reached Detroit. Jackson expressed the hope that Madison would "excuse the freedom of my remarks because you know the sincerity with which they are communicated."[75]

Progress on the campaign proved disappointingly slow to Jackson. On 22 November he wrote Mary that he had been in Zanesville, where he arrived "after a solitary journey of two days." He had advised Jonathan Jackson, his cousin, and his company to return home. Jackson took time to visit the grave of his mother, who had died the preceding 22 March, and admitted that "the tears blind me when reflecting upon her affection for me & . . . the heart which beat so warmly for a darling son is cold in the tomb."[76]

On the evening of 24 November Jackson returned to Franklinton with his brother Edward, who had been given a place equivalent to a surgeon's mate with Harrison's army. There Jackson learned that an expedition of 700 mounted men under Colonel John B. Campbell would leave shortly from Dayton, Ohio, for the upper Wabash country. By means of the expedition Harrison hoped to neutralize the Delaware and Miami Indians,

---

[74]Ibid.

[75]Ibid.

[76]Jackson to Mary S. Jackson, 22 November 1812, Meigs-Jackson Papers, BHPC. For the death of Jackson's mother, see Jackson to James Madison, 30 March 1812, James Madison Papers, Library of Congress.

who lived along the Mississinewa River and were in a position to disrupt the supply lines to a base Harrison was attempting to establish at the rapids of the Maumee River. Harrison gave Jackson permission to join the force.[77]

Jackson's presence on the Wabash expedition excited jealousy among some of its officers. According to Jackson, Campbell and Major James V. Bell complained to Harrison that "as theirs was a subordinate command & neither of them had the rank which I did, & altho I had no command, my *standing* was such as to induce a belief that whatever credit was acquired would be so divided as to assign a large share to me, & in so far diminish theirs." Although Harrison attempted to induce him to remain as a volunteer aide on his staff, Jackson considered the feeling against him an obstacle to his "going further or remaining longer" and returned home.[78]

Although disillusioned with his brief military career and despairing of success of Harrison's plans, Jackson allowed himself very little time for bitter reflection. He later declared to Dolley Madison that although he had not killed an enemy soldier, he was "daily spilling the blood of the deer" and that "I carried my Rifle all the way[,] threw away my cane & never enjoyed better health."[79] With the dream of military glory out of his system and his health much restored, Jackson was ready, and even eager, to turn his attention again to national politics.

---

[77]Jackson to Mary S. Jackson, 25 November 1812, Meigs-Jackson Papers, BPHC. For the expedition against the Indians on the Wabash, see, for example, Mahon, *War of 1812*, 71-73.

[78]Jackson to Dolley P. Madison, 11 December 1812, Jackson Family Papers.

[79]Ibid.

7 Industrial Entrepreneur and Patriot

During the two years following his duel with Joseph Pearson, John G. Jackson suffered a series of professional and personal disappointments that would have stifled the energies and ambitions of a less determined man. His successes as a member of the Virginia House of Delegates hardly compensated for his resignation from Congress, his failure to receive a coveted Virginia circuit judgeship, and the utter frustration of his desire for military action.

Fortunately, Jackson was able to turn his attention to private enterprises, which under wartime conditions assumed the character of great patriotic service. The Napoleonic Wars, the Embargo, the Non-Intercourse Act, and Macon's Bill Number 2 seriously curtailed imports from Europe, forcing Americans into domestic manufacture of many essential articles. In expanding his agricultural interests and establishing new industries in the Clarksburg area, Jackson identified himself with a rising economic nationalism in the West.[1]

Agricultural and industrial enterprises such as those in which Jackson engaged received encouragement and prospects of support from the highest authorities in government. Despite his deep attachment to agricultural

---

[1]Otis K. Rice, *The Allegheny Frontier: West Virginia Beginnings, 1730-1830* (Lexington: University Press of Kentucky, 1970) 309, 355-57; Reginald Horsman, *The Frontier in the Formative Years, 1783-1815* (New York: Holt, Rinehart and Winston, 1970) 160-65.

interests, Thomas Jefferson declared in his annual message to Congress on 8 November 1808 that manufacturing establishments then forming would, with protecting duties and other policies of the federal government, become permanent. Henry Clay, the Speaker of the House of Representatives, asserted that the farmer who manufactured most of his family's needs and squandered but little on "the gewgaws of Europe" represented "in epitome what the nation ought to do." James Madison informed Congress in 1815 that "in adjusting the duties on imports to the object of revenue the influence of the tariff on manufacturing will necessarily present itself for consideration."[2]

Jackson had "scarcely entered upon manhood when he conceived the idea of developing the resources" of the West Fork Valley in a manner that would make him its foremost industrial entrepreneur. Quite naturally, in a region where economic life still centered around rudimentary agriculture and the forests, Jackson's earliest industrial endeavors concentrated upon the operation of saw- and gristmills. In 1808 he acquired his first mill and adjacent lands on Coburn Run from Ephraim Frazier, who failed to meet his payments on a loan that Jackson had made to him four years earlier for purchasing the property. Jackson operated the mill from that time until his death in 1825.[3]

During the next few years Jackson constructed other mills on tributaries of the West Fork. On 18 September 1809 he informed the Harrison County Court of his intention to erect a water gristmill and dam on his land on Elk Creek, near the mouth of Murphy Run. The court granted his request for a writ of *ad quod damnum* for the confiscation of property needed for the dam, and the following year Jackson built a dam five feet high on Elk Creek. He constructed a millrace and a three-story building fifty-eight

---

[2]James D. Richardson, comp., *A Compilation of the Messages and Papers of the Presidents of the United States, 1789-1897*, 10 vols. (Washington DC: Government Printing Office, 1896-1907) 1:455, 567; James F. Hopkins, Mary W. M. Hargreaves, and Robert Seager, eds., *The Papers of Henry Clay*, 7 vols. (Lexington: University Press of Kentucky, 1959-) 1:460.

[3]"Harrison Co., Early incidents & Mineral developments," Meigs-Jackson Papers, Blennerhassett Historical Park Commission, Parkersburg, West Virginia (hereinafter cited as Meigs-Jackson Papers, BHPC); Harvey Harmer, *Old Grist Mills of Harrison County* (Charleston WV: Charleston Printing Company, 1940) 58-60.

feet by thirty-two feet and placed two waterwheels in operation.[4] On 20 May 1811 Jackson purchased from Stephen Dicks, a millwright from Pennsylvania, a forty-three-acre tract of land farther up Elk Creek, which included a gristmill constructed by Dicks in 1808. The following year he acquired another mill at Quiet Dell, also on Elk Creek, about four miles from Clarksburg, which Dicks had built in 1794.[5]

A visit to the handsome estate of General John Mason on Analostan Island in the Potomac River in the summer of 1813, where he observed the shearing of fine Merino sheep, convinced Jackson that his industries must include facilities for the processing of wool.[6] He converted the mill he had built on Elk Creek in 1810 into a cotton and woolen factory that would "subserve the interests of the community much more, than half a dozen water grist mills."[7] Jackson envisioned great profits in the production of wool. "Cloth makers in New England," he wrote his wife, "are making fortunes by giving 2 1/2 dollars for Merino & one dollar a pound for common wool." He proposed to buy all the wool he could get, as cheaply as possible, and cautioned Mary that "it is unwise to let the idea of high price go abroad."[8]

In order to set up a cotton and woolen factory, Jackson needed twelve to eighteen inches more water than a gristmill required. Believing that his rights to erect a dam may have lapsed because of his failure to put a gristmill into operation within the three years required and that backwater from the higher dam might injure a mill belonging to Stephen Dicks, Jackson

---

[4]Harrison County Court Minute Book, 1809-1810, 185, Harrison County Courthouse, Clarksburg, West Virginia; Henry Haymond, *History of Harrison County, West Virginia, from the Early Days of Northwestern Virginia to the Present* (Morgantown WV: Acme Publishing Company, 1910) 346-47.

[5]Harmer, *Old Grist Mills of Harrison County*, 85-86; Clarksburg *Telegram*, 12 February 1876.

[6]Jackson to Mary S. Jackson, 6 June 1813, Meigs-Jackson Papers, BHPC. For Mason's estate, see Elbridge Gerry, Jr., *The Diary of Elbridge Gerry, Jr.* (New York: Brentano's, 1927) 159.

[7]Harrison County Legislative Petition, 18 November 1813, Virginia State Library, Richmond.

[8]Jackson to Mary S. Jackson, 3 February 1814, Meigs-Jackson Papers, BHPC.

did not apply to the county court for a writ of *ad quod damnum*. Instead, on 18 November 1813 he petitioned the Virginia legislature to establish his mill dam and mills on the same footing as if they had been applied for "to drive carding, spinning, & fulling mills &c." He also sought permission to raise his dam as much as eighteen more inches, subject to the payment of such damages as a jury might decide. On 12 February 1814 the legislature authorized him to build and operate woolen, cotton, carding, and spinning machines and fulling and oil mills at his dam on Elk Creek, "which was heretofore established by the County of Harrison for a water grist mill." At the same time it granted his request to lay off a town for his workers, not to exceed fifty acres in area and to be known as "Mile's End," on his lands about one mile from Clarksburg.[9]

On 4 February 1814 Jackson visited the factory of Congressman Alexander McKim in Baltimore, where he engaged the services of two or three millwrights, two or three blacksmiths, a joiner, a saddler, and other artisans. When spring came he sent wagons drawn by oxen to Cumberland, Maryland, to transport heavy machinery he had purchased in Baltimore and ordered shipped to Cumberland. Tradition maintains that about one hundred men of the Clarksburg area, excited by the prospects of the new industry, went along to prepare the roads for their unusual burden. The machinery equipped not only a cotton and woolen mill, but also an iron furnace, a tannery, which Jackson had put into production in 1813, and other industries. Jackson expected the factory and a saltworks to bring in "a pretty smart revenue to me, or it would be idle to go on the way I do."[10]

By 1814 Jackson had several industries in operation at Mile's End. Among them were woolen and cotton mills, an extensive tannery, and a fulling mill. In addition, he had several gristmills and a saltworks nearing completion. When he was in Clarksburg, Jackson kept a close watch over

---

[9]Harrison County Legislative Petition, 18 November 1813; Virginia, General Assembly, *Acts, 1813*, 139, 145. Mile's End was usually referred to locally as "The Factory." Dorothy Davis, *John George Jackson* (Parsons WV: McClain Printing Company, 1976) 223.

[10]Jackson to Mary S. Jackson, 3 February 1814, Meigs-Jackson Papers, BHPC; Harrison County Personal Property Tax List, 1813, Virginia State Library; "Harrison Co., Early incidents & Mineral developments," Meigs-Jackson Papers, BHPC; Clarksburg *News*, 15 May 1886.

his industries. A large, vigorous man and an excellent horseman, he mounted his horse early each morning and rode three miles up the West Fork to the saltworks and from there across the hill to Mile's End on Elk Creek. On these daily journeys of inspection, Jackson carried with him "Old Skuller," his favorite rifle, and frequently added to the journeys' pleasure by killing deer.[11]

Of Jackson's enterprises, saltmaking was one of the most satisfactory. Encouraged by a thriving salt industry above Charleston on the Kanawha River and by the modest saltworks of John Haymond and Benjamin Wilson at Bulltown, on the Little Kanawha, since 1809, Jackson and his uncle, Edward, began to dig for saltwater on the West Fork in June 1813. They chose a site about three miles above Clarksburg and by dint of "great, industry and perseverance, & at vast expence [*sic*]" succeeded in obtaining a supply of saltwater in July 1814.[12] Jackson contracted with Jesse Evans of the Decker's Creek Iron Works near Morgantown for sixty large kettles, for which he paid seven hundred dollars. By March 1814 Evans had finished twenty-seven of the kettles, and in the midst of winter, Jackson sent his wagons for them at once.[13]

Although the brine obtained by Jackson was only about one-third as strong as that found in the Kanawha Valley, he believed that he could produce salt profitably by substituting water-driven pumping machinery for equipment operated by "a horse power." For that purpose he petitioned the Virginia legislature on 10 November 1814 for permission to build a mill dam not to exceed six feet in height above the low-water mark at his saltworks, with a slope of the width and angle required by law. Seeking to cast his request in the most favorable light possible, he stated that his "primary object" was to provide salt at a reasonable price to people of the area, who had depended on supplies from Winchester, and "check the speculations" by which they were compelled to pay two or three dollars more per bushel

---

[11]Clarksburg *News*, 15 May 1886.

[12]Harrison County Legislative Petition, 10 November 1814; Rice, *Allegheny Frontier*, 309-13.

[13]Jackson to Mary S. Jackson, 3 February 1814, Meigs-Jackson Papers, BHPC. For the Decker's Creek Iron Works, see Rice, *Allegheny Frontier*, 314.

at slaughtering time than in midsummer.[14] On 9 December 1814 the legislature granted Jackson's request to construct the dam, but it reduced the maximum height to which he might raise the structure to five feet. The Harrison County Court added its approval. On 15 May 1815 it granted him permission to build a dam five feet high across the West Fork River for the specific purpose of providing water for driving a pump and other machinery.[15]

Several years before the establishment of Mile's End, Jackson had developed plans for an ironworks in the West Fork Valley. He prospected the region for iron ore and had samples analyzed at Eastern furnaces. Hearing of Jackson's intentions, John Hayden, an experienced iron furnace operator of Uniontown, Pennsylvania, wrote Jackson that "there is the Best prospect of a plenty [of ore] Within that Neighborhood of any I Ever Saw in the West Country." Hayden expressed the hope that he might serve Jackson in some capacity, but Jackson's preparations for iron manufacture were evidently not sufficiently matured to require Hayden's services.[16]

In 1813 Jackson entered into a conditional agreement with Philip Bier for the construction of an iron furnace on land then belonging to John and George Devilbiss. He and Bier agreed to construct buildings, procure machinery, and set a furnace in operation, with Jackson assuming a two-thirds interest in the enterprise and Bier the remaining one-third. However, they failed to acquire the Devilbiss lands and dissolved their partnership.[17] For the moment Jackson's venture into the iron manufacturing business faltered.

During his absences for his congressional duties in Washington from 1813 to 1817, Jackson entrusted the management of his agricultural and industrial enterprises to various managers, but he frequently requested that

---

[14]Harrison County Legislative Petition, 10 November 1814; "Harrison Co., Early incidents & Mineral developments," Meigs-Jackson Papers, BHPC.

[15]Virginia, General Assembly, *Acts, 1814*, 132; Harrison County Court Minute Book, 1814-1816, 158, 189.

[16]John Hayden to Jackson, 30 March 1811, Meigs-Jackson Papers, BHPC; "Harrison Co., Early incidents & Mineral developments," ibid.

[17]Contract of Bier and Jackson, 19 October 1813, ibid.

his wife provide him with information on their performance.[18] He agreed that his uncle, Edward Jackson, who had a one-half interest in the saltworks, should be in charge of that operation, a decision he often regretted. On one occasion he wrote to Mary that Edward did not produce sufficient salt and that he was "always fooling around."[19] His uncle, he declared, "seems to be the most unlucky man in his movements I ever heard of—always tinkering at the Salt Works & doing nothing." To make matters worse, Jackson found it almost impossible to get precise information from Edward concerning production and other affairs at the saltworks.[20]

Despite his dissatisfaction with his uncle, Jackson kept him in charge of the salt operation. In January 1817, in his last year in Washington, he still complained that Edward had not kept his promise to write once a week with details of progress at the saltworks. The frustrated Jackson found it almost impossible to ascertain whether his manager was "boiling or boring, for I have not heard one word of the Salt Works since I left home." In desperation, he asked his wife to send a note to his uncle and request an answer by a servant. He wished to know the amount of salt produced each day since he left home, how much was then being made, the depth to which the wells had been bored, the state of the millwright work, how far his uncle could bore in one day, and why he did not move ahead with the boring in preference to everything else.[21]

For a time iron production proved even more disappointing than progress at the saltworks. After postponing work on an iron furnace, Jackson in 1816 "commenced and completed ready to go into blast a furnace for making iron metal with all the necessary buildings, and collected a large quantity of ore, coal" and other essentials. This furnace was located at the east end of Clarksburg just west of Stillhouse Run on the Philippi road.[22] More

---

[18]Jackson to Mary S. Jackson, 27 May 1813, ibid.

[19]Jackson to Mary S. Jackson, undated fragment of a letter, ibid.

[20]Jackson to Mary S. Jackson, undated fragment of a letter, [1815], ibid.

[21]Jackson to Mary S. Jackson, 25 January 1817, ibid.

[22]Jackson to James Madison, 15 October 1816, James Madison Papers, Library of Congress, Washington, D.C.; "Harrison Co., Early incidents & Mineral developments," Meigs-Jackson Papers, BHPC.

setbacks awaited Jackson. In January 1817, when Jackson was once more in Washington, Thomas Chapman, his overseer at the ironworks, wrote that he lacked a sufficient supply of ore and presented such a bleak prospect for the furnace that Jackson declared, "I almost fear that by some misconduct it will defeat my just expectations of realising [*sic*] profit commensurate to my fair claims."[23] Two weeks later Chapman informed Jackson that the furnace had become stopped up for want of water, causing Jackson to fear that it would have to "blow out."[24]

Jackson's greatest disappointment arose from the behavior of his young cousin and protégé, Jonathan Jackson, the son of his Uncle Edward. Jonathan, who assisted Jackson in his legal practice and looked after his business interests during his absences, proved unusually irresponsible in financial matters. His worst offense was a failure to settle his accounts from July 1815 through May 1816 as a federal collector of internal revenue, a position Jackson had obtained for him. Jackson refused to rescue Jonathan from his embarrassments and gave him such a lecture that he did not expect to see him again for some time. He replaced Jonathan with a trusted brother-in-law, Daniel Kincheloe.[25]

To meet the demand for laborers on his farms and in his expanding industries, Jackson drew from the local population, but he turned increasingly to Negro slavery. He purchased his first slave, Clayborne, from a local owner in 1801 for $640. The following year he bought three slaves—Esther, Harriet, and Charles—from Alexander McClelland. The slaves were born in Virginia, but McClelland took them to Pennsylvania, where he kept them about thirty-six hours. Informed that he had violated a Pennsylvania law of 1788, which held that any slave brought into the state should be free, McClelland sold the slaves to Jackson. The Negroes never made any attempt to obtain their freedom, but Jackson, probably in doubt about the

---

[23]Jackson to Mary S. Jackson, 11 January 1817, Meigs-Jackson Papers, BHPC. See also George Jackson to Mary S. Jackson, 18 February 1817, ibid.

[24]Jackson to Mary S. Jackson, 25 January 1817, ibid.

[25]Jackson to Mary S. Jackson, 17 February, 1817, ibid.; Jonathan Jackson to John G. Jackson, 27 February 1816, ibid.; U.S. Treasury Department, Miscellaneous Treasury Accounts, General Accounting Office, 1st Auditor's Office, National Archives, Washington, D.C.

legality of his purchase, sued McClelland for $452.50. On 20 August 1805 the Virginia District Court awarded him $137.85 and interest.[26]

Jackson gradually increased the number of his slaves. In 1809 he paid taxes on six blacks over twelve years old.[27] That year he attempted to purchase additional slaves from Hugh Nelson of Belvoir, Virginia, but Nelson had already sold them when Jackson made his inquiry. The following year he advertised in the Clarksburg *Bye-Stander* for Negro men and boys who were good farmers and either skilled at a trade or capable of learning one. In 1813, a year of considerable expansion of his industrial activity, Jackson owned twelve or thirteen slaves over twelve years old.[28]

His reliance upon slave labor caused Jackson considerable misgivings both with regard to its effectiveness and the problems of control over Negroes in an industrial environment. He wrote his wife in early 1814 that he hoped that he could obtain reliable men to oversee the slaves' work, "keep them away from us, & relieve us from a trouble—vexatious & perplexing. The Salt Works will be a fit place for several of them."[29]

Despite his apprehensions, Jackson continued to increase his stock of slaves. He made few purchases in 1816 because of the high prices then prevailing, but in 1817 he possessed thirty Negroes older than twelve. Of that number, twenty-seven were older than sixteen, with a total value of $18,050. At the time of his death in 1825, he held forty-one slaves, eight of whom were at his forge, fourteen at the iron furnace, fourteen at the dwelling house, and five at the saltworks.[30]

---

[26]Harrison County Court Minute Book, 1803-1805, 165-67, 245, 351-52; Davis, *John George Jackson*, 66, 356.

[27]Harrison County Personal Property Tax List, 1809. See also Harrison County Personal Property Tax Lists, 1801, 1802, 1804, 1805, 1807, 1810, 1811, 1812.

[28]Hugh Nelson to Jackson, 7 January 1810, John George Jackson Papers, Lilly Library, Indiana University, Bloomington; Clarksburg *Bye-Stander*, 2 October 1810; Harrison County Personal Property Tax List, 1813; Harrison County Tithable List, Book 2, 51, Harrison County Courthouse.

[29]Jackson to Mary S. Jackson, 3 February 1814, Meigs-Jackson Papers, BHPC.

[30]Jackson to Mary S. Jackson, 3 January 1816, ibid.; Harrison County Tith-

The Jackson slaves appear to have been a rather unruly lot. The difficulties probably arose in part from Jackson's prolonged absences from home during his service in the Virginia legislature and in Congress. Jacob Means, whom he employed as an overseer of his farms, wrote in November 1804 that one slave, Sam, had not finished the sowing of the grain, which he had been told to do, had "let the horses and cattle run in the orchard and in my [Means's] corn at the barn and destroyed it very much[,] and broke a number of your apple trees." Clayborne, another slave, had returned home after an absence of about six days "with the horses very pore and a sore back and denied having any mony [*sic*] or bills." Both Sam and Clayborne were very "sassy and say they will doo as they please for they was left to do their oan work there way." Moreover, Means wrote Jackson that the two blacks did not come home from nightly wanderings until breakfast and that when "I tell them they must not neglect their work they say if I strike them they will run away and that Is a fact for they have been gone every day."[31]

Some slave misbehavior involved infraction of the Virginia criminal code and intervention by legal authorities. In 1811 Jackson's slave June stole shirts from the house of James Pindall, a prominent Clarksburg attorney, and attempted to sell them at Jackson's saltworks. June then fled and was apprehended by Richard Dotson at his house in Wood County. He was tried for grand larceny and sentenced to death by hanging on 1 November 1811. Benjamin Wilson, Jr., a member of the Harrison County Court, which passed judgment on June, interceded with Governor George W. Smith to have him pardoned. Wilson declared that June had committed the theft while he was intoxicated and that otherwise he was "an industrious, trusty[,] dutiful[,] obedient slave."[32]

---

able List, 1817, Book 2, 200. For other information on the Jackson slaves, see also Harrison County Tithable Lists, 1812, 1814, 1815, 1818, 1819, 1821, 1822, 1823, 1824, Book 2, 9, 85, 109, 217, 236, 359, 427, 460, 533; Harrison County Personal Property Tax List, 1814; Inventory of the Estate of John G. Jackson, Harrison County Deed Book 3, 291-335, Harrison County Courthouse; "Harrison Co., Early incidents & Mineral developments," Meigs-Jackson Papers, BHPC.

[31]Jacob Means to Jackson, 7 November 1804, Meigs-Jackson Papers, BHPC.

[32]Transcript of Trial of June, Slave of J[ohn] G. Jackson, Virginia, Executive Papers, Pardon Papers, 1811, Virginia State Library; Benjamin Wilson, Jr., to George W. Smith, 20 September 1811, ibid.

The insubordination of the slaves frequently caused Mary Jackson deep anxiety. One such incident occurred in the summer of 1813, when Mary was eight months pregnant. Jackson apparently had suspicions that the difficulty arose from neglect or indiscretion on the part of Jonathan, who was looking after his affairs. He told Mary, "I'd rather that Jonathan were killed than that your fright should be any degree injurious."[33] Mary, who evidently had considerable compassion for the slaves, nevertheless, expressed concern about threats made by Chapman to sell some of those who had offended her. Jackson assured Mary that Chapman "only intended to intimidate, & make them obedient."[34]

By January and February 1817 Jackson himself had become convinced that he should sell some of the most recalcitrant blacks in order to induce the others to behave more properly. He urged Mary to have "fortitude & forbearance in relation to the vexation of business & our slaves" until he returned home from Congress.[35] Two weeks later he advised her to "relax in your cares," and if any slave gave trouble to "send for Sheriff Synott which I hope you will do, & have the first offender committed to jail until I return home."[36]

Ironically, the most serious charge ever made against a Jackson slave occurred shortly after he returned to Clarksburg from Congress. David, a slave belonging to Jackson, struck Isaac, a slave of Thomas Miller, on the head with a mattock and inflicted a fatal wound. On 15 July 1817 a court of oyer and terminer for Harrison County found David guilty of murder and sentenced him to be hanged on 29 August 1817.[37] Lemuel E. Davisson wrote William Robertson, the clerk of the Council of Virginia, that he did

---

[33]Jackson to Mary S. Jackson, 8 July 1813, Meigs-Jackson Papers, BHPC.

[34]Jackson to Mary S. Jackson, 16 February 1814, ibid. For a similar statement, see also Jackson to Mary S. Jackson, 20 January 1814, ibid.

[35]Jackson to Mary S. Jackson, 3 February 1817, ibid.; Jackson to Mary S. Jackson, 22 January 1817, ibid.; Jackson to Mary S. Jackson, 25 January 1817, ibid.; Jackson to Mary S. Jackson, 1 February 1817, ibid.; Jackson to Mary S. Jackson, 15 February 1817, ibid.

[36]Jackson to Mary S. Jackson, 19 February 1817, ibid.

[37]Report to Governor James E. Barbour, 22 July 1817, Virginia, Executive Papers.

not believe that evidence produced at the trial justified or proved the charge of premeditated murder. He stated that in an earlier trial for larceny David had had benefit of clergy and that this evidence had not been introduced at the trial. A deposition of Squire, another Jackson slave, stated that David and Isaac had been friendly until about an hour before the attack occurred. As a result, the sentence was not carried out.[38]

With Ohio and Pennsylvania less than seventy-five miles distant, Jackson's industrial slaves had unusual temptations to run away. In April 1822 he wrote to President James Monroe that "two valuable men[,] a Carpenter & Blacksmith[,] have ran [*sic*] away from me, & we look in the approaching season for several others to follow." He told Monroe that two years previously his brother, Edward B. Jackson, and his cousin, Jonathan Jackson, had each lost slaves who had fled to Ohio, where they found aid in escaping to Canada. Jackson believed that the assistance given the fugitives and their reception in Canada constituted an inducement to other slaves to follow their example and expressed the hope that the president might work out some agreement with Great Britain to prevent further encouragement of the practice.[39]

Jackson's difficulties with some of his industries and his slaves led him to declare, perhaps in a moment of dejection, "I am regretting very much that I have gone so largely into public works, but I must now make the best of them, either work[,] rent, or sell. I incline to the latter, & then I will retire from the vexations of business."[40] On another occasion, when he received notice of a six months' dividend of $525 on stock he held in the Bank of Marietta, he expressed the view that such investments were "much better than works of any kind."[41] Yet Jackson conceded that his industries had contributed substantially to such an increase in his wealth that he could consider renting or selling them in order that he and Mary might travel "and take some of the indulgences which my fortune entitles us to." At the

---

[38]Davisson to Robertson, 15 April 1817, ibid.; Deposition of Squire, August 1817, ibid.; Haymond, *History of Harrison County*, 228.

[39]Jackson to Monroe, 13 April 1822, John George Jackson Papers.

[40]Jackson to Mary S. Jackson, 1 February 1817, Meigs-Jackson Papers, BHPC.

[41]Jackson to Mary S. Jackson, 9 January 1814, ibid.; Jackson to Mary S. Jackson, 22 January 1817, ibid.

same time he ventured the opinion that "we may . . . spend of it freely, and there will be a large Estate for our children beside."[42]

Once Jackson's congressional career ended, he found more time for personal supervision of his agricultural and industrial enterprises. His numerous disappointments, British dumping of goods on the American market, and a declining economy that became evident in the Western country as early as 1817 caused him to decide against any immediate expansion of his operations.[43] By 1818, however, the iron furnace could produce enough metal for yearly local needs in only four weeks. To expand his markets, he sent Samuel Hart to Marietta and other Western towns, but he faced competition from ironmakers along the Ohio and evidently did not expand his sales greatly in that area.[44]

In February 1820 Jackson advertised that he had bar iron, iron castings, and pot metal for sale at his ironworks. Recognizing the effects of the Panic of 1819 and the shortage of money, which was chronic in the Western country, he expressed a willingness to accept corn, wheat, flax, bacon, linen, and other farm products in exchange for his metals. Two years later Jackson wrote his father that the "forge is now doing well, the Iron excellent. The Furnace will start in a few days. A great stock on hand & the ore excellent for Bar Iron."[45]

Production increased steadily at Jackson's ironworks. In one year he exported one hundred tons of iron castings valued at $1,860. He worked up most of the pig metal produced at the furnace into stoves and hollow ware, particularly cooking utensils, which he sold locally and down the West Fork and Monongahela rivers as far as Pittsburgh. His workmen dug ore and obtained limestone throughout the hills from Elk Creek to Ann

---

[42]Jackson to Mary S. Jackson, 20 February 1815, ibid.

[43]Rice, *Allegheny Frontier*, 313; Davis, *John George Jackson*, 271.

[44]Jackson to Charles Yancey, 30 January 1819, John George Jackson Papers; Samuel Hart to Jackson, 19 March 1818, Meigs-Jackson Papers, Ohio Historical Society, Campus Martius Museum, Marietta (hereinafter cited as Meigs-Jackson Papers, OHS-CMM).

[45]Clarksburg *Republican Compiler*, 18 February 1820; Jackson to George Jackson, 19 December 1822, Harrison County Circuit Court Records, Harrison County Courthouse.

Moore's Run. Nathan J. Davis recalled, when he was ninety years old, that most of the deer killed in Harrison County were shot with guns made of iron from Jackson's furnace. Ephraim Bee, of Doddridge County, and several other men made horseshoes, and Benjamin Scott supervised a number of hands in the manufacture of axes. Leonard Hoskinson, who rented the "Judge's Forge" after Jackson's death, declared that it produced iron of "a quality superior to any ever brought this side of the Mountains."[46]

Jackson's personal attention to his ironworks and other enterprises after he left Congress only partially explains their success. Also of importance was his increasing use of contracts with skilled craftsmen by which their own rewards were hinged to productivity. One such contract was with John Hugill, a master ironworker, whom Jackson employed as supervisor of his forge in late 1819. Under their agreement Jackson provided Hugill with a set of tools, boards, and cloths, kept him in iron and steel, and gave him a helper, probably a slave. Hugill agreed to furnish another set of tools and a helper to work in the shop and to keep up two fires. As he did with other essential craftsmen whom he employed, Jackson provided Hugill with a house, a garden plot, coal, and firewood.[47]

In 1823, when Jackson added nail-making to his ironworks at Mile's End, he contracted with James Trusdall, whom he met in Zanesville, Ohio, for the construction of the nail-cutting machine. Jackson sent a wagon to meet Trusdall and his family in Marietta, and, as was his custom with skilled supervisors, provided him with a house and garden free during his employment. Trusdall undertook the project at the "usual prices in the adjacent State, & Country" and accepted payment from Jackson "principally in the produce of his works, in necessaries for Trusdall's family, & a part in money for his wages."[48]

---

[46]Jackson to Charles S. Morgan, 5 January 1823, Charles S. Morgan Papers, West Virginia Department of Archives and History, Charleston; "Harrison Co., Early incidents & Mineral developments," Meigs-Jackson Papers, BHPC; Clarksburg *Intelligencer*, 16 July 1825; Clarksburg *News*, 15 May 1886; Wheeling *Register*, 23 September 1890.

[47]Contract between John G. Jackson and John Hugle [Hugill], 22 November 1819, Meigs-Jackson Papers, BHPC.

[48]Contract between John G. Jackson and James Trusdall, 4 March 1823, ibid.

Meanwhile, at his fulling mill Jackson had acquired the services of John T. Young, who remained with him until his death. He provided Young with a house and garden, fuel, dyestuffs, pasturage for his calves, and other necessities. In exchange, he required Young to keep an accurate set of books. Under the contract, Jackson received two-thirds of the profits and Young one-third.[49]

In contrast to the success of his ironworks and fulling mill, Jackson's salt wells began to decline. In 1822 the brine produced only seven and one-half bushels of salt a day instead of the twenty-one bushels it had yielded two years previously. In fact, in 1815 a single furnace had produced ten bushels per day. Nevertheless, William Rhodes, Jacob Willard, and Obediah Davisson, who rented the property after Jackson's death, expressed the belief that they could still manufacture enough salt to supply the West Fork Valley and prevent the drainage of money out of Harrison County.[50]

About the time his saltworks on the West Fork began to decline, Jackson turned his attention to potential salt-producing properties he owned jointly with his father near Zanesville, Ohio. In April 1821 he and his father entered into a partnership with John's brother, George Washington Jackson, who agreed to improve the land "by boring for salt water, [and] erecting [a] sawmill, suitable buildings for the works, and a good dwelling house for said George W[ashington] to reside in and carry on the works when completed." The contract also provided that George Washington should have one-third of the 150-acre salt tract and an allowance for his services, as well as stating that all would share expenses and profits equally.[51] Available records suggest that the venture failed, perhaps because salt from the Kanawha Valley and from new wells in the Pomeroy, Ohio, area was able to dominate Ohio Valley markets.[52]

---

[49]Contract between John G. Jackson and John T. Young, 25 March 1820, ibid. Prior to his arrangement with Young, Jackson had employed Horace Allen of New York as fuller. Davis, *John George Jackson*, 293.

[50]Jackson to George Jackson, 19 December 1822, Harrison County Circuit Court Records; Clarksburg *Intelligencer*, 25 June 1825, 2 and 9 July 1825.

[51]Jackson to George Jackson, 19 December 1822, Harrison County Circuit Court Records.

[52]Rice, *Allegheny Frontier*, 313.

Although his industries demanded more and more of his attention, Jackson never diminished his interest in agricultural pursuits. In 1811 he discharged tenants on five of his tracts in order that he might farm the lands himself and add to the supply of grain for his mills, but in later years his agricultural endeavors became increasingly adjunctive to his industrial enterprises.[53] His hired workers and slaves required substantial amounts of food products. A Beef and Pork Book, which Jackson kept for many years, showed that in 1822 he killed 64 hogs, weighing a total of 8,000 pounds. Yet such were the needs of his employees that he purchased an additional 39,500 pounds of pork, of which 10,000 were used at the iron furnace and 4,000 at the saltworks. Between 24 September and 19 December of that year he killed 40 beef cattle, and the previous year he slaughtered 46. He also provided corn, wheat, rye, oats, and other products for his workers.[54]

Meanwhile, Jackson continued to add to his landholdings. In 1809 he owned 3,494 acres in Harrison County valued at $28,962. Five years later he held 4,467 acres in the county. On 25 May 1814 he bought from his father, then living in Zanesville, Ohio, two tracts on Elk Creek, in and adjoining Clarksburg, for which he paid $10,000. By 1821 his holdings aggregated 7,046 acres, valued at $29,949.98, including buildings worth $5,399.50. His most valuable property was assessed at $12,537, of which $5,000 was for his dwelling.[55]

---

[53]Jackson to James Madison, 19 April 1811, James Madison Papers, Library of Congress.

[54]Jackson to Charles S. Morgan, 5 January 1823, Charles S. Morgan Papers. The Beef and Pork Book, which Jackson mentioned, is apparently no longer extant.

[55]For Jackson's Harrison County lands, see Harrison County Land Book, 1811, 27-28, Harrison County Courthouse; ibid., 1812, 34; ibid., 1813, 35-36; ibid., 1814, 36-37; ibid., 1819, 20-21; Harrison County Land Book Upper District, 1821, 13; Harrison County Land Book Lower District, 1821, 12; "Schedule of Lands, Slaves, & other things the property of J. G. Jackson—Annexed to his Will [1809]," Meigs-Jackson Papers, OHS-CMM; George Bryan to John G. Jackson, 31 July 1815, Jackson Family Papers, Virginia Historical Society, Richmond; Indenture between George Jackson and John G. Jackson, 25 May 1815, Harrison County Deed Book 21, 17, Harrison County Courthouse.

Extensive as they were, Jackson's Harrison County properties constituted but a small portion of his landed wealth. In 1809 he paid a direct tax on 38,492 acres recorded in the District Court of Monongalia for lands in Harrison and Wood counties, which represented a one-fourth interest in a 155,768-acre property of which Jackson's deceased mother-in-law, Mary Payne, owned a one-fourth interest and Jonathan Dayton the remainder. In addition, Jackson owned 6,793 acres in military lands in Ohio, the most valuable of which lay along the Muskingum River and were worth five dollars per acre. In 1809 Jackson's total holdings amounted to 48,904 acres and were valued at $71,396.[56]

George Jackson acted as agent for John's Ohio properties. Between 1 August 1806 and 26 May 1815, he sold nineteen tracts of land and transacted other business for his son, amounting to $15,573.55. During the same period John sold lands and conducted other business, mostly in Harrison County, for his father, for a total of $15,449.63. When the two settled their accounts, George Jackson paid his son the balance of $123.92 due him in limestone lands in Harrison County. Between 19 June 1819 and 5 March 1823, George Jackson transacted additional business for John, including the sale of seven tracts and five lots valued at $5,404.85. John disposed of Virginia lands belonging to his father, who remained indebted to him for $1,304.85 when they again settled their accounts.[57]

As the foremost entrepreneur of the West Fork Valley, Jackson had a keen appreciation of the close relationship between industrial development and adequate banking facilities. He evidently took the initiative in the formation, by written compact, of a company known as the Farmer's Bank of Virginia on 15 August 1814. Located at Clarksburg, the organization had capital of $120,000. Its stated purpose was to render "pecuniary aid" to the people of northwestern Virginia, since the branches of the Bank

---

[56]"Schedule of Lands, Slaves, & other things the property of J. G. Jackson—Annexed to his Will [1809]," Meigs-Jackson Papers, OHS-CMM. A facsimile of this document is in Davis, *John George Jackson*, 329-40.

[57]Statement of Accounts Settled, George Jackson and John G. Jackson, 26 May 1815, Meigs-Jackson Papers, BHPC; Statement of Accounts Settled, George Jackson and John G. Jackson, 5 March 1823, ibid. See also George Jackson, Power of Attorney to John G. Jackson and Edward B. Jackson, 27 May 1815, Meigs-Jackson Papers, OHS-CMM.

of Virginia generally refused to lend money to persons living in isolated areas.[58]

On 10 December 1815 the promoters of the Farmer's Bank of Virginia asked the legislature to approve a charter for an institution called the Virginia Saline Bank, with capital of $300,000. The stated purpose of the institution coincided so perfectly with the activities of Jackson that it must be assumed that Jackson was its chief architect. The promoters pointed out that "valuable wells of salt water, and mines of Iron Ore," as well as "inexhaustible bodies of Stone coal and timber," existed in the vicinity of Clarksburg. They expressed a desire to promote the improvement of the Monongahela River; the manufacture of salt, woolen and cotton goods, and other articles; and the encouragement of agriculture.

The petitioners declared that Western residents suffered great inconvenience because they had to rely upon paper issued by banks in Ohio and Pennsylvania as a circulating medium. As a result of the policies of those banks, specie was "continually Vanishing from the circulation [in the West Fork Valley] and burying itself in the Vaults of the numerous Banks of Ohio and Pennsylvania." Without waiting for legislative action, the stockholders of the bank proceeded on the assumption that the charter would be forthcoming.[59]

The General Assembly rejected the petition for incorporation of the Virginia Saline Bank, but the indomitable Jackson prepared another memorial for the next session. It asked for a charter for a bank with capital of $150,000, either as a substitute for the Virginia Saline Bank or to be connected with it. The sixty-odd petitioners pointed out that "no person in this quarter of the State now has, or ever had a note discounted by either of the established Banks in this Commonwealth" and that the branch bank at Winchester flatly refused to make loans to persons living so far distant. They stated, "Since the declaration of the late war a Spirit of improvement

---

[58]Harrison County Legislative Petition, 10 December 1815. Several writers have stated that the Virginia Saline Bank had its origins in 1812, but they cite no evidence. See, for example, Haymond, *History of Harrison County*, 403; Boyd B. Stutler, "Money Is What You Make It," *West Virginia Review* 10 (May 1933): 226.

[59]Harrison County Legislative Petition, 10 December 1815.

has been manifested amongst us . . . and given a new spring to its industry and enterprise."[60]

The legislature continued to reject the petitions of its promoters, but the Virginia Saline Bank remained in operation. Jackson, who held 600 of its 12,500 shares of stock, was one of the principal investors in the bank. His grandmother, Elizabeth Cummins Jackson, owned 100 shares. The establishment by the legislature in 1817 of the Northwestern Bank of Virginia at Wheeling, with authorization to set up branches at Wellsburg, Morgantown, and Clarksburg, obviated the need for the Virginia Saline Bank, and it, like other wildcat banks, proved short-lived.[61]

In addition to his holdings in the Virginia Saline Bank, Jackson had connections with other banking institutions. In 1812 he became an attorney for the Bank of Zanesville, of which his father served as a director. In November 1818 the Virginia Board of Public Works named him as its representative on the Board of Directors of the Northwestern Bank of Virginia at Wheeling.[62] He may also have served as a director or attorney for the Bank of Marietta, in which he was a stockholder.[63] When he sold his house in Washington following his retirement from Congress in 1810, he accepted as payment from the Metropolis Bank, the purchaser, 200 shares of stock valued at $40 per share in lieu of cash. In 1817 he invested $5,000 in stock of the newly rechartered Bank of the United States.[64]

---

[60]Harrison County Legislative Petition, 28 October 1816.

[61]Haymond, *History of Harrison County*, 403. For the establishment of the Northwestern Bank of Virginia, see Rice, *Allegheny Frontier*, 329; Charles H. Ambler and Festus P. Summers, *West Virginia, the Mountain State*, 2d ed. (Englewood Cliffs NJ: Prentice-Hall, Inc., 1958) 128.

[62]Certificate of Appointment of J. G. Jackson as Attorney for the Bank of Zanesville, 2 March 1812, Meigs-Jackson Papers, BHPC; Jackson to Bernard Peyton, 30 November 1818, Virginia, Board of Public Works Records, Monongalia Navigation Company Records, Virginia State Library.

[63]See, for example, L. Barber to John G. Jackson, 7 April 1814, Jackson Family Papers.

[64]Jackson to Mary S. Jackson, 9 April 1812, Meigs-Jackson Papers, BHPC; Jackson to Mary S. Jackson, 22 January 1814, ibid.

While he was making remunerative investments, Jackson also became involved in the shaky financial affairs of his brother-in-law, Richard Cutts of Massachusetts. During the War of 1812 Cutts speculated heavily in shipbuilding enterprises of a dubious nature and suffered severe financial losses. Apparently given to extravagant modes of life, he borrowed money freely, including about $5,000 from James Madison, another brother-in-law. Jackson endorsed a note for $6,000, which Cutts obtained from the Metropolis Bank in 1817, and Return Jonathan Meigs, Jr., acted as surety for another loan, which Cutts received from the Farmers and Mechanics Bank of Georgetown in 1819. Failing to recover his financial losses, even with support from friends and relatives, Cutts declared bankruptcy. Even then he was unable to escape commitment to a debtors' prison and the sale of his Washington properties. At the sale of Cutts's Washington assets, Madison purchased both his house and furniture and made them available to his family.[65]

Jackson and Meigs paid dearly for their friendship with Cutts. In 1823 Jackson learned that "Cutts is doing nothing, and never will, to pay his old debts or indemnify his endorsers" and that he would not apply any of his income from a government position Madison had obtained for him to "old scores" any more than he had "before he took benefit of the insolvent law."[66] The banks holding the Cutts notes later filed suits against the Meigs and Jackson estates. Meigs, who had endorsed notes totaling $4,500, still owed $4,117.98, including interest. Most of his property, including his house in Marietta, was sold to satisfy the claim against him.[67] Jackson, fortunately,

---

[65]Richard Cutts to Jackson, 22 May 1817, John George Jackson Papers; Washington *National Intelligencer*, 22 December 1825; Ralph Ketcham, *James Madison: A Biography* (New York: The Macmillan Company, 1971) 618. For the Madison purchases, see Thomas Monroe to Jackson, 30 September 1823, John George Jackson Papers; Dolley P. Madison to Jackson, 4 January 1825, Breckinridge-Watts Papers, Alderman Library, University of Virginia, Charlottesville.

[66]Thomas Monroe to Jackson, 30 September 1823, John George Jackson Papers.

[67]Thomas Monroe to Dr. Bradley, 12 September 1825, John George Jackson Papers; Sophia Meigs to Mary S. Jackson, 18 May 1825, Meigs-Jackson Papers, BHPC; Sophia Meigs to Mary S. Jackson, 3 June 1825, ibid.; Schedule of Provisions and Other Property [left to Sophia Meigs], 18 July 1825, ibid.; Washington *National Intelligencer*, 22 December 1825; Marietta *American Friend, & Marietta Gazette*, 10 April 1830.

left a sufficiently large estate that his obligations to the Bank of the United States were settled without such devastating effects.[68]

Adequate land and water transportation was as vital to Jackson's industrial and agricultural enterprises as banking facilities. In fact, to a considerable extent his own interests lay behind his legislative and congressional efforts to obtain road and river improvements. When the Harrison County Court decided on 17 June 1816 that it could not afford to build a bridge across Elk Creek, where a mill dam had destroyed the fording place, Jackson offered to build it himself. In accordance with a petition that Jackson addressed to the legislature, the county court agreed to assign him all the tolls that he might legally collect, pay him an additional $120 annually, and at the end of twelve years purchase the structure from him at a fair market price. On 7 December 1816 the General Assembly also gave Jackson permission to erect a toll bridge across the West Fork River at Clarksburg, and the Harrison County Court authorized a writ of *ad quod damnum* for the necessary lands. Jackson failed, however, to complete the work within the time allotted, and by agreement with the county court he surrendered his rights.[69]

One of Jackson's enduring civic interests, unrelated to his business enterprises, concerned Randolph Academy. In 1809 he served as president of its Board of Trustees, and in 1818 he accepted the position of treasurer. When the academy began to experience financial difficulties, the trustees named Jackson and Thomas P. Moore to seek an endowment from the legislature. Efforts to gain further legislative support proved unsuccessful, and in June 1822 Jackson served on a committee to contract for the completion of the log structure in which the academy was housed with funds that might be raised locally.[70]

---

[68]Virginia, Superior Court, Fourth District, Chancery Orders, 21 October 1826, No. 3, 135, 230-34, filed with the Harrison County Circuit Court Records.

[69]Harrison County Legislative Petition, 11 November 1816; Jackson to Court of Harrison County, 20 May 1822, Jackson Family Papers; Virginia, General Assembly, *Acts, 1816*, 110-11; Harrison County Court Minute Book, 1816-1818, 220, 222; ibid., 1818-1820, 164.

[70]Minutes of the Board of Trustees of Randolph Academy, 1803-1851, Typescript, West Virginia Collection, West Virginia University Library, Morgantown; Harrison County Court Minute Book, 1818-1820, 70.

Almost as a last-ditch effort to save Randolph Academy, Jackson turned to the collection of surveyors' fees, which the legislature had assigned to the school by the terms of its charter but which few of the surveyors had ever remitted. He instituted a suit for $62.23 against Robert Triplett, a surveyor who had failed to make payments to the academy. The Virginia Circuit Court, on 23 May 1823, ordered Triplett to pay the amount due with interest from 1 January 1820. However, such measures could not stem the decline of the academy, and by the mid-1820s it became "dormant for want of funds."[71]

For all his business interests, political responsibilities, and civic activities, Jackson found time to enjoy life. His house, the most elegant in Clarksburg, reflected the cultivated tastes of a country gentleman. In 1809, when he faced the possibility of death in the duel with Joseph Pearson, Jackson made an inventory of his property. Among his household effects he listed fifty-one articles of silver—including a coffee pot, a teapot, a sugar bowl, spoons, forks, tumblers, and other items—in addition to seventeen pieces of silver plate. While he was in Congress in 1813, he wrote Mary that he had bought some silverware in Georgetown worth $367. The purchases included six silver tumblers, $54; one silver milk bowl, $60; one "*superb*" silver coffee pot, $95; two silver pitchers, $94; four plated candlesticks, $23; one plated snuffer and tray, $11; and one set of elegant knives, forks, tablespoons, dessert spoons, and a carver, all with ivory handles, $30.[72]

Harrison County tithable lists and the inventory of Jackson's estate shed additional light upon the elegancies of his household. In 1815 the tithable list included among Jackson's numerous furnishings two bookcases, one sideboard, thirteen chairs ornamented with gold, twelve sets of window curtains, mirrors, a pianoforte, silver pitchers, and other articles. Personal

---

[71]Virginia, Eleventh Circuit Court, Chancery Orders, No. 2, 198, 246, filed with Harrison County Circuit Court Records; Rice, *Allegheny Frontier*, 238-40; Charles H. Ambler, *A History of Education in West Virginia from Early Colonial Times to 1949* (Huntington WV: Standard Printing and Publishing Company, 1951) 75-76, 107-108.

[72]"Schedule of Lands, Slaves, & other things the property of J. G. Jackson—Annexed to his Will [1809]," Meigs-Jackson Papers, OHS-CMM; Jackson to Mary S. Jackson, 3 July 1813, Meigs-Jackson Papers, BHPC.

property listed in the inventory of his estate included, in addition, dinner tables, card tables, tea tables, a desk, a Venetian carpet, and silverware worth more than $400, including a punchbowl worth $55, chinaware, an ice cream freezer, and a silver watch.[73]

Jackson's library also reveals intellectual interests befitting his position. Comprised of 725 volumes at his death, it covered a wide range of subjects. Jackson chose his books with great care. In 1810, shortly before his second marriage, he wrote Mary Meigs that he had been adding a "few choise [*sic*] books" to his collection "hitherto made both extensive & valuable, & as I delight much in reading & being read to in turn prepare yourself to do penance in that way when Heaven hasten the epoch when you are mine." Even when he was in Washington, where social opportunities existed in abundance, Jackson frequently spent his evenings in his room reading from such works as the writings of Sir Walter Scott—whom he regarded as one of the greatest writers of England—William Shakespeare, and Oliver Goldsmith.[74]

For many men the successes incident to a diversity of agricultural and industrial enterprises, a remunerative law practice, accumulating landed properties, and civic responsibilities would have provided all the ingredients needed for a rewarding life. Jackson, with his boundless energy and unquenchable ambition, needed more. With respect to his industrial establishment, he wrote James Madison, to whom he often confided his thoughts, "I am vexed that I have a wish beyond it, but dame nature is to blame[,] not I[;] she infused the fire [of politics and public service] & death alone can extinguish them."[75] When he returned to Washington in 1813 after three years' absence, Jackson was again in his element. During this

---

[73]Harrison County Tithable List, 1815, Book 2, 109; Inventory of the Estate of John George Jackson, Harrison County Will Book 3, 291-335.

[74]Inventory of the Estate of John George Jackson, Harrison County Will Book 3, 311-26; Jackson to Mary S. Meigs, 14 April 1810, Meigs-Jackson Papers, BHPC. See also Jackson to Mary S. Meigs, 24 May 1810, ibid.; Jackson to Mary S. Jackson, 3 June 1813, ibid.; Jackson to Mary S. Jackson, undated fragment of a letter, ibid.

[75]Jackson to James Madison, 19 April 1811, James Madison Papers, Library of Congress.

second period of service in Congress, which encompassed some of the most exciting and critical events in the history of the young republic, he would reach the zenith of his career as a statesman.

8 Wartime Congressman

On 25 May 1813 John G. Jackson returned to the House of Representatives as congressman from the First District of Virginia. He wrote President James Madison that he had left his home for Washington with some reluctance, evidently because of his wife's pregnancy. Jackson was convinced, however, that the welfare of the country required strong congressional support for the Madison administration. He had consented to become a candidate because he believed that he was the only Republican capable of defeating the Federalist incumbent, Thomas Wilson of Monongalia County, who in 1811 had won the congressional seat controlled by the Jackson family since 1795.[1]

The election, held in April 1813, confirmed Jackson's assessment of the political situation and resulted in a dramatic Republican victory in a district in which Federalism remained a substantial force. Jackson received 1,134, or nearly sixty percent, of the 1,870 votes cast for congressman and carried every county in the district with the exception of Wilson's home county of Monongalia.[2]

---

[1]Jackson to James Madison, 19 April 1813, James Madison Papers, Alderman Library, University of Virginia, Charlottesville.

[2]In the election Harrison County cast 549 votes for Jackson and 205 for Wilson; Monongalia County, 221 for Jackson and 383 for Wilson; Ohio County, 199 for Jackson and 116 for Wilson; and Brooke County, 165 for Jackson and 32 for Wilson. Jackson to James Madison, 19 April 1813, James Madison Papers, Alderman Library; Jackson to Madison, 3 May 1813, James Madison Papers, Library of Congress, Washington D.C.; Daniel Porter Jordan, Jr., "Virginia Congressmen, 1801-1825" (Ph.D. dissertation, University of Virginia, 1970) 407.

Jackson's victory in the election of 1813 rested not only upon his personal popularity but also upon his stout defense of the nation's rights and honor in the War of 1812 and the events preceding that conflict. He set the tone for the coming campaign in a speech at Clarksburg on 4 July 1812. He declared that the British paper blockade of enemy ports had provoked honest indignation throughout the world, but that impressment of American seamen stood "first on the list of [American] grievances" and was "unequalled in its wanton cruelties." According to Jackson, upwards of 5,000 American citizens had been impressed into British service, "torn from their country, from the liberty which they so highly value, and all the tender ties of nature." Jackson insisted that if the government did not protect the rights of these individuals, "the constitution is broken—and the whole fabric of government is dissolved."

In assertions clearly calculated to evoke the patriotism of western Virginians, Jackson charged that the British government was deliberately attempting to destroy the American union. He called upon all Americans to "rally round the constituted authority," for theirs was "the last asylum of liberty," and to defend their rights against all who would encroach upon them. At the same time he threatened that if the French government did not cease its hostile actions against the United States, "war will and must be declared against France also."[3]

As the campaign advanced, Jackson concentrated attention upon those Federalists who criticized the foreign policy of the Madison administration. He singled out for special excoriation the "criminal" action of Federalist members of Congress who had earlier issued a "joint address" to their constituents to protest the declaration of war against England. In a democratic system, he declared, the majority must govern, and the government "is at an end the moment it is overawed by a faction." He continued, "[W]ith a divided people we cannot make an impression upon his [England's] conduct toward us."[4] By way of contrast, in an address to voters of Wheeling, he stressed the evils of impressment. He "vindicated the course

---

[3]John G. Jackson, *Oration Pronounced at Clarksburg, on the Fourth Day of July, 1812, and Thirty-Seventh Year of American Independence* (Clarksburg WV: F. & A. Britton, 1812) 4-8.

[4]John G. Jackson, undated address, "To the People," John George Jackson Papers, Lilly Library, Indiana University, Bloomington.

taken by our government, and claimed, in the strongest language, every privilege of American native citizens" for naturalized persons.[5]

Although Jackson undoubtedly looked forward to the first session—a special one—of the Thirteenth Congress, which convened on 24 May, he delayed his departure from Clarksburg at the urging of his young wife, who was then in her seventh month of pregnancy.[6] Mary had given birth to their first child, a daughter, either in late March or on 1 April 1811, but she evidently lived only a short time. In November 1811 Mary was expecting again, but the absence of any records concerning the second birth suggests either that she had a miscarriage or that, like other Jackson children, the child lived but a brief time.[7] Jackson attempted to allay Mary's apprehensions concerning her third pregnancy and promised her that he would return to Clarksburg before the child was born.[8]

Jackson arrived in Washington on 24 May and took rooms, as usual, at Mrs. Suter's boardinghouse. He still hoped to sell his Washington residence, but popular fears of a British invasion made property sales in the capital city almost impossible. On the day of his arrival he dined with the Madisons and promised to return the next day. The following evening he attended a large party given by the Madisons. Among the guests were the Russian and French ministers and Madame Betsy Bonaparte, whose low-cut dress Jackson considered in extremely poor taste. "Delicate minds," he wrote Mary, "are always shocked at such indiscretions. They prefer to imagine invisible charms to seeing them displayed to the gaze of all."[9]

---

[5]St. Clairsville *Ohio Federalist*, 26 May 1813.

[6]For Mary's pregnancy, see Jackson to Mary S. Jackson, 27 May 1813, Meigs-Jackson Papers, Blennerhassett Historical Park Commission, Parkersburg, West Virginia (hereinafter cited as Meigs-Jackson Papers, BHPC). See also Jackson to Mary S. Jackson, 6 June 1813, ibid.; Jackson to Mary S. Jackson, 24 June 1813, ibid.

[7]Jackson to James Madison, 1 April 1811, James Madison Papers, Library of Congress; Dolley Madison to Jackson, 10 April 1811, John George Jackson Papers; James Madison to Jackson, 12 April 1811, ibid.; Jackson to Mary S. Jackson, 28 November 1811, Meigs-Jackson Papers, BHPC; Return Jonathan Meigs, Jr., to Jackson, 23 December 1812, John George Jackson Papers.

[8]Jackson to Mary S. Jackson, 27 May 1813, Meigs-Jackson Papers, BHPC.

[9]Ibid.

When Jackson took his seat in the House on 25 May, old colleagues, including John W. Eppes, a son-in-law of Thomas Jefferson, greeted him with warmth and cordiality.[10] Equally gratifying was the fact that he found the Madison administration somewhat stronger than it had been in the waning months of the president's first term. The recent elections had given the administration 22 Senate votes it could count on with some certainty, although 14 Senators were in most cases hostile; and there were 114 supporters in the House of Representatives compared with 68 opponents. Although the military campaigns continued to be embarrassingly ineffective, antiwar extremists had suffered defeats of their own at the polls, particularly in New York, and could find little reason for hope that the Federalist party might be restored to national power.[11]

Madison's message to Congress on 25 May was rather bland in nature, neither bold nor apologetic. Perhaps the most encouraging note was the announcement of a Russian offer to mediate in the war between the United States and England, a proposal received coldly in England but characterized by John Quincy Adams, the American minister to Russia, as "a new evidence of the czar's friendship" for the United States. Otherwise, as Henry Adams observed, the message had "the merit of directing Congress strictly to necessary business."[12]

One of the most urgent matters facing the House concerned wartime financial measures proposed by Secretary of the Treasury Albert Gallatin, who had recently been named, with James A. Bayard, to assist Adams in St. Petersburg in the anticipated peace negotiations with England. Gallatin himself had already worked out arrangements for a loan of sixteen million dollars with John Jacob Astor, Stephen Girard, and David Parish, New York and Philadelphia bankers. His proposed revenue measures included a direct tax of three million dollars and imposts on salt, licenses, spirits,

---

[10]*Annals of Congress*, 13th Cong., 1st sess., 107; Jackson to Mary S. Jackson, 27 May 1813, Meigs-Jackson Papers, BHPC.

[11]Henry Adams, *History of the United States of America*, 9 vols. (New York: Charles Scribner's Sons, 1909-1911) 7:49-51.

[12]Ibid., 54. Madison's address is in James D. Richardson, comp., *A Compilation of the Messages and Papers of the Presidents, 1789-1897*, 10 vols. (Washington DC: Government Printing Office, 1896) 1:526-30.

carriages, auctions, and sugar refineries, as well as a stamp tax, together with the machinery for assessment and collection.[13]

Although he gave consistent support to the administration, Jackson took little part in the debates on Gallatin's proposals. Adhering to his Jeffersonian principles, he opposed an amendment to the direct tax bill to include "tools of trade, beasts of the plow, arms, household utensils and apparel" among taxable commodities.[14] After the defeat of an amendment to allow drawbacks on exports of spirits distilled from foreign materials, he nevertheless voted with the majority for the direct tax and for taxes on sugar, distilling of spirituous liquors, sales at auctions, and carriages. Keeping his promise to Mary to return to Clarksburg for the birth of their child, he left Washington on 15 July and did not vote on the final bills imposing levies on salt and stamp taxes on bank notes, promissory notes, and other negotiable paper. Had he been present, he probably would have opposed part of the bills, since he spoke in favor of confining the tax to bank notes alone.[15]

During the special session of Congress, Jackson displayed an unusual restraint in responding to criticisms of the administration. On 10 June Daniel Webster, beginning his long congressional career as a representative from New Hampshire, offered five resolutions, all implying that the administration had allowed itself to be duped into believing that Napoleon's Berlin and Milan decrees had been repealed. The resolutions called upon the president to disclose the time and circumstances under which the United States had been apprised of the action of the French government on 28 April 1811, which purportedly repealed the earlier decrees. Federalists and Republicans, for a variety of reasons, combined to vote overwhelmingly for disclosure. Even Jackson, sensitive to charges that he was pro-French, favored the resolutions.[16]

---

[13]Adams, *History of the United States*, 7:44-46, 55.

[14]*Annals of Congress*, 13th Cong., 1st sess., 331-32.

[15]Ibid., 391, 393, 405-12, 431-32, 439-42, 449-55.

[16]Adams, *History of the United States*, 7:55-58. For Jackson's vote on Webster's resolutions, see *Annals of Congress*, 13th Cong., 1st sess., 150-51, 302-303, 308-10.

Three days after Webster presented his resolutions, President Madison took to his bed with a dangerous remittent fever, and for the next five weeks doubts existed concerning his recovery. On the evening of 16 June Jackson sat with him for more than two hours. When his condition later became worse, Jackson, at the request of Madison's family, spent the night at the White House. "It was wished," he wrote Mary, "that I should stay there in consequence of his alarming illness the night before. I lay on a bed in an adjacent room with my clothes on & altho ready had no occasion to be with him." Jackson also visited Eppes, who was confined to his bed with a rheumatic condition.[17]

With both the president and Eppes (who was chairman of the House Ways and Means Committee) ill, the pace of events in the House of Representatives slowed somewhat. Jackson found himself longing to be at home with Mary and wondering why he allowed his ambition to intrude upon his desires for the simple pleasures of life. Partly to assuage his loneliness, he went horseback riding with his friend, Congressman Thomas Gholson, Jr., of Virginia; visited with Samuel H. Smith, the editor of the Washington *National Intelligencer*, and his wife, the former Margaret Bayard; and called upon General John Mason at his estate on Analostan Island in the Potomac. He also rode to Georgetown, where he purchased silverware costing $367 for his home in Clarksburg.[18] Although he preferred reading in his room to attendance at some of the social affairs, he occasionally found the parties exhilarating. Of a "brilliant" party given by Louis Sérurier, the French minister, he wrote Mary, "Lamps were hung on all the adjacent trees (& he lives in a grove) which made the scene quite a fairy land. They danced & talked 'till 11 o'clock. The furniture, painting of Buonaparte &c &c are the most splendid I ever saw. Gold with him supplies the place of silver, & all is rich."[19]

---

[17]For an account of Madison's illness, see Ralph Ketcham, *James Madison: A Biography* (New York: The Macmillan Company, 1971) 560-62. Jackson's visits are noted in Jackson to Mary S. Jackson, 17 June 1813, Meigs-Jackson Papers, BHPC; Jackson to Mary S. Jackson, 24 June 1813, ibid.

[18]Jackson to Mary S. Jackson, 3 June 1813, Meigs-Jackson Papers, BHPC; Jackson to Mary S. Jackson, 6 June 1813, ibid.

[19]Jackson to Mary S. Jackson, 24 June 1813, ibid.

For Jackson, the glitter of Washington social life never relieved the distresses occasioned by the war and attacks upon the administration. On 29 June Federalist Congressman Timothy Pickering presented a memorial of the Massachusetts legislature opposing the war. According to Pickering, France was the real enemy and England was simply defending herself against an "unjust and iniquitous system" created by Napoleon. Since England had repealed her Orders in Council by negotiation and the United States had never declared to the British that impressment of American seamen constituted grounds for war, Pickering argued that reasons for the war were "wholly inadequate." Ranging into unrelated areas, he maintained that the United States had been better off before the acquisition of Louisiana, the projected reduction of Canada, and the seizure of West Florida, and held that the provinces would drain the blood of the country and require a large standing army. To needle him, or perhaps as a tactic of contempt, Jackson complained that he could not hear the memorial when it was presented because Pickering's back was toward him. He asked that the clerk read it again. The Speaker decided against another reading, but when the House took up the memorial on 8 July, it voted by a large majority to postpone consideration until the December 1813 session of Congress.[20]

Far more serious in Jackson's view was a speech on 9 July by Congressman William Czar Bradley, a Republican of Vermont, who delivered a scathing attack upon the military conduct of the war. Declaring that "almost every paper which is daily laid upon our tables teems with some tale of disaster and disgrace," Bradley called for the appointment of a committee "to inquire into the causes which have led to the multiplied failures of the arms of the United States on our Western and Northwestern frontier" and authorization for the committee "to send for persons and papers."[21]

Springing to the defense of the government, Jackson branded Bradley's resolution the "most impolitic in relation to the situation of the country and of the national affairs, that was ever submitted to Congress." He agreed with Bradley that Congress had not only the right but also the duty to institute an inquiry "if they discover any gross and manifest mismanagement of the arms of the country." But with only two weeks left in the ses-

---

[20]*Annals of Congress*, 13th Cong., 1st sess., 332-44, 403-404.

[21]Ibid., 413-15.

sion and the necessity for months of work by the committee, he could not see that an investigation was either expedient or practical. Moreover, Jackson contended that Bradley had really implicated the officers of the army rather than officials of the government. The military officers should not be condemned unheard, he maintained; however, any summons to those in the field could only produce chaos and demoralization in the army. Opposed to an inquiry until the campaigns then in progress had ended or to any action while Congress was not in session, he called for postponement in considering the resolution.[22] Jackson's forceful remarks bolstered arguments set forth by Republicans Ezra Butler of Vermont, Samuel Hopkins of Kentucky, Adam Seybert of Pennsylvania, and Thomas Gholson, Jr., of Virginia. On the motion of John W. Taylor of New York, the House voted 76 to 67 to table Bradley's resolution.[23]

Unlike those congressmen inclined to fruitless and damaging debate on past mistakes and failures, Jackson, in at least one respect, sought to draw the attention of the House to the future needs of the country. Already he sensed a new direction in political and economic affairs and a need for increased authority for the federal government. As a Jeffersonian Republican, however, he appears to have had serious doubts about the constitutional authority of Congress to enact the broad economic legislation that he considered essential to a strong and healthy nation. His proposal to remove any uncertainties by constitutional amendment reflected not only his own convictions but also those of Madison and Eppes and anticipated recommendations and suggestions made later by the president in his forward-looking Seventh Annual Message to Congress in December 1815.[24]

On 10 July 1813 Jackson proposed four amendments to the Constitution that would give the federal government unequivocal power to lay ad valorem export duties, build roads and canals in any state, subject to its consent, and establish a national bank with branches in any state or terri-

---

[22]Ibid., 416-17.

[23]Ibid., 415, 418-21.

[24]For Madison's Seventh Annual Message, see Richardson, comp., *Messages and Papers of the Presidents*, 1:562-69. The views of Eppes are set forth in Norman K. Risjord, *The Old Republicans: Southern Conservatives in the Age of Jefferson* (New York: Columbia University Press, 1965) 152.

tory of the United States. He declared that he knew that "many persons in the nation believed that Congress [is] already clothed with these powers; but it is equally true that a great portion, also, deny the authority; whilst almost all, I believe, agree that it is proper and necessary to possess it." Jackson's proposed amendments were tabled by the House, which was preoccupied with the war, eager to get away from the hot, sultry Washington summer, and not at all certain that it did not already have the authority that Jackson desired.[25]

With nearly three weeks remaining in the special session of Congress, Jackson left Washington on 15 July for Clarksburg. His wife gave birth to a daughter, Sophia, on 18 July.[26] Since the journey between Clarksburg and Washington usually required a week, Jackson evidently did not reach home until after the birth of the child.

At Clarksburg, Jackson continued to keep in close touch with political affairs. He urged Madison, who slowly recovered from his fever, to remain at Montpelier until "the billious [*sic*] season shall have passed by in order to confirm you against the danger of a second attack." He also advised the president against trying to placate his political enemies in making appointments of assessors and collectors of internal revenue in the First Congressional District of Virginia. Instead, Jackson recommended Dr. William Williams, his brother-in-law, for the district composed of Harrison, Wood, and Randolph counties, and William McKinley, his longtime political ally, for the district made up of Monongalia, Ohio, and Brooke counties.[27]

As the autumn passed, Jackson made plans to return to Washington for the second session of Congress, which convened on 6 December. He expected to take Mary and his young daughter with him, but Mary began to plead for a postponement of their departure, first on the ground that Sophia was not well and later out of a desire to spend Christmas in Clarks-

---

[25]*Annals of Congress*, 13th Cong., 1st sess., 430-31.

[26]Dorothy Davis, *John George Jackson* (Parsons WV: McClain Printing Company, 1976) 221, 378n.

[27]Jackson to Madison, 4 September 1813, James Madison Papers, Library of Congress.

burg. Yielding to his wife's entreaties, Jackson agreed to remain at home until late December.[28]

Jackson knew that Mary's reluctance to go to Washington sprang from timidity and apprehension at the thought of mingling in Washington society. In June 1813 he had written her that he regretted that "you will urge upon me one argument against coming here which you know does not in fact exist, & by depreciating yourself in your own estimation unavoidably do so in mine. You assert that your simple manners &c unfit you for the circle of high life." Jackson even threatened that he would "at once resign & encounter all the odium of the measure" unless Mary agreed to join him.[29]

When Mary proved adamant in her refusal to accompany him, Jackson set out for Washington with his son, John Jay. The midwinter journey was unusually tiring, and Jackson suffered pains in his left leg, which "was swelled & troublesome." On the second night, "in crossing a bridge over a small creek," he wrote Mary, "my horse fell in & pitched forward & got me fast. I struggled to get out & he made several efforts also, & at the moment I got clear he fell through the bridge into the water." After considerable maneuvering, which necessitated throwing off all the top of the bridge, both horse and rider were extricated. Except for spraining both thumbs and sustaining another small injury, Jackson escaped unharmed.[30]

Jackson reached Washington early on the morning of 3 January. Mrs. Suter's boardinghouse, where he again took lodgings, was filled with military men. After breakfast he called on the Madisons, where he found Payne Todd, Dolley's son by her first marriage, and Lucy Washington. The following day he took his seat in the House of Representatives.[31]

On 5 January 1814 Jackson again brought up his proposed amendments to the Constitution. When the House took them up, some three weeks later, he declared that the time had come when "a decision . . . outliving the present distinctions of party" must be made "upon grounds applicable to the fundamental principles of our Government." Although he regarded the Constitution "as the sublimest effort of man to preserve his

[28]Davis, *John George Jackson*, 223-24.

[29]Jackson to Mary S. Jackson, 17 June 1813, Meigs-Jackson Papers, BHPC.

[30]Jackson to Mary S. Jackson, 5 January 1814, ibid.

[31]Ibid.; *Annals of Congress*, 13th Cong., 2d sess., 844.

rights," Jackson believed that amendments which had the sanction of reason and propriety should be adopted "with promptitude and alacrity."[32]

In setting forth his arguments for a tax on exports, Jackson elucidated some of his own views on the nature of the Constitution and demonstrated the progress he had made toward becoming an economic nationalist. He held that the reason for prohibiting a tax on exports could not be determined from the writings and speeches at the time of the adoption of the Constitution, but attributed it to a general fear that the new government would annihilate state sovereignties. In words that might well have been uttered by Madison himself, Jackson declared that "it was the policy of that period, and a wise one too, to grant no more than was essential to set the machinery of Government into motion, and to provide for enlarging the grant by incorporating the power of amendment, to be used as experience and propriety might require." He contended that export duties would not adversely affect any economic group in the country, but would fall exclusively upon the foreign consumer. He pointed to the example of England, which laid export taxes on all products and manufactures of the nation, and declared that the United States must have similar powers in order to bring about "a perfect reciprocity."[33]

Jackson proposed to apply revenue derived from the export tax to construction of roads and canals, which would consolidate the various sections of the country in interest and feeling and break down geographical distinctions. "By mixing together," he asserted, "we shall lose those prejudices which names alone have excited; we will form early attachments and connexions, and become in fact, as in name, one family and one people." He envisioned "new cities, towns, and villages, springing up as if by magic, in regions where the voice of civilizations has scarcely been heard" and "the whole interior smiling under the influence of a system which dispenses almost equal value to the labor of man wheresoever employed and all the conveniences of life in every quarter."[34]

With respect to a national bank, Jackson declared that "it is now admitted on all hands" that the fiscal operations of the government required

---

[32]*Annals of Congress*, 13th Cong., 2d sess., 849, 861, 1191.

[33]Ibid., 1191-92.

[34]Ibid., 1193.

banks and that common prudence revealed the advantages of a centralized institution. He noted, however, that there were those who had denied the power of Congress to establish the first national bank and that "General Washington [had] doubted much and hesitated for several days before he gave his approbation to the law establishing the United States Bank." Jackson therefore concluded, "It is better to acquiesce in a construction contended for by those who deny the authority, than to assert and exercise it." He reminded his colleagues that the Constitution represented a limited grant of power to the federal government and that at least one-half of the first twelve amendments to the Constitution were designed to prohibit the exercise of powers not granted by it.[35]

When the House on 31 January again took up his amendments, Jackson strenuously resisted efforts by fellow Republicans Gholson, Robert Wright of Maryland, and William Findley of Pennsylvania to defer action upon them. Despite his pleas that the two houses of Congress act quickly and refer them to the state legislatures (several of which were then in session) for early decision, the House voted 63 to 55 to postpone consideration.[36] In its divided state, the only positive step the House could agree to take was consideration of a bill introduced by John C. Calhoun to establish a national bank in Washington, D.C., a move that evaded the constitutional issue and contributed virtually nothing to the alleviation of the nation's financial troubles.[37]

Meanwhile, Jackson spoke forcefully on matters arising immediately from the war. He strongly endorsed a resolution of Congressman Thomas Robertson of Louisiana on 21 January 1814 for an inquiry into the expediency of enacting a law establishing the right of expatriation for native American citizens. Jackson took the view that since the Constitution gave the power of naturalization, it was illogical to deny its counterpart to Americans. Wartime conditions, he believed, made some provision essential. He pointed out that an ill-disposed citizen going to Canada and re-

---

[35]Ibid., 1193-95.

[36]Ibid., 1195, 1197.

[37]Ibid., 1235, 1578-85, 1860-62; Risjord, *Old Republicans*, 152-53.

turning could claim, upon detection, that he had been expatriated; but if he were tried as a spy, he could allege that he was an American citizen.[38]

Jackson's opposition proved decisive in blocking a congressional investigation into the Blue Lights. These signals by fire had allegedly been sent from the shores at or near the harbor of New London, Connecticut, to the British blockading squadron off the coast. Although "testimony the most irrefragable" had proved that the enemy had been apprised of the condition and movements of American ships under the command of Commodore Stephen Decatur at that port, Jackson did not desire that the House become a court of inquiry or judicature for criminal offenses. Instead, he favored a thorough investigation by the United States attorney of the district in which the offense had occurred. His convincing arguments killed any congressional investigation, and the House by a vote of 89 to 42 tabled the motion.[39]

Criticisms of the government, sometimes vicious in character, continued to permeate the debates in the House of Representatives. A resolution for an inquiry into the conduct of the war, introduced by Bradley of Vermont on 20 December, passed by the overwhelming vote of 137 to 13.[40] Two weeks later Federalist Daniel Sheffey of Virginia attempted unsuccessfully to attach a rider to a bill for encouraging enlistments, which would have limited any troops raised to the defense of the territory and frontiers of the United States. Jackson voted with the opposition.[41]

More serious was a memorial from the Maryland House of Delegates, which came before the House of Representatives on 2 February. The memorial characterized the United States government as hardly more powerful than that under the Articles of Confederation and charged it with inadequate measures for the protection of its citizens, particularly those of Maryland, who were exposed to enemy attack by virtue of their proximity to the federal capital. It called for "a speedy restoration of the blessings of

---

[38]*Annals of Congress*, 13th Cong., 2d sess., 1094-95, 1097.

[39]Ibid., 1123-28. The most detailed discussion of the Blue Lights is in Irving Brant, *James Madison, Commander-in-Chief, 1812-1836* (New York: The Bobbs-Merrill Company, Inc., 1961) 227-37.

[40]*Annals of Congress*, 13th Cong., 2d sess., 819-22.

[41]Ibid., 939.

peace, and an essential change in that mistaken policy whose effects are now so unhappily to be seen in the privations and afflictions of the land." Declaring that the administration had been the victim of frauds perpetrated by the French government, the petition suggested that the United States had erred in going to war with England and that a propitious moment for reconciliation had arrived.[42]

Jackson took the occasion of the debate on the Loan Bill of 1814 to deliver a wide-ranging address, one of the most statesmanlike of his career, in which he responded to the mounting criticisms of the administration. Believing it incumbent upon members of Congress to "venture occasionally upon a larger view of our affairs than would be strictly admissable, if the argument were to be solely intended for this House,"[43] he obviously addressed his remarks to the nation, as well as to Congress. He dealt with the origins of the war, the justice of its continuance, and the mode of waging it, which had constituted the major bases for attacks upon the government.

With respect to the genesis of the war, Jackson dwelt at considerable length upon British interferences with American shipping and damages to the mercantile interests. He held that Americans derived their right to navigate the ocean "from the recognition of their character as an independent people, and the munificence of a beneficent God who made the sea free to all." Yet, declared Jackson, they were "required by Great Britain, who had usurped dominion over it, to carry their cargoes to a British port, land them there, and pay tribute for a license to carry them to their place of destination."

Jackson asserted that the United States had repeatedly stated its determination to protect its rights and had informed both England and France that it would engage in war against one of them if the other repealed its hostile acts. The British had refused to accept this offer. In what may have been one of his weakest arguments, Jackson countered opposition charges that Madison had naively accepted the *promise* of repeal of the Berlin and Milan decrees by Napoleon for the *fact* of repeal and so had precipitated

---

[42]Ibid., 1206-1209. Jackson's vote against the petition is recorded in ibid., 1228.

[43]Ibid., 1472.

the American war with England. In defense of the administration, he declared that without trust among nations, "all of the advantages of civilization would be lost to the present generation, and we should be thrown back into the dark ages" and forced to rely upon the deplorable doctrine that "no reliance could be placed except on the sword of our own."

Violations of property rights, Jackson contended, remained "of most subordinate importance in the scale of national wrongs endured by the United States." He reiterated a position he had consistently held, that "the rights of persons are more invaluable than the rights of property" and that the "violations of personal rights merit the prompt interposition of the Government; whilst spoliations of property admit of dilatory adjustment." Holding that "the rights of persons . . . constitute the key-stone of the arch of our political edifice," he considered it unthinkable that under the American government "a freeman can be despoiled of his liberty, or a citizen can be torn from his country, without producing more excitement than the capture of a bale of cotton or a barrell of flour."[44]

Without equivocation, Jackson reaffirmed his belief that "impressments of our citizens are most certainly a primary cause of this war." He noted that Washington himself had branded the practice "an outrage not to be endured" and had threatened reprisals. Moreover, the Federalists John Marshall and Rufus King, as secretary of state and minister to England, respectively, had spoken forcefully against impressment; and Thomas Jefferson had made its cessation a sine qua non for negotiation with the British. Jackson admitted that Washington, Adams, and Jefferson had not gone to war because of it and defended their policies as correct for the struggling new nation. Unfortunately, the government had sought redress in vain and had finally been driven to declare war for "free trade and sailors' rights." Jackson contended that nearly all of the impressed sailors had become naturalized American citizens and were therefore entitled to the full protection of the American government, whose primary duty was "to preserve the immunities of persons and rights of property inviolate."[45]

Jackson rejected the Federalist argument that American refusal to accept the treaty negotiated with Great Britain by William Pinkney in 1806

---

[44]Ibid., 1472-77.

[45]Ibid., 1477-78.

had produced the war. He declared that by accepting the demands of the British "we should, after having become the scorn and derision of the world, by refusing to fight for our rights and honor, have been compelled at last to fight for our existence as a nation." He compared the American situation to that of Poland, whose partition other rulers had justified on the ground that its principles of freedom constituted a danger to the crowned heads of Europe. As a course of action for the United States, he recommended the advice of Polonius to his son, "Beware of entrance on a quarrel; but, being in, be firm, and then thy enemy will beware of thee."[46]

In his second point Jackson offered justification for the continuance of the war. He stressed that the British had repealed their Orders in Council—the basis for much Federalist clamor for the war's end—on the condition that British vessels and goods be freely admitted to American ports; but they had coupled the repeal with an assertion of the right of the British government to issue the orders. Moreover, the British government had adamantly refused to negotiate the question of impressment on any basis.

Jackson reminded his colleagues that Czar Alexander I of Russia had agreed to Russian mediation of the war and had accepted an American mission, one member of which was a distinguished Federalist. He charged that while opponents of the administration believed that the Russian mediation was sanctioned by Great Britain, they had favored its acceptance by the United States as "wise, pacific, and just." Then, "when Great Britain rejected it, they too condemned it, as an imposition, which the Executive had practised, knowing it must necessarily fail." The response to the Russian offer, Jackson asserted, stamped with "eternal infamy" the allegations by critics that the adminstration was under the influence of France.[47]

The third point considered by Jackson dealt with the conduct of the war. He vehemently rejected contentions, made even before the war began, that the conflict was really for conquest rather than the protection of American rights. "Canada," he declared, "as a territory is not worth one cent to us—I would not have it." Speaking as "a Western man," Jackson claimed that the United States had sufficient territory for many years to come. When emigrants from the Northern and Eastern sections of the

---

[46]Ibid., 1478-84.

[47]Ibid., 1486-88. For the treaty, see Ketcham, *James Madison*, 447-51.

country—Federalists strongholds—moved into the Western lands, they would discover that the jealousies that "wicked and designing men are industriously exciting are unfounded and unjust." Surely when these sectional animosities were extinguished, the country would acquire a national character. On the other hand, Jackson stressed British incitement of the Indians to "deeds of blood" for extension of the war into Canada. He scoffed at the notion that the British could not restrain the Indians and branded any resort to a purely defensive plan of operations by the United States as "most absurd, humiliating, and destructive."[48]

Jackson reserved some of his most bitter invective for Federalists who charged that the Russian mediation had grown out of fraud and trickery by the administration and that Americans were fighting against the land of their fathers. He rebuked those who had attempted to dissuade citizens from entering the army, opposed the lending of money and, in the case of one member, even intimated that the money would not be repaid. To them he thundered, "You, that have everything to gain by vigilance, are sleeping at your posts, while the great majority, who apprehend no danger, alone are vigilant! You might as well tell me that the lamb is vigilant and the wolf sleepeth." Their threats of resistance to policies destructive of their commerce he met with a challenge: "Let treason rear its head, it will and must be put down though it have a thousand heads."[49]

Because of the encouragement given to the enemy by domestic opponents of the war, Jackson believed it might "require a seven years drubbing to beat John Bull into his senses." Nevertheless, he opposed further peace overtures to the British government. Rather, he continued, "let Greek meet Greek," and "in the mighty tug of war, the conquered will preserve his honor." Extending his comparison of the circumstances of the United States to those of ancient Greece, he warned that what the power of Xerxes could not accomplish when Greece was united was easily affected by Philip of Macedon when a fractious spirit prevailed, and "the grandeur and glory of the Republic fell." The lesson for the United States, Jackson declared, was obvious.[50]

---

[48] *Annals of Congress*, 13th Cong., 2d sess., 1490-92.

[49] Ibid., 1495-97.

[50] Ibid., 1499-1502.

In other actions Jackson also gave strong support to the administration and the prosecution of the war. He consistently voted for appropriations for the military establishment, strengthening the nonintercourse laws, and support of the Yazoo claims, positions that accorded with his views during his previous service in Congress.[51]

Always a welcome guest to the Madisons, and with numerous social invitations from both government officials and foreign diplomats, Jackson found Washington society congenial. He was elated when Madison told him, on 24 February, that he would submit the name of Return Jonathan Meigs, Jr., Mary's father, to the Senate for postmaster general. Already, Meigs's cousin Clara and her husband, Congressman John Forsyth of Georgia, had entered Jackson's circle of friends. Jackson confessed to Mary, however, that Forsyth, while a fine man and an excellent orator, was "rather attentive . . . to the Ladies for a married" man, though Jackson acknowledged that he himself was "quite fastidious on that score."[52]

Mary's refusal to join him in Washington sorely disappointed Jackson. On 20 January he wrote her that he expected to travel to Clarksburg to pick up her and young Sophia about 20 February. He reminded Mary that the baby, then seven and one-half months old and not yet weaned, could be left at home, if she preferred, since Pat could give her milk. Mary, nevertheless, remained adamant in her determination to remain at Clarksburg.[53]

Scarcely less vexing to Jackson was the irregularity of Mary's letters, although he continued to write frequently. On one occasion he missed his

---

[51]Ibid., 87, 933, 979, 1049, 1093, 1113, 1122, 1131, 1134, 1144, 1248, 1264, 1772, 1803, 1807, 1830, 1831. Jackson's position on the Yazoo claims is set forth in ibid., 1856, 1858-59, 1868, 1891, 1894, 1912, 1917-19.

[52]Jackson to Mary S. Jackson, 27 January 1814, Meigs-Jackson Papers, BHPC; Jackson to Mary S. Jackson, 24 February 1814, ibid.; Jackson to Mary S. Jackson, 6 March 1814, ibid. Meigs assumed office in March 1814.

[53]Jackson to Mary S. Jackson, 20 January 1814, ibid.; Jackson to Mary S. Jackson, 27 January 1814, ibid.; Jackson to Mary S. Jackson, 30 January 1814, ibid. Even Mary's parents were surprised that she did not accompany Jackson to Washington. Her father told her that he would have arranged for her mother to have visited her had he known that she remained at home. Return Jonathan Meigs, Jr., to Mary S. Jackson, 15 January 1814, ibid.

dinner in order to read one of her letters that arrived late. Jackson used nearly every stratagem he could devise either to get Mary to Washington or at least to encourage her to write more often. He told her, "The life I lead is truly distressing. I mope over the newspapers every evening, grow heavy, go to bed & read myself asleep; in the morning read & write until breakfast, as soon as it is over the hour of meeting arrives, I go to Congress[,] set [*sic*] there until 4 oClock[,] get dinner about dark, & thus day after day passes away."[54] His letters dwelt upon his desire to be with Mary rather than "languishing away my life in this cheerless, *artificial* world of gaiety & politeness, where the true character is hid & we know little of the true tempers of those we meet with." He frequently mentioned gifts that he had purchased for her, including on one occasion six yards of levantine silk for a dress.[55] Since Jackson did not vote on any question after 8 April, there is reason to believe that he left for home a full ten days before Congress adjourned, perhaps on an impulse to get back to his wife and children.[56]

At home, Jackson watched with a troubled heart as the fortunes of war reached their lowest point for the young republic. With the defeat of Napoleon in Europe, the British were in a position to turn their full might against the United States. American victories at Lundy's Lane and Plattsburg, which thwarted any invasion from Canada, and the defeat of other British forces at Baltimore could not conceal the danger to the nation. During the summer of 1814 the British burned the Capitol in Washington. New England Federalists and other dissidents made plans for the Hartford Convention, which would strike at the very foundations of the Union; and the government, in serious financial straits, reached the limits of its borrowing power under existing legislation. Under these dire circumstances President Madison, on 8 August 1814, called Congress into an early session, to meet on 19 September.[57]

---

[54]Jackson to Mary S. Jackson, 3 February 1814, ibid.

[55]Jackson to Mary S. Jackson, 16 February 1814, ibid.

[56]*Annals of Congress*, 13th Cong., 2d sess., 2002, 2031; Jackson to Mary S. Jackson, 9 January 1814, Meigs-Jackson Papers, BHPC.

[57]The situation with respect to the war in the summer of 1814 is detailed in Adams, *History of the United States*, 8:1-148.

Happily for Jackson, Mary and his children were with him when he returned to Washington. He and Mary took rooms at Mrs. Suter's establishment, where the Meigs family also lived. Among her other boarders were Congressman John W. Eppes, William McCoy, John Sevier, John Rhea, and Perry Humphreys. Jackson placed his daughter, Mary, in Miss Taylor's school, but she joined the family on Friday of each week and remained for the weekend.[58]

Finding their building in ashes, the result of the burning of Washington by the British, members of Congress met temporarily in the building used by the Post and Patent Office, the only public structure not burned. The House of Representatives, by a vote of 79 to 37, set up a committee to inquire into the expediency of removing the seat of government, while Congress was in session, to some other place of greater safety and less inconvenience than Washington. On 3 October, with the Speaker breaking a tie, the House voted for removal. Believing that to leave Washington would cause a further loss of popular confidence, Madison flatly refused to vacate the capital. Jackson stoutly defended the president in his decision. By mid-October even the Federalists conceded that removal of the capital was highly unlikely.[59]

Amid great discomfort, Congress heard the president's annual message, the most significant part of which dealt with the bleak fiscal condition of the government. George W. Campbell, secretary of the treasury, and James Monroe, secretary of war, revealed the true extent of the financial crisis. Campbell asserted that the government would require approximately fifty million dollars in additional money in the coming year, and he made it clear that he had no suggestions as to where it might be raised.

Faced with this disturbing prospect, the Senate approved the appointment of the unpopular but able Philadelphia lawyer, Alexander J. Dallas, as secretary of the treasury. Although Eppes advanced a fiscal proposal that, in some essentials, had originated with Thomas Jefferson, his father-in-law, the House on 24 October accepted in principle an administration plan, the

---

[58]Jackson to Mary S. Jackson, 24 January 1815, Meigs-Jackson Papers, BHPC; Davis, *John George Jackson*, 239-40.

[59]Madison's views on the removal of the capital are set forth in Ketcham, *James Madison*, 586-87. For the actions of the House, including Jackson's attitude, see *Annals of Congress*, 13th Cong., 3d sess., 312, 322, 341, 344, 356, 376, 394-96.

heart of which came from Dallas. Like Eppes, Dallas advocated doubling taxes in order to produce twenty-one million dollars; but in sharp contradiction to the old Virginia philosophy, he recommended the establishment of a national bank with capital of fifty million dollars. Of that amount, forty-four million dollars might be subscribed in government bonds and the remaining six million dollars in specie. The bank would at once lend the government thirty million dollars.[60]

The Dallas plan created a dilemma for Republicans who had until then advocated a strict construction of the Constitution. Jackson, who had long since recognized the need for increasing the powers of the central government, on 27 September returned to his effort to amend the Constitution by giving Congress authority to levy an export tax, construct roads and canals in the states, and establish a national bank. Countering an argument by Jonathan Fisk, a Republican from New York, that the existence of a national bank for twenty years through the action of Congress constituted an affirmation of its power to charter a bank, Jackson declared that "it is a fortunate thing for this country that Congress is not enchained by precedent in its legislation," for "if the Constitution be violated to-day, it is no reason why it should be violated to-morrow."

Since many of the states had denied that Congress possessed the power to establish a national bank, Jackson reasoned, "it would be respectful at least to consult their opinions on the subject." He did not profess to say whether Congress already had such authority, but he believed that it should have and that it was necessary "to place that power beyond question or doubt." In support of Jackson, Wright of Maryland pointed out that he had voted against the national bank on the ground that it was unconstitutional and that even the president had denied the constitutionality of the old bank. Following Wright's remarks, the House voted 61 to 53 to refer Jackson's motion to the committee of the whole.[61]

On 30 September the House took up Jackson's proposed amendment relating to a national bank. Jackson maintained that the value of a central bank had been demonstrated "by every day's experience" and that all parties agreed upon its necessity for the "convenience of our fiscal operations."

---

[60]Adams, *History of the United States*, 8:239-42, 245-50.

[61]*Annals of Congress*, 13th Cong., 3d sess., 324-26.

Since the only question lay in its constitutionality, it was best "to make assurance doubly sure" by presenting the matter to the state legislatures, many of which had denied that Congress had authority to charter a bank, and to receive "at their hand, by liberal grant" a power so essential to the welfare of the country.[62]

Samuel McKee, a Kentucky Republican, spoke against the amendment. He drew attention to the deep interest of many legislators in state banking establishments, the inevitable deterioration of state stocks and curtailment of revenues on which many states depended, and the opposition to a national bank based on reservations regarding its expediency.[63]

Responding to McKee's remarks, Jackson, himself a major stockholder in the newly formed Virginia Saline Bank at Clarksburg and in the Metropolis Bank in Washington, contended that once the indispensable utility and value of a national bank were established, the honor and patriotism of the state legislatures would assure its support. He rejected McKee's argument that adoption of his proposal would be tantamount to an admission that Congress did not have the power to establish a central bank. Admitting that "the most virtuous men" might differ in their conception of the Constitution, he again warned that "if one violation were to be made a precedent for a subsequent and analagous [*sic*] violation, the Constitution would become a matter of convenience, instead of an instrument of obligation."

Jackson insisited that Congress should not deny the country the advantages of a national bank and should remove its own scruples by applying to the states for a grant of power. The House, however, by a vote of 86 to 44, defeated his proposed amendment. Opponents included representatives of state banking interests and others, both Federalist and Republican, who feared that the amendment would raise a question about the constitutionality, which they considered already settled in favor of a bank. On 12 October Jackson, who found it necessary to make a journey home, moved to postpone consideration of his remaining proposals until the first Monday in December.[64]

---

[62]Ibid., 335-36.

[63]Ibid., 336-37.

[64]Ibid., 338, 339, 385.

On or about 5 November Jackson left Washington with his wife and baby and Mary's mother. Mary was then in her sixth month of pregnancy and insisted that the child be born at home. Jackson's daughter, Mary, remained in school. His wife survived the arduous journey without mishap, but Jackson sustained injuries when one of his horses "fancied a nap in the street" between Washington and Georgetown.[65]

On 13 November, about a week after Jackson left Washington, Eppes dispatched an urgent letter, which reached him at Westernport, Maryland, a stopping place on his way home. Eppes wrote that "for some days after you left us our Table was dreary and silent" and suggested that Jackson return as soon as possible since "your presence here will be necessary." He informed Jackson that the proposal to establish a national bank had already been before the House once and that major tax bills would be considered the following week.[66]

The bill for chartering a United States Bank with capital of fifty million dollars, to which Eppes alluded, was reported by a House committee on 7 November during Jackson's absence. Because of a provision that allowed the president to use his discretion to suspend specie payments, the House rejected the bill. The Senate then took the initiative in formulating a bank bill, which embodied essentially the recommendations of Dallas. Jackson, who returned to Congress on 2 January, opposed all moves by the House to recommit the bill to the Senate or to table it, although he voted with the majority on 5 January to amend it by reducing the capital stock of the bank to thirty million dollars, of which the government might subscribe five million dollars.[67]

---

[65]Jackson's date of departure for Clarksburg is suggested by the fact that he is not recorded as voting in Congress after 5 November. *Annals of Congress*, 13th Cong., 3d sess., 540. See also Davis, *John George Jackson*, 240.

[66]Eppes to Jackson, 14 November 1814, John George Jackson Papers.

[67]For the establishment of the House committee to consider the national bank, see *Annals of Congress*, 13th Cong., 2d sess., 1956. Convenient summaries of the progress of the bank bill in the House of Representatives may be found in Adams, *History of the United States*, 8:245-62, and Risjord, *Old Republicans*, 155-57. Jackson's voting record on the various aspects of the bank bill may be traced in *Annals of Congress*, 13th Cong., 3d sess., 496, 499, 1030-31, 1041-42, 1043-44, 1080-83, 1150-52, 1168.

The bill, as finally enacted, forbade the United States Bank to lend more than five hundred thousand dollars to the government, or to buy government indebtedness, and also deprived the president of the authority to suspend specie payments. Jackson's failure to vote on the bill reflected the opposition of both Madison and Dallas, who considered it merely as a means of curbing state banks and as of little value in disposing of the bonds of the United States.[68] His abstention, therefore, served as a harbinger of Madison's veto.

On 4 February 1815 the somewhat dispirited Madison administration received the joyful news of Andrew Jackson's dramatic victory over the British at New Orleans and on 13 February the long-awaited tidings of the signing of the Treaty of Ghent, but its troubles were not over. Critics now complained that the treaty contained no guarantees against a renewal of the detested practice of impressment. Entering the arena in defense of the government, Jackson accused one critic, Federalist Richard Stockton of New Jersey, of trying "to throw the firebrand of discord" into the House. Moreover, Jackson expressed surprise that those who had earlier favored withdrawing from the war before impressment had ceased should now object to the treaty. He declared that no right had been yielded by the treaty and that every assertion to the contrary was incorrect.[69]

Jackson's elation at "the glorious news from [New] Orleans" did not lessen his interest in military matters. As a member of the Military Affairs Committee, he reported a bill on 14 January to provide uniformity in the organization and staffing of the various state militia forces. In an unsuccessful attempt to have the House consider the establishment of one or more military schools and naval academies, he gave additional evidence of his growing nationalism.[70]

Other actions of Jackson indicate not only survivals of Republican traditions regarding military affairs, but also an awareness of war-weariness

---

[68]Kendric C. Babcock, *The Rise of American Nationality, 1811-1819*, vol. 13 of *The American Nation: A History*, ed. A. B. Hart, 28 vols. (New York: Harper & Brothers, 1904-1918) 221-23.

[69]*Annals of Congress*, 13th Cong., 3d sess., 1250-51.

[70]Jackson to Mary S. Jackson, 4 February 1813, Meigs-Jackson Papers, BHPC; *Annals of Congress*, 13th Cong., 3d sess., 1164.

among his constituents and the desire of Americans to return to peacetime pursuits immediately upon the conclusion of a war. On 17 February he submitted several resolutions calling upon the House to instruct the Military Affairs Committee to inquire into and report on the extent to which the armed forces could be reduced without detriment to the public interest and into the possibility of reducing the navy on the Great Lakes. He asked Madison not to detain the 20th Virginia Brigade, of which he had been a brigadier general, in an inactive state at Norfolk; for many of these men, "who never saw a case of fever & ague or bilious fever, until they reached that quarter, were the first victims to the insalubrity of the climate." He also cautioned the president that if he ordered additional Western men to Norfolk, "the enemies of the Government will have the gratification to see Virginians refusing obedience to the constituted authorities, in a quarter where their friends have been hitherto predominant."[71]

A testimony to Jackson's catholicity of interests, even in the midst of national crisis, lay in his strong support of a proposal that Congress purchase the library of Thomas Jefferson. Opponents of the purchase objected to the cost, questioned the value of the selections, and maintained that too many works were in foreign languages or dealt with philosophical matters. Jackson opposed moves to amend the bill by restricting the negotiators to the acquisition of such parts of the library as they deemed appropriate and to limit the price to $25,000. His vigorous stand contributed to the failure of both amendments.[72]

Following Mary's return to Clarksburg, Jackson lived much as he had during the previous session of Congress. He spent most of his evenings at his lodgings, where he read or talked and played backgammon with Eppes. He frequently went to Miss Taylor's school and brought his daughter Mary to his quarters. He wrote his wife that his face was "as round & chubby as Toby's [a term Jackson commonly used when referring to any of his unborn children]."[73]

---

[71]*Annals of Congress*, 13th Cong., 3d sess., 1071, 1102, 1103, 1164-65; Jackson to Madison, 10 January 1815, James Madison Papers, Library of Congress.

[72]*Annals of Congress*, 13th Cong., 3d sess., 398-99.

[73]Jackson to Mary S. Jackson, 24 January 1815, Meigs-Jackson Papers, BHPC; Jackson to Mary S. Jackson, 7 February 1815, ibid.; Jackson to Mary S. Jackson, 28 January 1815, ibid.

Jackson was elated on 30 January, when he received a letter from Dr. William Williams, his brother-in-law, informing him that Mary had given birth to a son on 24 January. He declared, "I am all impatience to know what kind of boy he is, large or small, black eyes or blue, white hair or red, who does he look like &c."[74] About two weeks later he wrote Mary that when "my fingers unveiled the little lock of hair [which she had sent him] shorn from the stranger they thrilled with delight."[75] Although he and Mary had decided upon the name of John George for the boy, they yielded to the preference of his daughter Mary and called him George John.[76]

As the session of Congress drew to a close, Jackson looked forward with unusual anticipation to his return to Clarksburg. When Congress adjourned on 3 March, he set out immediately for western Virginia. Although the spring elections kept him away from home on several occasions during the ensuing weeks, his thoughts were with his family. Tell "my sweet little Sophy," he wrote Mary, "she shall set [*sic*] at the table constantly when I return & George shall have a (pop) Gun."[77] With the war over, his political prospects bright, most of his industries on a firm basis, and his family life seemingly secure, Jackson had reached a high plateau in human happiness.

---

[74]Jackson to Mary S. Jackson, 7 February 1815, ibid. See also Jackson to Mary S. Jackson, 30 January 1815, ibid.

[75]Jackson to Mary S. Jackson, 19 February 1815, ibid.

[76]Jackson to Mary S. Jackson, 14 February 1815, ibid.

[77]Jackson to Mary S. Jackson, 8 April 1815, ibid.

9 Postwar Congressman

By the middle of February 1815, John G. Jackson had decided to seek reelection to Congress. On 28 January he wrote to his wife that "the letters I receive almost compel me to run."[1] Convinced that his presence would "be of vast importance in almost every point of view that can be imagined," he told her more explicitly three weeks later, "I have decided to . . . run for Congress." Remembering the lonely hours in his Washington lodgings during previous sessions, however, Jackson wrote her, "I swear by all that is sacred, you shall come with me[;] if I come & and you do not, I will not." Perhaps to reconcile Mary to the idea of another term, he promised her that "if I am elected, before the period ends, we will make our eastern visit, & take some of the indulgences which my fortune entitles us to."[2]

Once he made his decision, Jackson lost no time in beginning his campaign. He set its tone in an address entitled "Fellow Citizens of Tyler County." Unable to attend the election there, Jackson issued a written statement in which he declared that he had heeded the call of the people "at the last Election [1813] from that retirement which I had voluntarily chosen" because of the belief that their votes for him spoke "a language of patriotism, of devotion to American freedom."[3]

---

[1]Jackson to Mary S. Jackson, 28 January 1815, Meigs-Jackson Papers, Blennerhassett Historical Park Commission, Parkersburg, West Virginia (hereinafter cited as Meigs-Jackson Papers, BHPC).

[2]Jackson to Mary S. Jackson, 20 February 1815, ibid.; Jackson to Mary S. Jackson, 28 January 1815, ibid.

[3]Jackson's address to "Fellow Citizens of Tyler County," 29 March 1815, John George Jackson Papers, Lilly Library, Indiana University, Bloomington.

In his address Jackson took full advantage of the discomfiture of Federalists who had opposed the War of 1812. "The men who called themselves the Peace-party," he asserted, "might have desired peace most sincerely," but "their conduct defeated the object of their professions—like the ferry-men in our flatboats[,] if they looked one way they certainly rowed the other." He accused them of having done everything possible "to paralize [*sic*] the national arm, poison the national confidence, & jeopardize the national existence." Because of their destructions, the British had seen "whole states refusing to obey the constituted authority" and numerous citizens in other states "either openly espousing the cause of the enemy, or denouncing their own government." Turning to Federalist charges that the nation had lost even more through the peace treaty, Jackson emphatically denied that anything substantial had been conceded by the Madison administration. On the contrary, he held that much had been gained by depriving the British of the free navigation of the Mississippi River and the right to trade with the Indians of the United States. "Humanity will rejoice," he told the Tyler County voters, "at this event, for all the indian [*sic*] wars owe their origin to british [*sic*] interposition."

Whether he was unable to envision the coming Era of Good Feelings or desirous of keeping divisions alive for election purposes, Jackson, in closing his address, expressed the belief that the return of peace would bring "a more vindictive war of party" and his hope that he might provide an antidote for its poison. He also held out a prospect that within a year most of the wartime taxes might be repealed. Finally, in asking the support of the freemen of the county, he declared that he had "represented the people with a zeal which no man ever doubted, & with a fidelity which my enemies never questioned."[4]

With the Federalists dispirited and his own popularity at its zenith, Jackson had no serious opposition in his quest for reelection. In Ohio County, which he carried by a vote of 408 to 23, his expected opponent, Noah Zane, actually voted for Jackson, and Philip Doddridge, his arch political enemy, did not appear. Even in Monongalia County, where the Federalists usually showed their greatest strength, he received 132 votes to 7

---

[4]Ibid.

cast in opposition.[5] Returned to office with a near-unanimous mandate of the people of his district, Jackson triumphantly wrote President James Madison that "here the Feds backed out & even voted for me, this looks a little suspicious[.] Yet I hope that I have given them no excuse to distrust my patriotism."[6]

Despite his joy over his victory, Jackson had no desire to return to Washington immediately. News of "the astounding events in Europe," in which Napoleon returned to the throne of France with "the acclamation of the French people," presented a new aspect of world affairs. Nevertheless, Jackson saw no danger that Great Britain would provoke a new war with the United States. He counseled Madison against suggestions advanced by some newspapers that the president should call Congress into session.[7]

When the time came for Jackson to leave Clarksburg to attend the Fourteenth Congress, Mary was again nearing childbirth. Congress convened on 4 December, but Jackson remained at home for the birth of his daughter, Madisonia, in late November or early December and did not take his seat in the House until 15 December.[8] Mary's father and mother evidently stopped in Clarksburg on their way to Washington from Marietta and took the one-year-old George John with them. George John died in

---

[5]Richmond *Enquirer*, 19 April 1815, 6 May 1815; Daniel Porter Jordan, Jr., "Virginia Congressmen, 1801-1825" (Ph.D. dissertation, University of Virginia, 1970) 412.

[6]Jackson to Madison, 8 May 1815, James Madison Papers, Library of Congress, Washington, D.C. The lack of opposition to Jackson may have stemmed in part from the fact that Virginia Federalists had a more nationalistic attitude than those of Massachusetts and in part from common interests of the Western sections, which transcended party lines. Norman K. Risjord, "The Virginia Federalists," *Journal of Southern History* 33 (November 1967): 512-17; Otis K. Rice, *The Allegheny Frontier: West Virginia Beginnings, 1730-1830* (Lexington: University Press of Kentucky, 1970) 355-59.

[7]Jackson to James Madison, 8 May 1815, James Madison Papers, Library of Congress.

[8]Jackson to James Madison, 15 October 1815, ibid.; *Annals of Congress*, 14th Cong., 1st sess., 387.

Washington shortly afterward.[9] A few days after he arrived in Washington, John made a hasty journey back to Clarksburg, probably to break the bitter news and try to console Mary. His friend, John W. Eppes, who had "followed [two children] to the grave" and understood Jackson's own grief, wrote him, "Our fates have been in some respects similar. Each has met and survived the severest trial to which man in his life can be subjected. It is not philosophy or strength of mind but time and tears, nature's grand restoratives, which enable us again to value life."[10]

On 2 January 1816 Jackson was back in Washington. He gave up the lodgings he had taken for his family at a Mr. Campbell's on Pennsylvania Avenue and took bachelor quarters at O'Neal's.[11] Without delay he resumed his place in the House of Representatives, where his views remained tuned to the ideas and principles that guided the Madison administration. By then fifteen years of Republican leadership, in the opinion of one scholar, had "harnessed the Hamiltonian engine, not by destroying, aimlessly and dogmatically, everything the Federalists had done, but by subjecting the bank, the debt, the armed forces, and the federal service to mild Republican guidance." In doing so, leaders made the popular will and public utility the tests of programs and institutions rather than "visions of Augustan grandeur."[12] Although Jackson, like Madison, had trimmed his political sails to centralizing tendencies that he would have found unacceptable earlier, he nevertheless retained a strong sense of the limiting powers of the Constitution.

In one respect, at least, Jackson found himself somewhat at variance with the administration and with interpretations of the Supreme Court. The divergence concerned the power and function of the House of Represen-

---

[9]In accounting for the death of George John Jackson in Washington, D.C., I have followed what appears to be a very reasonable assumption advanced in Dorothy Davis, *John George Jackson* (Parsons WV: McClain Publishing Company, 1976) 251-52. For the burial of the child, see Sophia Meigs to Mary S. Jackson, 11 May 1820, Meigs-Jackson Papers, BHPC.

[10]Eppes to Jackson, 10 February 1815, John George Jackson Papers.

[11]Davis, *John George Jackson*, 253.

[12]Ralph Ketcham, *James Madison: A Biography* (New York: The Macmillan Company, 1971) 603-604.

tatives vis-à-vis those of the chief executive and the Senate in the making of treaties. Jackson ably set forth his views in a speech on 13 January 1816, during the debates on the treaty of commerce with Great Britain. The commercial convention, signed on 3 July 1815, had failed to break down British restrictions upon her colonial trade, particularly that of the West Indies, and had given British shipping an advantage, estimated to be worth six million dollars a year, in the carrying trade between the United States and the islands. Jackson held that stipulations in the treaty exempting British vessels from paying duties in American ports contravened an act of Congress and could not be operative.

Jackson drove to the heart of a significant constitutional question by asserting that treaty-making power was restricted and that the authority of the president and Senate in regulating American commerce with foreign nations was subject to the subsequent sanction of Congress. Without the latter, trade agreements had no validity, because the Constitution provided that "Congress shall have the power to regulate commerce with foreign nations." Jackson believed that the Constitution gave the direct power to Congress and gave only subordinate power to the president and the Senate, and that by inference only.[13]

Although he admitted that there could be no treaties except through the executive agency, Jackson contended that "when the treaty embraces a subject requiring legislation, either by a promise to pay money, or that a law shall cease to operate, in all cases Congress must act to render the treaty effectual." He conceded that during a war the president, as commander-in-chief, might suspend hostilities, or with the consent of the Senate terminate them, since a treaty of peace abridged no power, violated no right, and required no legislation. All that it did was to promise that the president, to whom power was given by the Congress to wage war, would no longer prosecute it. Jackson's condemnation of the commercial treaty with England, however, arose from his conviction that "it exercises all the functions of legislation—it repeals an act of Congress."[14]

To the contention that a refusal of Congress to carry the treaty into effect constituted a violation of national faith, Jackson answered that if

---

[13]*Annals of Congress*, 14th Cong., 1st sess., 662-65.

[14]Ibid., 665-66.

Congress were bound on all treaty questions, "we are a mere registering body; we ought to go home, and no longer presume to be a deliberative assembly." Such a restriction would not "palsy the Executive arm of the Government," Jackson contended, but even "if this consequence were to follow," it might yet be a "better evil than to annihilate the legislative body."[15]

Jackson took issue with an assertion of Federalist Joseph Hopkinson of Pennsylvania that a commercial treaty required no sanction and that it repealed laws in conflict with it. He held that such a proposal usurped the powers of Congress and that it was the duty of members to "stand here as the sentinels of the people to challenge all hostile attempts to invade their liberties, all hostile attacks subversive of the Constitution." He would not allow the Senate to legislate without the House, "the favorites of the Constitution," to which it had entrusted the purse strings of the nation.[16]

With respect to the contention that the treaty was promulgated by the president as a valid and binding instrument requiring no legislation, Jackson quoted Madison's message to Congress on 22 December 1815, in which he recommended "such legislative provisions as the convention may call for on the part of the United States." Jackson then asked, "Why recommend to us legislative provisions at all, if none were necessary, and he considered them unnecessary?"[17]

Jackson rejected the proposition that sufficient security against the abuse of executive power lay in the force of popular opinion. He declared, "I bow to the public opinion, revere it, and the politician who defies its mandates will sooner or later be prostrated by it. The *vox populi* is emphatically the *vox dei*." Jackson overcame whatever doubts he had relating to constitutionality, possibly after talking with Madison himself, and in the end voted with the majority to approve the treaty of commerce.[18]

As wartime concerns subsided, Jackson's thoughts, like those of other congressmen, turned increasingly to domestic affairs. Fortunately, an abatement in party strife following the termination of the war provided a

---

[15]Ibid., 668.

[16]Ibid., 669-70.

[17]Ibid., 670-71.

[18]Ibid., 671, 674.

new nationalistic atmosphere conducive to the resolution of significant issues. Moreover, the Fourteenth Congress had a statesmanlike quality unequalled since the First Congress. As Henry Adams observed, the people of the United States, under the stress of war, had sent their most able and most vigorous men to Washington, and in dealing with postwar domestic problems Madison himself displayed a capacity for leadership that he had been unable to exert during the war years. In his Seventh Annual Message to Congress, Madison addressed the significant issues facing the country, including the military establishment, banking and currency, the tariff, and internal improvements. During the last two years of his administration, nearly every month saw the end of a difficulty or the solution of a problem.[19]

Perhaps none of the points raised by Madison in his Seventh Annual Message excited more interest on Jackson's part than that relating to the construction of roads and canals. On 23 March 1816 Jackson reported for the House committee charged with consideration of the portion of the presidential message of 12 March dealing with the laying out and construction of the National Road from Cumberland, Maryland, to the Ohio River. The report pointed out that on 1 May 1802 Congress had authorized the formation of the state of Ohio, with the stipulation that the state could not tax federal lands within its borders. Congress, however, provided that the federal government would apply one-twentieth of the proceeds from the sale of its lands in Ohio to the building of a public road from navigable water emptying into the Atlantic Ocean to the Ohio River. By 1816 it had appropriated $410,000 for the road, but $101,513.65 remained unexpended. Jackson asked that Congress make a further appropriation of $300,000 from land revenues.[20]

In an eloquent plea for completion of the highway, Jackson expressed regret that work on the road had been delayed for more than nine years, since its completion would bind the Ohio and lower Mississippi valleys to the Atlantic seaboard. "Good roads," he declared, "have an influence over physical impossibilities. By diminishing the natural impediments, they bring

---

[19]Henry Adams, *History of the United States of America*, 9 vols. (New York: Charles Scribner's Sons, 1909-1911) 9:106-108, 138, 142. See also Ketcham, *James Madison*, 601-605.

[20]*Annals of Congress*, 14th Cong., 1st sess., 1250-51.

places and their inhabitants nigher to each other. They increase the value of lands, and the fruits of the earth in remote situations, and by enlarging the sphere of supply, prevent those sudden fluctuations of prices, alike prejudicial to the grower and consumer." Jackson held that apart from the economic benefits that roads fostered, they "promote a free intercourse among the citizens of remote places, by which unfounded prejudices and animosities are dissipated, local and sectional feelings are destroyed, and a nationality of character, so desirable to be encouraged, is universally inculcated."[21]

The proposed appropriation aroused opposition, particularly by Congressman William Gaston of North Carolina. Jackson, Henry Clay, and John Randolph, however, held that an appropriation from the fund already set aside constituted a solemn obligation of the government. Also persuasive were declarations that the thirty miles of the route completed between Cumberland and the Ohio River was "the most excellent road which had ever been built in America." Clay himself remarked that he had seen many turnpikes, "as well in Europe as in this country, but had never travelled on so fine a road as the thirty miles of the Cumberland turnpike which were finished." The House thereupon agreed to the appropriation of $300,000, which made possible the completion of the National Road to Wheeling in 1818.[22]

Like most congressmen, Jackson had developed a considerable aversion to the existing direct tax. Soon after his reelection to Congress, he wrote Madison that he saw no advantage to the collection of the tax by the federal government when it would have to be repaid to the states. Jackson declared that Virginia had advanced substantial sums of money for militia called out and placed at the disposal of the federal government and that when accounts were settled her claim would be "as urgent & as equitable . . . as any that can be presented at the Treasury." Assessment of a direct tax, however, would add almost insuperable burdens to those already faced

---

[21]Ibid., 1252-54. See also Walter Lowrie and Walter S. Franklin, eds., *American State Papers: Documents, Legislative and Executive, of the Congress of the United States . . . 1809-1823*, 7 vols. (1832-1861; Wilmington DE: Scholarly Resources, 1972) 2:300-302; Philip D. Jordan, *The National Road* (Indianapolis: The Bobbs-Merrill Company, 1948) 88.

[22]*Annals of Congress*, 14th Cong., 1st sess., 1306-1307.

by the state, and Jackson asserted that he "entertain[ed] no doubt that Congress will if possible dispense with the tax altogether in the future."[23]

Although Jackson favored the outright repeal of the tax, on 3 February 1816 he supported a motion, which passed 109 to 16, to reduce the annual amount of the direct tax to three million dollars and to limit it to one year. With consistency, he voted for a proposed amendment by William Mayrant of South Carolina to reduce the tax to two million dollars. Following several other unsuccessful efforts to limit or repeal the tax, Jackson, probably seeing no likelihood of an acceptable alternative, voted with the majority to continue it.[24]

Jackson favored import duties instead of the direct tax to raise needed revenue. Brushing aside John Randolph's argument that the burden of import duties fell upon the poor and the Southern slaveholders, on 23 January Jackson voted for an amendment to the revenue bill to raise existing duties by fifty percent, unless a new tariff schedule were adopted by 30 June 1816, when the wartime double duties would expire. Jackson opposed proposals that fell short of such levels, including those to set the tariff on imports at twenty-five percent for two years after 30 June and then reduce it to twenty percent or to fix it at twenty-five percent for the next three years. He also objected to a duty on cotton and woolen goods at twenty percent ad valorem as well as to the assessment of certain cotton cloths at twenty-five cents per yard even though they cost less than that amount.[25]

Although Jackson generally couched his arguments for the tariff increases in terms of revenue needs, there can be no doubt that, with his industrial interests, he fully comprehended the protective aspects of substantial augmentation of existing import duties. The Tariff of 1816 is commonly regarded as the first protective tariff in American history. Henry Clay has justly received credit for its enactment; however, Jackson, with his steadfast refusal to revert to low prewar levels of tariff revenue, also made

---

[23]Jackson to Madison, 8 May 1815, James Madison Papers, Library of Congress.

[24]*Annals of Congress*, 14th Cong., 1st sess., 863-64, 875, 916, 967-69.

[25]Ibid., 737, 1315, 1325-27, 1348, 1350-51. For Randolph's arguments, see also Adams, *History of the United States*, 9:112-16.

an important contribution to the history of protectionism as a major factor in American tariff policy.

Jackson was one of the first congressmen to advocate a revenue structure based in part upon the ability of citizens to pay. He offered an amendment to the report of the Ways and Means Committee to retain duties on household furniture and gold and silver watches as a means of reducing the direct tax from three million dollars to two million dollars. Jackson declared, "A system of taxation to be just, must draw, from every part of the community, a sum in proportion to their wealth and income." He pointed out that his proposal, which undoubtedly appealed to Western interests, constituted a tax on expenditures, an excellent measure of wealth, and not on basic necessities, which adversely affected the poor. His amendment, however, received only 64 votes out of a total of 154.[26]

Along with internal improvements and the protective tariff, the establishment of a national bank was one of the hallmarks of the nationalism that influenced legislation in the postwar years. Jackson had long been an advocate of a national bank and of constitutional amendments that would place the authority of Congress to create such a bank beyond the shadow of a doubt. Supporters of a national bank beat down efforts of a few opposing Federalists—led by Daniel Webster—and strict constructionists among the Republicans—the most prominent of whom was John Randolph—to prevent establishment of such an institution. On 14 March 1816 Jackson had the pleasure of voting with a majority of the House to create the second Bank of the United States.[27]

Like all congressmen, Jackson had to form opinions and respond to scores of routine matters. He voted against a Post Office bill, presented by Representative James Tallmadge of New York, forbidding carrying of the mails on the Sabbath and then, with some inconsistency, spoke against extending the current session of Congress to 21 April to include a Sunday, claiming that he did not favor "legislating on the Sabbath, except in case of great emergency." In keeping with his perennial interest in military affairs, he voted for a bill for the organization of a general staff for the army. Probably one of his most interesting assignments included service on a

---

[26]*Annals of Congress*, 14th Cong., 1st sess., 939, 952-56.

[27]Ibid., 1210-11.

committee to advise the architect of the Capitol, Benjamin H. Latrobe, on alterations in plans for the House of Representatives and modifications for the Supreme Court.[28]

Jackson did not anticipate the violent criticism that would descend upon him when he was named a member of a House committee, established on 4 March, to study a change in the mode of compensating the members of Congress. Its task was to determine a gross payment for each session to each member and to suggest ways "to compel the punctual attendance of members of Congress during the session." Other members of the controversial committee were Richard Mentor Johnson of Kentucky, probably the most popular man in the House, Thomas P. Grosvenor of New York, John McLean of Ohio, Timothy Pitkin of Connecticut, Daniel Webster of New Hampshire, and John B. Yates of New York.[29]

At the time of the establishment of the committee, the salaries and allotment for travel of senators and representatives remained at six dollars per diem for each day that Congress was in session and six dollars for each twenty miles of travel between their homes and Washington, as they had been set by the First Congress. Some conservative members held that the pay was sufficient. Joseph Desha of Kentucky pointed out that after taking care of boarding expenses a congressman might carry home as much as $450 in savings from a typical session.[30]

The Fourteenth Congress undertook a new salary arrangement in the so-called Compensation Bill. In the House, Johnson assumed the risk of exciting the displeasure of the people. Through him the House committee reported that a flat, annual salary of $1,500 would be equivalent to the rate then in effect. The bill was presented on 6 March and debated for two days, with John Randolph and John C. Calhoun among its most ardent champions. It moved through the House with unusual rapidity and passed on 8 March by a vote of 81 to 67. The Senate also passed it with no difficulty, and the president signed it into law.[31]

---

[28]Ibid., 1133, 1150, 1250, 1277.

[29]Ibid., 1130-34.

[30]Adams, *History of the United States*, 9:119-21.

[31]*Annals of Congress*, 14th Cong., 1st sess., 1188.

Most congressmen anticipated some criticism, but few were prepared for the storms with which the electorate greeted the legislation. On 19 September 1816 President Madison wrote Jackson from Montpelier, "We have not yet heard whether you are to be included in the Index Expurgatorius to which the Compensation bill has given rise. The loud reports from other quarters & silence as to yours, is a favorable augury."[32] However, Madison's optimism with respect to Jackson's situation was entirely unwarranted. Jackson learned almost immediately that his support of the Compensation Bill had been a mistake and had stirred up much opposition in his district. He told the president that all of his "personal & political popularity" had been barely enough to offset the hostility toward the bill in the local elections of 1816. Jackson believed that the only thing that had prevented more attacks upon him was his repeated assertion that he did not intend to run for reelection to Congress in 1817. Obviously looking forward to devoting greater attention to his industries and agricultural endeavors, he assured Madison, "I shall be perfectly willing that the day which closes your political life, shall terminate mine also."[33]

Jackson had little time to reflect on the mistake of supporting the Compensation Bill. Following the death of George John in December, his wife became exceedingly depressed. She refused to leave Clarksburg, and during January and February 1816 she would not even write to Jackson. Her attitude evidently troubled her father and mother. Jackson talked with Meigs, whom he considered a friend, and very likely her parents also interceded with Mary. Jackson continued his entreaties to his wife, but not until 8 March did she write to him and dispel the "doubt and gloom" that had surrounded him.[34] Although Congress did not end its work until 30 April, Jackson neither spoke nor voted after 15 April.[35] Very likely he returned to Clarksburg, perhaps to restore harmony to his domestic affairs and to mollify constituents critical of the Compensation Bill. Most of the following summer Jackson attended to family matters and looked after his

---

[32]Madison to Jackson, 19 September 1816, John George Jackson Papers.

[33]Jackson to Madison, 15 October 1816, James Madison Papers, Library of Congress.

[34]Jackson to Mary S. Jackson, 8 March 1816, Meigs-Jackson Papers, BHPC.

[35]For Jackson's last recorded vote, see *Annals of Congress*, 14th Cong., 1st sess., 1376.

industrial establishments.[36] He wrote Dolley Madison for advice about the education of his daughter Mary. Evidently he had considered sending Mary to a school in Philadelphia, but Lucy Washington Todd, Dolley's sister, had suggested a school in Bethlehem, Pennsylvania.[37]

Hoping that his wife Mary would accompany him to Washington when the new session of Congress convened on 2 December, Jackson purchased a coachee before he left the capital in the spring of 1816 for her to "travel down in, next winter." Once again, however, Mary remained at home. On 13 October she gave birth to a daughter, but the child lived only a few weeks. Because of Mary's health and that of the infant, Jackson again delayed his departure for Washington. On 20 December, Sophia Meigs, cognizant of the pressures that Mary exerted upon Jackson, wrote her daughter that he was needed in the House of Representatives and that she hoped he would soon return.[38]

When Jackson took his seat on 2 January 1817, a month after Congress had convened, the House was engaged in a full-scale debate on amendments to the enormously unpopular Compensation Bill, passed at the previous session. On 17 January, by a vote of 91 to 81, it defeated a bill, supported by Jackson, providing compensation for members of Congress at the rate of six dollars per day and travel allowances of six dollars for each twenty miles from Washington. The House also beat down successive attempts to fix the rates at ten dollars, nine dollars, and eight dollars, with Jackson opposing all except the last. It finally passed the onus of legislating the politically dangerous question to the next Congress by voting, 104 to 62, to suspend repeal of the existing act. Jackson, who had become very sensitive to the feelings of his constituents on the matter, voted with the minority.[39]

---

[36]See, for example, Jackson to James Madison, 15 October 1816, James Madison Papers, Library of Congress.

[37]Jackson to Dolley Madison, 6 September 1816, Jackson Family Papers, Virginia Historical Society, Richmond.

[38]Jackson to Mary S. Jackson, undated fragment of a letter, Meigs-Jackson Papers, BHPC; Sophia Meigs to Mary S. Jackson, 20 December 1816, ibid.; Davis, *John George Jackson*, 260.

[39]*Annals of Congress*, 14th Cong., 2d sess., 406, 574, 609, 612, 637-38, 691-92, 701-702, 706.

As he anticipated retirement from Congress at the end of the session, Jackson once again pressed for federal road construction, a matter of perennial concern to the Western country. On 11 January 1817, in keeping with the principle by which a portion of the receipts from federal land sales in Ohio was applied to roads, he offered resolutions that the Committee on Roads and Canals consider the opening of two new highways. One road, which he had proposed at the previous session, would lead from Washington, Pennsylvania, via present Wellsburg, West Virginia, to the Sandusky River at or near Fort Stephenson. The other, to be financed from lands sold in the new state of Indiana, would extend from Winchester, Virginia, to the Indiana border by way of the mouth of the Muskingum River and Chillicothe. The House accepted the resolutions, but the committee recommended only one road, to be built from the terminus of the Cumberland Road, at Wheeling, (West) Virginia, to the Indiana border, a route not proposed by Jackson.[40]

Never deviating in his advocacy of improved transportation, Jackson cast one of his major votes in favor of Calhoun's Bonus Bill, which would have set aside the bonus to be paid by the United States government to the states as an internal improvement fund. Jackson must have suffered keen disappointment when Madison, whom he had almost unfailingly supported, vetoed the bill on constitutional grounds.[41]

Despite his arguments that good roads would foster a feeling of nationalism, Jackson's own sectional antipathies died slowly. On 30 January, in a rather wide-ranging comment during the discussion of a bill dealing with commerce with Great Britain, he again lashed out at the commercial interests of the Northeast. He declared that in 1806 the merchants had united in urging Congress to take stern measures against British violations of American rights, but when, after much forbearance, the government went to war against Great Britain, they "abandoned its cause, and traitorously turned their force and power against the country." Now, he asserted, the merchants, caring for nothing but their own selfish interests, opposed any agreement conducive to the national welfare because it might interfere

[40]*Annals of Congress*, 14th Cong., 1st sess., 1254; *Annals of Congress*, 14th Cong., 2d sess., 464-65, 746.

[41]*Annals of Congress*, 14th Cong., 2d sess., 922-23; Adams, *History of the United States*, 9:148-53.

with their profitable carrying trade. As to the agriculturists, their interests were never consulted. "They were," Jackson declared, "the great passive beast of burden, bearing all the weight imposed upon it, and asking nothing in return of the Government, in their boldest prayer, but to be left alone." He would have continued, he said, but had to "yield to the pressure of a severe cold" and declined further remarks on the subject.[42]

Jackson's attack upon the merchants opened a veritable Pandora's box and drew a spirited response from Rufus King of Massachusetts. Sensitive to charges of disloyalty by New England, King launched a counterattack against Virginia. He attributed to John Randolph a declaration that in 1799-1800 Virginia had constructed an armory for the purpose of resisting federal authority.[43] In the ensuing exchanges, Randolph asserted that the armory had indeed been built to furnish patriotic citizens with arms with which to resist usurpations of the Adams administration and the Alien and Sedition laws. Randolph declared that the "State of Virginia was disposed to stand on the bank of the Potomac, and defend that parchment [the Constitution] against the bayonets of those who were willing to burn that parchment at the point of a bayonet."[44]

Jackson then reentered the verbal battle, with both King and Randolph as antagonists. He insisted that he was a young legislator in Richmond at the time and had a clear recollection of the circumstances surrounding the building of the armory in the Virginia capital. Governor James Wood's purpose had been simply to obtain good arms instead of the inferior ones the Swann firm of Boston had supplied from the refuse of Europe. Jackson stated that even though Governor James Monroe's administration had seen party spirit raised to a high level, he had never heard any person avow any intention of resisting federal authority with force.[45] Randolph countered with the assertion that the quality of arms obtained had not been a consideration in the construction of the armory, but that Virginia's "long-headed and clear-sighted" leaders simply did not consider it proper for her to be dependent upon contracts the federal government

---

[42] *Annals of Congress*, 14th Cong., 2d sess., 792-93.

[43] Ibid., 793.

[44] Ibid., 795.

[45] Ibid., 796-98.

might stop. He further declared that Alexander Hamilton practiced "high-toned politics; we were afraid of him."[46]

Other matters that claimed Jackson's attention included a bill introduced by Lewis Condict of New Jersey to provide vaccination against smallpox for members of the armed forces of the United States and for citizens of the country. Surprisingly, the usually progressive Jackson vehemently opposed the measure on the ground that no part of the Constitution specifically granted such authority and that "no such power could be inferred from the general [welfare] clause of the Constitution." Although both Condict and Wright argued that the Constitution did confer such authority both through the power of Congress to raise money for the army and navy and the general welfare clause, opponents brought about the defeat of the bill by a vote of 88 to 57.[47]

On 12 February 1817, as the session approached a close, Jackson moved that the Senate be notified that the House was ready to open and count the electoral votes for president and vice-president of the United States. Members of the Senate came to the House chamber, and the President of the Senate took his seat beside the Speaker of the House. Jackson and Pitkin of the House and Nathaniel Macon of the Senate were designated tellers and occupied seats in front of the Chair. The President of the Senate broke the seals of the official communications and handed the results to the tellers. In accordance with the results, Jackson on 21 February offered a resolution calling for the appointment of a committee to notify James Monroe and Daniel D. Tompkins officially of their election as president and vice-president, respectively. The Speaker appointed Jackson and Pitkin to represent the House on the committee.[48]

Jackson's part in heralding the beginnings of a new administration provided a fitting close to his own public life in the nation's capital. He was certain to miss his associations with the powerful figures in national affairs and the close ties he had formed with the Madisons. On 26 January, for instance, he had dined with the President and First Lady and a small party, which included Commodore and Mrs. Stephen Decatur. The previous

---

[46]Ibid., 798-99.

[47]Ibid., 467-71.

[48]Ibid., 943, 944.

evening he had dined with the French minister "in grand stile [*sic*]." He thought that the French "entertain[ed] elegantly," but he was somewhat shocked by the dress of the wife of the British minister, Sir Charles Bagot, whose "neck [was] bare almost to the waist." Jackson wrote Mary that the president appeared remarkably well and "looks to the close of his great career with delight unaccompanied by a single regret." Weary with a cold and the harshness of the Washington weather, Jackson himself felt a loneliness and expressed to Mary the hope that he would never be away from home so long again.[49]

Unlike Madison, Jackson left Washington with some feelings of bitterness. "What have I got for my career [of] so many years," he asked, "but wounds and curses & delapidations [*sic*] of private funds?"[50] As early as 5 January, when he sent his son, John Jay, back to Clarksburg, he told his wife that he was keeping his horse, "Potomac," to have him for riding and to avoid detention when Congress adjourned.[51] Jackson wrote Mary, "I have not received much solicitation from the district to become a Candidate" again,[52] and told her to "indulge no fears about my offering for Congress again[.] That question is decided & not subject to revision for some years at least when the fruits of our industry will afford without personal care an ample income."[53]

When Jackson departed from Washington, he was a seasoned veteran of the halls of Congress and a politician of discernment. For nearly fifteen years he had been near the centers of state and national power. He had begun his career as an ardent supporter of Thomas Jefferson and had given even more undeviating allegiance to Madison and his administration. During those years of service his views changed substantially. For him, the War of 1812 and the factionalism that it engendered "taught a lesson never to be forgotten," and by the time his legislative career came to an end he was

---

[49]Jackson to Mary S. Jackson, 27 January 1817, John George Jackson Papers.

[50]Jackson to Mary S. Jackson, 15 February 1817, Meigs-Jackson Papers, BHPC.

[51]Jackson to Mary S. Jackson, 5 [6] January 1817, ibid.

[52]Jackson to Mary S. Jackson, 11 January 1817, ibid.

[53]Jackson to Mary S. Jackson, 17 January 1817, ibid.

convinced that a strong central government was essential.[54] At the same time, he had seen much of what he had fought for accomplished. He took heart in observing the war brought to a close without the loss of national honor, the establishment of a national banking system, the increasing acceptance of the principle of federal aid to internal improvements, and the emergence of a genuine national feeling.

In the relatively placid Era of Good Feelings, ushered in by the Monroe administration, Jackson, always the political warrior, might have found congressional service less appealing. Certainly he had never been a close political associate of the new president, and he could hardly have expected to play as significant a role in the House of Representatives as he had enjoyed during the Madison years.

---

[54]Jackson to Madison, 9 December 1821, John George Jackson Papers.

10 The Monongalia Navigation Company

When John G. Jackson completed his second period of service as a congressman in the spring of 1817, he had wearied of politics and was ready, at least for a time, to give his undivided attention to his business enterprises. Contrary to custom, he took little part in the congressional campaign in his district in the April 1817 elections, and his seat fell to James Pindall, a Federalist. The succession of Pindall, a personal friend, rather than a political enemy, such as Philip Doddridge, must have ameliorated any feelings of regret that Jackson experienced in leaving the halls of Congress. Jackson must also have taken comfort in the reelection of his brother, Edward Brake Jackson, to the Virginia House of Delegates, to which Edward had first won election in 1815.[1]

Jackson knew that the success of his business ventures hinged largely upon adequate transportation facilities, and for years he had labored to improve communications in the West Fork Valley. In 1811 he served on a committee of the Virginia House of Delegates to consider ways of effectively removing obstacles to navigation from the West Fork of the Monongahela River. As a congressman, he had fought vigorously for completion of the National, or Cumberland, Road to Wheeling.[2]

---

[1]Daniel Porter Jordan, Jr., "Virginia Congressmen, 1801-1825" (Ph.D. dissertation, University of Virginia, 1970) 416; Virgil A. Lewis, *Second Biennial Report of the Department of Archives and History of the State of West Virginia* (Charleston: n. p., [1908]) 122.

[2]Virginia, House of Delegates, *Journal, 1811*, 38; Walter Lowrie and Walter S. Franklin, eds., *American State Papers: Documents, Legislative and Executive of the Congress of the United States . . . 1809-1823*, 7 vols. (1832-1861; Wilmington DE: Scholarly Resources, 1972) 2:300-302.

Following the War of 1812 Jackson, for whom the West Fork had become an economic lifeline, conceived perhaps the most ambitious plans for river improvement to emerge from west of the Allegheny Mountains. The West Fork and Monongahela rivers were the natural link between Clarksburg and the National Road, some fifty miles to the north, as well as Clarksburg's outlet to the Ohio Valley. Knowing that the West Fork could not provide sufficient water for navigation in all seasons, in the autumn of 1815 Jackson drafted a petition to the Virginia General Assembly seeking the formation of a company with authority to construct a canal to divert waters of the Buckhannon River, a tributary of the Tygart Valley River, itself a branch of the Monongahela, to Elk Creek and thence to the West Fork.[3]

The General Assembly failed to act upon Jackson's petition, which bore the signatures of numerous prominent citizens of the West Fork Valley. Undaunted, Jackson prepared a second memorial, signed by twenty-three residents of Clarksburg and dated 19 November 1816, for presentation to the following legislature. The new petition asked permission to form a company to improve the West Fork by "individual efforts." It stated that a public meeting held at Clarksburg on 18 October 1816 revealed no "diversity of opinion" among the people of the area with respect to the proposed improvements.[4]

With Jackson's guidance, "individual efforts" grew into a corporate structure. Upon the recommendation of the Virginia Board of Public Works, the General Assembly on 29 January 1817 approved the organization of the Monongalia Navigation Company, with capital stock of $100,000, which on 19 February 1818 was raised to $150,000. The state agreed to subscribe $60,000 of the original amount.[5] Some question arose as to whether the carelessly drafted law creating the company required individual stockholders to pay their full subscriptions before the state in-

---

[3]Harrison County Legislative Petition, 28 October 1815, Virginia State Library, Richmond.

[4]Harrison County Legislative Petition, 19 November 1816.

[5]Virginia, General Assembly, *Acts, 1816*, 103-110; Virginia, General Assembly, *Acts, 1817*, 119; Virginia, Board of Public Works, Journal C, 133, Virginia State Library (hereinafter cited as BPW Journals).

vested any part of its share. At Jackson's behest the Board of Public Works declared it would follow the general policy laid down in the act of the legislature of 5 February 1816, which created the Board, and subscribe the state's share as soon as one-fifth of the private stock had been paid in or secured.[6]

From the outset John G. Jackson and other members of the Jackson family held a controlling interest in the $90,000 of privately owned stock. John, the prime mover in the company throughout its existence, took $33,600. His brother, Edward B., subscribed $10,000, and his cousin, Jonathan, took another $10,000. Other major stockholders included Benjamin Wilson, Jr., with $10,000; Jacob Israel, $7,500; James Pindall, $3,000; Joseph Israel, $2,500; Daniel Kincheloe, Jackson's brother-in-law, $1,900; and David Hewes, $1,500.[7] The influence of the Jacksons appeared likely to become even greater when on 30 March 1818 John was appointed a member of the Virginia Board of Public Works, which had jurisdiction over all internal improvement companies.[8]

---

[6]Jackson to James P. Preston, 22 July 1818; Monongalia Navigation Company Records, in Virginia, Board of Public Works Records, Virginia State Library (hereinafter cited as MNC Records); BPW Journal B, 3, 7; Virginia, *A Collection of All Laws and Resolutions of the General Assembly of Virginia, Relating to the Board of Public Works; The Report of the Commissioners Appointed to Review Certain Rivers Within the Commonwealth in 1812; The Reports of 1814-15, from the Committee on Roads and Internal Navigation, to the Legislature; and the Several Annual Reports of the Board of Public Works to the General Assembly of Virginia up to 1819* (Richmond: Shepherd and Pollard, 1819) 28-29.

[7]A list of stockholders, with the amounts subscribed by each, dated 22 December 1818, is in the MNC Records.

[8]Virginia, Board of Public Works, Letterbook A (June 1816-April 1832) 17, Virginia State Library (hereinafter cited as BPW Letterbook A). Jackson accepted this appointment with "sentiments of distinguished respect." Jackson to Bernard Peyton, 30 March 1818, MNC Records. Whether because of the pressure of other duties or public criticism, Jackson served as a member of the Board of Public Works for only one year. For the elections to the Board of Public Works by the General Assembly on 4 February 1819, when Jackson's term ended, see, for instance, BPW Journal B, 41.

The preponderant involvement of the Jackson family in the company produced immediate repercussions in the local community. Benjamin Wilson, Jr., often a bitter political and business rival of John, became the most vociferous critic of the Jacksons' dominance in company affairs and of the plan advanced for the improvement of the West Fork River. On 26 December 1818 Wilson declared that in consequence of the composition and plans of the company "several thousand dollars of stock was given up or relinguished [*sic*], in disqust [*sic*]" and that it would be "imprudent" for the public to advance any money for the project.

Wilson also suggested improprieties. He objected to John's membership on the Board of Public Works at the same time that he exercised such an influence in the Monongalia Navigation Company. He charged that the "day after it was announced that the publick money was to come" Jonathan Jackson had tried to buy Wilson's stock, and similar overtures had been made to Edwin S. Duncan, a small stockholder. Wilson further declared that George I. Davisson, a member of the Virginia Senate, had been named a director of the company in order to "soften the Execution of his threats at Richmond this winter."[9]

An article by "Argus," possibly Wilson himself, in the Morgantown *Monongalia Spectator* expressed the same concern that Wilson had voiced earlier. Commenting upon the article, "Gisco," in the same newspaper, charged John G. Jackson—who had been chosen president of the company—and his relatives with attempts to control the organization. "Gisco" contended that the company funds should not be deposited in the Virginia Saline Bank at Clarksburg, which, he held, was also actually under the control of Jackson, even though he was not a director. Calling upon the Jacksons to reduce their stock to the level of other major investors, "Gisco" deplored the fact that "the very brightest prospects" were dampened "by family hatreds, by personal quarrels, and by the unbounded and pecuniary ambition, which like the head of Medusa chills and petrifies all before it."[10]

George I. Davisson, a minor stockholder, refuted the charges made by Wilson and his supporters. In a letter to the Board of Public Works, Davisson denied that Wilson possessed "either theoretical, or practical

---

[9]Wilson to Isaac Morris, Jr., 26 December 1818, MNC Records.

[10]Morgantown *Monongalia Spectator*, 9 January 1819.

knowledge, of navigation," as he had claimed, and accused him of "a personal and political hostility to some of the Directors of the Board [of the company], who have been patriotic, in fostering, and promoting this great, and desirable object, by subscribing, & vesting, a great portion of their estates, in this enterprize [*sic*]." Davisson dismissed fears of misapplication of funds, which Wilson professed, by declaring that such apprehensions would be considered groundless by all who knew the directors of the company.[11]

On 28 January 1819 the Board of Public Works considered the letter of Davisson and one from Wilson and concluded that it had no authority to pass judgment on the plan of the Monongalia Navigation Company for improving the West Fork River and "no discretion to refuse" its authorized subscription of $60,000 to the project.[12] It referred the questions to the General Assembly, which on 10 March 1819 suspended any contribution by the state until the principal engineer of the Board of Public Works could complete a survey of the West Fork River.[13]

Not unexpectedly, John G. Jackson, always a fiery protagonist, rose to the defense of the company. He noted that Wilson had favored incorporation of the company, acted as a commissioner for receiving subscriptions of stock, subscribed $10,000 himself, served as a director, explored a portion of the river for locks and dam sites, and "never found any fault . . . except that the affairs of the company were not conducted with sufficient vigor." He echoed a charge made by Davisson that Wilson had become angry because the stockholders, concerned about Wilson's alleged mismanagement of the Virginia Saline Bank, which he served as president, had refused to elect him a director of the company.

Jackson justified his own sizable holdings in the company by answering that he had made clear from the beginning that he would take all stock not sold at the time the subscription books were closed. He vehemently denied that he and his family sought to monopolize the stock of the company for speculative purposes. He pointed out that four of the directors were Federalists and that three of them, George I. Davisson, Lemuel E. Davisson, and Edwin S. Duncan, were closely related to Wilson through

---

[11]Davisson to Board of Public Works, 23 January 1819, MNC Records.

[12]BPW Journal B, 37.

[13]BPW Journal C, 133.

marriage. If the directors tended toward any corruption, as Wilson feared, "it would be in the power of one honest man among them to sound the alarm & thwart it." Jackson declared, "Were it not that to abandon the scheme would be to succumb to the charges exhibited, I would most willingly retrace my steps." He branded Wilson an Argus, who pretended to guard the public treasury against "peculation," but who had himself, according to court records, on several occasions engaged in fraudulent or unsavory practices.[14]

The discord among the stockholders of the company aroused previously disinterested residents of the West Fork Valley to the implications of improvements to the West Fork and resulted in public meetings in several towns.[15] At Bridgeport, a few miles from Clarksburg, opponents of the company attacked provisions of the act that gave it authority to condemn dam sites and that allegedly failed to safeguard the public against control of the river by individuals "who may be influenced by motives not always pure." Participants expressed concerns over destruction of fording places and declared that the dams proposed would create great bodies of stagnant water that would become health hazards. "We shall in the already long list of our ills," ran one objection, "have pale faces, the personifications of Billious [*sic*] and intermittent fevers, instead of the ruddy and healthy complexions with which we are now blessed."[16]

Some of the same complaints appeared in petitions to the legislature in December 1819. In addition to the usual protests against threats to health, one of the memorials charged that the law creating the company interfered with property rights and incorporated "a Body of Men over whom the Law has but little controul [*sic*]." It gave power to a few "Stockholders who may hold a large number of Shares to procure their own election as Directors and to condemn Mill Seats[,] erect Dams and Build water works and create

[14]Jackson to Charles Yancey, 30 January 1819, John George Jackson Papers, Lilly Library, Indiana University, Bloomington. See also Jackson to unidentified addressee, 29 January 1819, Meigs-Jackson Papers, Blennerhassett Historical Park Commission, Parkersburg, West Virginia (hereinafter cited as Meigs-Jackson Papers, BHPC).

[15]Clarksburg *Independent Virginian*, 18 August 1819, 1 September 1819.

[16]Ibid., 1 September 1819.

to themselves an undue Monopoly not intended by the Law."[17] Jackson and his supporters scored a victory when the House of Delegates rejected the petitions on the ground that they were "unsupported by evidence, and . . . unfounded."[18]

Following the action of the House of Delegates on 22 January 1820, the Board of Public Works ordered Thomas P. Moore, its chief engineer, to survey the West Fork River to determine "the best and most desirable" method of improving the stream.[19] Moore made his examination in the summer of 1820. His report emphasized that towns along the Monongahela and Ohio rivers and across the Allegheny Mountains to the Atlantic coast, some 250 to 350 miles distant, constituted the chief natural markets for the West Fork Valley. Transportation costs made the marketing of grains unprofitable, and they most often served as feed for horses, cattle, and hogs, which were sent to Eastern markets on hoof. At certain seasons of the year, river conditions permitted the shipment of hogs, boats, planks, and staves downstream, but otherwise the only major exports were likely to be salt from John G. Jackson's wells and iron products from his establishment near Clarksburg. Although Moore believed that "the demands of the country imperiously require that some improvement should be made in the navigation of the river," he concluded that a proposal of the Monongalia Navigation Company to erect twenty-six dams at a cost of about $97,000 was impractical. Instead, he recommended the construction of seven locks and dams at a cost of $32,000.[20] Acting upon the engineer's reports, on 20 December 1820 the Board of Public Works found that "under existing circum-

---

[17]Harrison County Legislative Petition, 15 December 1819. The name of Benjamin Wilson, Jr., appears first on this petition. Similar petitions, dated 8 December 1819, contain the names of more than two hundred residents of Harrison and Monongalia counties.

[18]BPW Journal D, 122.

[19]BPW Journal B, 239.

[20]Virginia, *Fifth Annual Report of the President and Directors of the Board of Public Works, to the General Assembly of Virginia* (Richmond: Thomas Ritchie, 1820) 35-45. At this time at least five private dams had been erected on the West Fork River. Ibid., 35-36. Harrison County Legislative Petition, 6 December 1804; Harrison County Legislative Petition, 10 November 1814.

stances it is neither necessary or expedient" for it to subscribe $60,000 "or any other sum" to the capital stock of the Monongalia Navigation Company. It therefore rescinded its resolution of 5 November 1818 authorizing its president to make the subscription.[21]

Pursuant to the new developments, the General Assembly on 2 March 1821 reduced the capital stock of the company to $35,000 and stipulated that it must complete its work by 2 March 1826 or forfeit its rights.[22] The directors of the Monongalia Navigation Company accepted the changes, and on 11 June, Jackson, as president, requested the Board of Public Works to subscribe two-fifths of the stock and to appoint four directors of the company as provided by law. Jackson explained that because so many people "have imagined that injury, rather than benefit, would result from improvements on the river," it had become more difficult to raise $35,000 than it had been in the past to obtain $100,000. He believed that the aid of the Board of Public Works would identify the interests of the company with those of the Commonwealth and place its concerns "above the danger of the little chicane which sometimes mars the successful progress of institutions merely private."[23]

Although the Board of Public Works subscribed 140 shares of stock, valued at $14,000, difficulties yet lay ahead for Jackson and the company. Land purchases for dam sites were delayed when Thomas M. Randolph, the president of the Board of Public Works, informed the legislature that a proposal to increase the capital stock should have further study. Moreover, Edwin S. Duncan, a director of the company and a member of the state Senate, objected to the erection of mills at company dam sites as a violation of its charter. Duncan's position received reinforcement on 18 February 1822 when the Committee on Roads and Internal Improvements of the House of Delegates condemned the construction of mills by the company as "an improper diversion of the [internal improvement] fund from the objects for which it was created." The committee recommended that

---

[21]BPW Journal C, 133.

[22]Virginia, General Assembly, *Acts, 1820*, 87-89.

[23]Jackson to Board of Public Works, 11 June 1821, MNC Records. For a typical complaint by a small mill owner, see the memorial of Jacob Polsley, Monongalia County Legislative Petition, 13 December 1821, Virginia State Library.

the House call upon the Board of Public Works to protect the state against such use of its resources.[24]

Jackson bitterly denounced not only his critics but also members of the Board of Public Works who gave credence to their charges. He branded Duncan as "wholly destitute of those ideas of correctness, which characterise [*sic*] the intercourse of Gentlemen." He declared, ". . . until I saw his Letter I did not conceive that he would play the part of a blind infuriated Sampson [*sic*], to pull down the edifice which crushed his own reputation in its fall, for the dying gratification of involving mine in a common ruin." He had hoped that the Board of Public Works would have "the magnanimity to retract its error" as soon as it was pointed out, but he concluded, "I ascribed to them a virtue to which they are strangers." He concluded his refutation of the charges against him by threatening to "lay the whole case before the People, & if I do, whilst I will avoid setting down aught in malice, so help me God, I will nothing extenuate. My accusers, witnesses & all can be stript of their little brief authority, & be held answerable, with me, at one common tribunal—the bar of public opinion."[25]

In the face of mounting obstacles, Jackson convened a meeting of the stockholders of the Monongalia Navigation Company on 20 April 1822 to consider the desirability of surrendering the charter of the company. The stockholders voted against giving up the charter. Instead, they granted a committee of Duncan, Daniel Morris, and Jacob Coplin, all appointees of the Board of Public Works, the power to enter into a contract with Jackson to build the necessary dams, locks, and slopes, with a sawmill at each dam.

---

[24]BPW Journal C, 285-87; Virginia, House of Delegates, *Journal, 1821*, 189; Virginia, *Sixth Annual Report of the President and Directors of the Board of Public Works, to the Legislature of Virginia* (Richmond: Thomas Ritchie, 1821) 13, 60-62. Duncan, who married a niece of Benjamin Wilson, Jr., was a member of the Virginia House of Delegates from Randolph County in 1812-1813 and of the state Senate from 1821 to 1824. For sketches of his life, see Henry Haymond, *History of Harrison County, West Virginia, from the Early Days of Northwestern Virginia to the Present* (Morgantown WV: Acme Publishing Company, 1910) 138-39; Geo[rge] W. Atkinson, ed., *Bench and Bar of West Virginia* (Charleston WV: Virginian Law Book Company, 1919) 18; "Edwin S. Duncan," *West Virginia Historical Magazine* 2 (April 1902): 74-76.

[25]Jackson to Charles S. Morgan, 29 January 1822, Charles S. Morgan Papers, West Virginia Division of Archives and History, Charleston.

The contract, signed on 26 April 1822, specified that Jackson should receive $21,000 in four equal installments, payable at the end of sixty days, six months, and nine months, and upon completion of the work. Jackson agreed to complete one-half of the work by the end of 1822 and the remainder by 1 December 1823.[26] Ironically, the contract made the state and its representatives, including Duncan, parties to the same practices for which his opponents had earlier condemned Jackson.

In order to expedite fulfillment of the contract, on 17 June 1822 the directors requested the stockholders to pay installments of seventeen percent each on their stock on 26 June 1822, 26 October 1822, and 26 January 1823. They made an exception in the case of Jackson. Since his payments would immediately be returned to him, the directors allowed him to give a receipt to the company treasurer, who then charged the sums against his contract. Significantly, the Board of Public Works complied with the requisitions made upon the stockholders.[27]

The action of the directors soon led to new accusations of improprieties, most of them leveled at Jackson. On 10 August 1822 Duncan resigned his directorship in protest over the conduct of company affairs, and Edward B. Jackson succeeded him. Duncan severely criticized ambiguities in the legislation relating to the Monongalia Navigation Company and accused Jackson of giving receipts to individual stockholders for amounts they had subscribed in order to obtain release of state funds, when in reality "no consideration actually passed between said Jackson & said stockholders." He contended that Jackson, who then held 135 of the 210 shares of stock

---

[26]Minutes of the Monongalia Navigation Company, 16 and 20 April 1822, in Return of the State of the Monongalia Navigation Company on the 30th Day of November, 1822, MNC Records (hereinafter cited as MNC Return . . . 1822, MNC Records). See also BPW Journal D, 124, 180-83; Virginia, *Seventh Annual Report of the President and Directors of the Board of Public Works, to the Legislature of Virginia* (Richmond: Thomas Ritchie, 1822) 26-27.

[27]Minutes of the Monongalia Navigation Company, 17 June 1822, MNC Return . . . 1822, MNC Records; BPW Journal D, 183-85; Virginia, *Seventh Annual Report of the Board of Public Works*, 29. For action of the Board of Public Works, see Bernard Peyton to John Sommerville, 17 October 1822, BPW Letterbook A, 41, 129; James Brown, Jr., to John W. Williams, 29 July 1824, ibid., 186-87; BPW Journal C, 51.

in private hands, could not only appoint five of the nine directors of the company but, as president, could refrain from calling meetings of the directors and, therefore, control decisions regarding fulfillment of the contract. Inconsistently, Duncan, who himself had been a party to the contract that he now so bitterly denounced, declared that he had "no belief that John G. Jackson would avail himself of the advantages he possesses in this ill formed association to commit the fraud suggested," but he considered it unwise to place such a strain upon "the mere integrity of one man."[28]

Benjamin Wilson, Jr., also seized the opportunity to strike once more at his old adversary. Writing to Philip Doddridge, then a prominent member of the House of Delegates and a perennial political enemy of Jackson, that the legislature had once "Broke in upon it and may do so again," Wilson proposed a special commission to study the need for improvement of the West Fork and the activities of the Monongalia Navigation Company.[29] Wilson also complained to the Board of Public Works that Jackson's stock in the company enabled him to dominate the Board of Directors and that he had allegedly issued receipts to stockholders "who has [*sic*] never actually paid one Dollar in Specia [*sic*]," but had merely provided goods and services. He again circulated petitions against the company and personally drew up one signed by Clarksburg residents.[30]

Jackson and his supporters again rose to the defense of the company and its procedures. They circulated petitions opposing any move to repeal the charter of the Monongalia Navigation Company. On 30 November 1822 the directors reported to the Board of Public Works that Jackson had actually spent $11,068 on river improvements. Although admitting that the procedure was not in "express accordance" with the letter of the act by which the state quota was demandable, they defended the payment by some

---

[28]Minutes of the Monongalia Navigation Company, 10 August 1822, MNC Return . . . 1822, MNC Records; Duncan to Board of Public Works, 10 December 1822, MNC Records; Virginia, House of Delegates, *Journal, 1822*, 52-53.

[29]Wilson to Doddridge, 23 November 1822, MNC Records. For a sketch of Doddridge, see Atkinson, ed., *Bench and Bar of West Virginia*, 127-28.

[30]Wilson to Board of Public Works, 23 November 1822, MNC Records; Virginia, House of Delegates, *Journal, 1822*, 54; Harrison County Legislative Petition, 9 December 1822.

stockholders in labor and materials as "a mutually convenient and beneficial" arrangement because of the "absence of a sound circulating money medium." Finally, they expressed confidence that "from his known ability" and the progress of his own enterprises the company could "safely rely" on Jackson's assurances that he would satisfactorily complete the contract.[31]

Jackson also endeavored to justify the need for river improvement in a letter to Charles S. Morgan, a member of the House of Delegates from Monongalia County. He declared that in 1822 alone he exported more pork, beef, wheat, rye, oats, linsey, linen, and other articles than Wilson had sent out in thirty years. "I have therefore a right to say the Country are identified in interest with me," he asserted, and all would suffer until "a keel navigation *up* & down stream, at all seasons" was available. Jackson saw no conflict of interest in his holding a contract from the company which he served as president and principal stockholder, contending that, like judges, he could simply refrain from voting on questions affecting him personally.[32]

Although the legislature found the charges against Jackson "unsupported by evidence" and rejected petitions for dissolution of the company, the Board of Public Works, irritated by a letter from Jackson to the legislature complaining of its conduct, undertook a review of its own. On 13 February 1823 it unanimously condemned Jackson's preponderant influence in the company and his ability to judge the amount and quality of the work he performed under his contract with it. The Board of Public Works expressed the belief that the funds of the company had been misapplied, since no stockholder had paid as the law required, and that the only money in company hands, that paid by the Board itself, had apparently been applied to a contract that had been violated. Regarding reasons for Jackson's failure to complete one-half of the work in 1822 as "insufficient," it refused to pay the third installment of seventeen percent on its stock until the public engineer certified that Jackson had made improvements valued at $10,500.[33]

---

[31]Harrison County Legislative Petitions, 4 November 1822, 11 December 1822; BPW Journal D, 177-79.

[32]Jackson to Morgan, 5 January 1823, Charles S. Morgan Papers.

[33]Virginia, House of Delegates, *Journal*, 1822, 143; BPW Journal D, 120, 127-30.

Deeply concerned about the turn of events, Jackson asked Caesar A. Rodney, a longtime friend and a former attorney general of the United States in the administrations of Jefferson and Madison, to present his case to the Virginia legislature. He also made plans to go to Richmond himself to defend his position, but apparently he never carried out either plan.[34]

On 15 November 1823 Jackson addressed a defense of his procedures and progress to the directors of the Monongalia Navigation Company. He attributed delays in the work on the river to time spent getting materials and "in conciliating and explaining away the absurd prejudices, with which the People had been impressed," the necessity of making excavations from nearly solid rock at some places and building cribs of hewn timber where river banks were sandy or loamy, and the fact that writs of *ad quod damnum* had not been issued for the last of the dam sites until 27 June 1823. Despite these handicaps, Jackson asserted, he could have completed the work had not the unprecedented high waters in May, June, and July 1823 and unseasonably cold weather from 12 August to 18 October made it impossible to keep men at work.[35]

As a major stockholder in the Monongalia Navigation Company, Jackson declared that he had a desire "to see the work faithfully executed, & with proper uniformity." He could see no reason why the stockholders, the Board of Public Works, or anyone else should care whether he was paid in materials, labor, pledges of stock, or other commodities as long as he executed his contract. He attributed the animosity against him to "the violence to which Political zeal carried its votaries in times past" and to the fact that a "majority of the Directors never were my personal or political friends." In order to clear himself of the charges against him and to obtain release of state funds, Jackson called upon the Board of Public Works to dispatch its engineer to inspect the river immediately to determine whether work to the value of $10,500 had been completed.[36]

---

[34]Jackson to Rodney, 8 January 1823, Gratz Collection, Historical Society of Pennsylvania, Philadelphia.

[35]Jackson to Directors of the Monongalia Navigation Company, 15 November 1823, MNC Records.

[36]Ibid.; Jackson to James Brown, Jr., 19 October 1823, ibid.; BPW Journal D, 222.

Less than a month later, with pressures upon him mounting, Jackson resigned the presidency of the Monongalia Navigation Company. Attacks upon him, nevertheless, did not abate. Benjamin Robinson, a Harrison County member of the House of Delegates, viciously charged that Jackson hoped to live in affluency by draining off the profits of the company to himself. During the "latter end of Christmas week" of 1823 one of the company's mills was destroyed through violence.[37]

Responding to Jackson's pleas for an official inspection of his work in order that he might be paid money allegedly due him, the Board of Public Works on 31 January 1824 instructed Claudius Crozet, the public engineer, to make an examination of the West Fork improvement his "first duty."[38] Upon completing the examination, made in May and June, Crozet reported that, although an unprecedented flood in which the river had risen to a height of thirty feet had made the project "very unfavorable," Jackson had complied with his contract. The Board of Public Works thereupon authorized payment to Jackson.[39]

The financial affairs of the company remained precarious. At the end of 1824, $21,350 of the authorized capital stock of $35,000 had been requisitioned from the stockholders, and $19,618, much of it apparently in goods and services, had been paid in. The final installment of the state's share, amounting to $6,100, would fall due in 1825. On the other hand, the company had expended $18,918 on the river, with the improvements

---

[37]Jackson to James Brown, Jr., 17 November 1823, MNC Records; Benjamin Robinson to President of the Board of Public Works, 5 December 1823, ibid.; Jackson to Thomas P. Moore, 5 January 1824, ibid.

[38]BPW Journal D, 256. Earlier, on 30 October 1823, the ex-officio Board had refused to send out the public engineer on "any informal call," such as Jackson requested. Ibid., 273-74. As late as 27 November 1823, the ex-officio Board of Public Works considered it "inexpedient" to send Crozet to make the inspection, but it agreed to refer the matter to the next general meeting of the board. Ibid., 221, 222. Jackson's insistence upon an inspection is set forth in Jackson to Thomas P. Moore, 3 May 1824, ibid.

[39]Virginia, *Ninth Annual Report of the President and the Directors of the Board of Public Works, to the General Assembly of Virginia, Twentieth December, 1824* (Richmond: T. W. White, 1825) 16-21, 282-83.

far from complete and no tolls yet collected.[40] To make matters worse, in November 1823 John Sommerville, the treasurer of the company, after failing to pay over and account for $1,000 advanced by the state for its stock, had become personally "Insolvent."[41]

Affairs of the Monongalia Navigation Company took a dramatic turn with the death of John G. Jackson on 28 March 1825. On 20-21 June the Board of Directors held a one-day meeting to consider the new situation. One member, probably William Martin, offered a resolution that the Board of Directors immediately institute suits against the Jackson estate for any money due the company because of Jackson's failure to complete his work and also against Sommerville and his sureties for misappropriated funds. Declaring it inexpedient to complete the project, he also moved to allow the charter of the company to expire.[42]

Before the question was called on the resolutions, James Pindall read a letter from Mary S. Jackson, the widow and administratrix of Jackson, for whom he served as agent.[43] Acting upon the advice of Edward B. Jackson, who warned that some of the directors were capable of "carrying hostility to a man in his grave," Mrs. Jackson had already put twenty-five men to work in an attempt to fulfill her late husband's contract.[44] The member presenting the resolutions, however, insisted that the directors act upon them before considering Mrs. Jackson's letter, and all were adopted. Thereupon, Pindall read another letter in which Mrs. Jackson asked that the engineer of the Board of Public Works evaluate the work done by Jackson. If

---

[40]John W. Williams to James Brown, Jr., 13 January 1825, MNC Records; Virginia, *Ninth Annual Report of the . . . Board of Public Works*, 57, 178.

[41]William A. Harrison to Second Auditor [James Brown, Jr.], 20 March 1825, MNC Records.

[42]Jonathan Jackson to James Brown, Jr., 28 June 1825, MNC Records; George I. Davisson to James Brown, Jr., 21 June 1825, ibid.

[43]Jonathan Jackson to James Brown, Jr., 28 June 1825, ibid.; Proceedings of the Stockholders of the Monongalia Navigation Company, 1 July 1825, ibid.

[44]Memorandum from Edward B. Jackson to Mary S. Jackson, 6 July 1825, MNC Records. Jackson, Allen, Leonard Hoskinson, its superintendent, and William Martin and Jacob Israel of the Board of Directors inspected the works on 13 June 1825. Ibid.

he had been overpaid, his estate would make restitution of the difference to the state, but if he had done more work than he had been paid for, his estate would be reimbursed. The directors rejected her offer. They also turned down her request that they appoint a committee to discuss with her the status of the contract and to ascertain "whether it could not be satisfactorily adjusted without a lawsuit."[45]

Even after his death, John G. Jackson remained the towering figure in the Monongalia Navigation Company. In 1825 his widow held approximately $14,000, or about two-thirds, of the privately owned stock. In an apparent effort to remove the "obnoxious" directors and replace them with men willing to rescind the resolutions adopted on 20 June, she transferred some of her shares to persons friendly to her interests.[46] At a meeting of the stockholders on 1 July, only Edward B. Jackson and William L. Jackson of the old owners and James McCally, Thomas Synott, Charlton Shephard, and Henry Caruthers of the new ones appeared to vote. They agreed to seek legislative permission for the company to sell its properties, settle its accounts with Mrs. Jackson with respect to her husband's contract, and take steps to secure the improvements against damage pending their sale. After adopting a resolution that persons hostile to the interests of the company should not be elected to its Board of Directors, they chose five directors representing individual stockholders from their own number, with each one except William L. Jackson voting for himself.[47]

The new Board of Directors met on 4 July and elected McCally president for the ensuing year. Edward B. Jackson read a scathing statement, a copy of which was sent to the Board of Public Works. Detailing the history of the company and endeavoring to vindicate his deceased brother's ac-

---

[45]Jonathan Jackson to James Brown, Jr., 28 June 1825, ibid.; Edward B. Jackson's Statement attached to Minutes of Monongalia Navigation Company, 4 July 1825, ibid. (hereinafter cited as Edward B. Jackson's Statement . . . 4 July 1825). For Mary S. Jackson's proposal to continue work on the West Fork until it was completed, see also Clarksburg *Intelligencer*, 2 and 9 July 1825.

[46]George I. Davisson, Daniel Morris, and Jacob Israel to Board of Public Works, 12 July 1825, MNC Records. The amount of Mary S. Jackson's stock is noted in Edward B. Jackson's Statement . . . 4 July 1825, ibid.

[47]Proceedings of the Stockholders of the Monongalia Navigation Company, 1 July 1825, ibid.

tions, he declared that the "suing mania" could benefit only Benjamin Wilson, Jr., and Edwin S. Duncan. He contended that the directors had allowed his brother to proceed with his contract after the time of its expiration without "a murmur or complaint" and that John believed that a tacit agreement existed between him and the company for the extension. Daniel Morris and William Martin, directors representing the state, angrily denounced the statement. Martin committed his objections to writing and resigned his office.[48]

In another letter to the Board of Directors, Mary S. Jackson, on the advice of her counsel, claimed the balance due her late husband, since the former directors had refused to allow her to complete the work her husband had undertaken. Leonard Hoskinson, whom she engaged to appraise the work completed as well as that remaining to be done, estimated that $3,000 would be adequate to fulfill the contract and that $18,000 should be paid for the portion completed. The new directors dropped plans for a lawsuit against the Jackson estate and took steps to reach an "amicable" settlement with Mrs. Jackson.[49]

Unable to obtain guidance from the Board of Public Works as to whether it should proceed with the contract signed with John G. Jackson or bring suit against his estate, the company at a 29 August meeting with only five directors, representing private stockholders, present, made plans to terminate its activities. The directors named a committee, consisting of Davisson, Morris, and Synott to draw up a petition to the legislature seeking permission to dissolve the company and to distribute the proceeds from the sale of its lands, houses, and other works to the stockholders in proportion to the amounts they had paid in.[50]

---

[48]Minutes of the Monongalia Navigation Company, 4 July 1825, ibid., Edward B. Jackson's Statement . . . 4 July 1825, ibid. For the complaints of the state's directors, see George I. Davisson, Daniel Morris, and Jacob Israel to Board of Public Works, 12 July 1825, ibid.

[49]Minutes of the Monongalia Navigation Company, 12 July 1825, ibid.; Mary S. Jackson to President and Directors of the Monongalia Navigation Company, 4 July 1825, ibid.

[50]Minutes of the Monongalia Navigation Company, 4 and 11 July 1825, 27 and 29 August 1825, ibid. See also James McCally to President and Directors of the Board of Public Works, 22 November 1825, ibid.

The directors also set up a committee, made up of McCally, Shephard, and Israel, to seek an accommodation with Mrs. Jackson along the lines she had proposed on 21 June. The committee referred the dispute to the decision of Joseph Johnson and Benjamin Reeder, representing Mrs. Jackson and the Board of Directors, respectively. On 22 November the directors approved all committee reports by a one-vote margin, the private stockholders voting aye and those appointed by the state voting nay.[51]

Affairs of the company moved toward a denouement, with almost no prospect of overcoming the difficulties before the expiration of its charter on 2 March 1826. Claudius Crozet, the public engineer, who personally inspected the West Fork River in the summer of 1825, maintained that Jackson had complied with the terms of his contract, but that works "of a much more substantial nature should have been constructed."[52] The Board of Public Works, perhaps bewildered by the whole affair, declared on 16 January 1826 that "from the contrariety of opinion existing among the Directors of that Company, there are some points on which it would be difficult, if it were important, to come to any satisfactory conclusion." It recommended to the legislature that the state sever its connection with the company upon the expiration of its charter and appoint an agent to take care of its interests in the property and improvements.[53]

The Monongalia Navigation Company suffered a slow and painful death. The legislature defeated a bill for its dissolution, and on 24 January 1826 the Board of Public Works appointed two of its most severe critics, Wilson and Duncan, to its Board of Directors. On 8 September 1826 Edward B. Jackson, the company's staunchest supporter, died suddenly at

---

[51]Minutes of the Monongalia Navigation Company, 29 August 1825, 22 November 1825, ibid.

[52]Minutes of the Monongalia Navigation Company, 22 November 1825, ibid.; James McCally to the President and Members of the Board of Public Works, 22 November 1825, ibid. Crozet's report is in Virginia, *Tenth Annual Report of the President and Directors of the Board of Public Works, to the General Assembly of Virginia, Seventeenth January, 1826* (Richmond: Shepherd and Pollard, 1826) 225-26.

[53]BPW Journal E, 11.

Bedford Springs, Pennsylvania.[54] In December its opponents declared to the legislature that they had "borne the deprivation of their rights, the sacrifice of their interests and endangering of their health" through the activities of the company, which they charged had been designed for "private emolument and not public utility." They declared that much property had been "sacrificed under the hammer" and that there had been more cases of bilious fever during the past three years than in the preceding twenty.[55]

The last major defense of John G. Jackson, who continued to be the target of most of the attacks, fell to John J. Allen, who on 11 November 1824 had married Jackson's daughter Mary.[56] Allen, later a judge of the Virginia Supreme Court of Appeals, recounted the history of the company in detail. He declared that "the knowledge that I have obtained of Judge Jackson's affairs has convinced me, that he has made nothing by the contract, on the contrary, it has been a serious injury to his fortune." Allen asserted that Jackson looked "to the value of the works when finished . . . for remuneration" and added that "the sacrifices of health & fortune must be borne, but I cannot silently witness an attempt to add to this, the loss of his fair name."[57]

On 17 January 1827 the Board of Public Works considered a letter from Wilson and Morris calling for the forfeiture of the Monongalia Navigation

---

[54]Virginia, House of Delegates, *Journal, 1825*, 161. For the deaths of Edward B. Jackson and, on 26 March 1826, Jonathan Jackson, see Haymond, *History of Harrison County*, 382; Dorothy Davis, *History of Harrison County, West Virginia* (Clarksburg WV: American Association of University Women, 1970) 159, 419.

[55]Monongalia [actually Harrison] County Legislative Petition, 19 December 1826.

[56]Allen became the agent of Mary S. Jackson following the death of James Pindall on 22 November 1825. For biographical sketches of Allen, see Davis, *History of Harrison County*, 158-60; Haymond, *History of Harrison County*, 384-85; Atkinson, ed., *Bench and Bar of West Virginia*, 19. Allen's marriage to Mary Elizabeth Payne Jackson is noted in Dolley Madison to John G. Jackson, 27 November 1824, John George Jackson Papers

[57]Allen to unidentified addressee, undated letter, Mary Allen Cassady Collection, Fincastle, Virginia.

Company to the state and the institution of a suit against the Jackson estate for the recovery of money received by Jackson from the Board of Public Works. Because of legal questions raised by their request, the Board of Public Works submitted the matter to the General Assembly. Pending legislative action, it sought an opinion from the attorney general as to its own course.[58]

In conformity with an opinion of the attorney general, rendered more than a year later, the Board of Public Works on 20 October 1828 arranged for the commonwealth attorney for the Superior Court of Harrison County to file "an information in nature of a 'quo warranto' . . . for the purpose of enforcing a forfeiture of the rights of the Monongalia Navigation Company to the State." It requested William A. Harrison, an attorney closely identified with company affairs, to cooperate with the prosecuting attorney of the court "to bring [the matter] to a speedy termination."[59] Oddly enough, however, available records suggest that the case against the company may never have been prosecuted.[60]

Edwin S. Duncan struck the final blow to the Monongalia Navigation Company on 29 January 1831. As a member of the Board of Public Works, he moved the adoption by that body of a resolution that, if it became expedient, would vest the real and personal property of the company in the state Internal Improvement Fund, to be disposed of as the Board of Public Works might prescribe.[61] Nearly six years after John G. Jackson's death his most ambitious enterprise also suffered its demise.

---

[58]BPW Journal E, 46, 56. For the demands of Wilson and Morris, see their letter to John Tyler, 2 September 1826, MNC Records.

[59]BPW Journal E, 107, 112, 140-41; James Brown, Jr., to William A. Harrison, 30 October 1828, BPW Letterbook A, 219.

[60]Records of the Harrison County Circuit Court from the summer of 1829 to the middle of 1830 are no longer in existence. Yet, no suit was brought against the estate of John G. Jackson during the first eight or nine months after the appointment of Harrison to work with the prosecuting attorney. Moreover, the journals of the Board of Public Works, the instigator of the proposed action against the company, are silent on the progress or outcome of any suit.

[61]BPW Journal E, 208.

In assessing Jackson's connection with the Monongalia Navigation Company, his vision must be weighed against his methods. Time proved the merits of his idea, and, to a considerable extent, the shortsightedness of his detractors. On the other hand, as an excellent lawyer and later a judge, Jackson should have been especially sensitive to the conflicts of interest and questions of public morality. With his multiple positions as member of the Board of Public Works, president and member of the Board of Directors of the company, and construction contractor, he laid himself open to charges of corruption and to popular censure.

These charges, however, need not have been laid upon Jackson alone. Edwin S. Duncan, also a competent lawyer and jurist, Daniel Morris, later a member of the House of Delegates, and Isaac Coplin, all representing the state on the Board of Directors of the company, entered into the contract with Jackson and mentioned no conflicts of interest. When accusations later centered about Jackson, they remained discreetly silent about their own responsibilities. The Board of Public Works also on several occasions declined to intervene in the affairs of the company and at least during its early years bore some culpability for failure to give diligent oversight to its affairs. Although Jackson's conduct cannot be entirely condoned, the misfortunes of the Monongalia Navigation Company arose in part from a collective guilt that embraced not only Jackson but also the Board of Public Works and even some of Jackson's most implacable foes.

11 Constitutional Reform in Virginia

The question of constitutional reform troubled Virginia politics throughout the first half of the nineteenth century. The frame of government of the state, adopted in 1776 under the stress of wartime necessities, placed serious restrictions upon democracy in the form of limitations upon the franchise, unequal representation of constituencies in the General Assembly, and county governments that were in effect closed corporations. It enabled powerful agrarian leaders of the Tidewater and Piedmont sections to dominate the government of the state, which became more and more incompatible with the needs and ideals of the Valley and the trans-Allegheny regions.

John G. Jackson appears to have been the first trans-Allegheny political leader to embrace the cause of constitutional reform in Virginia, and it remained a cause worthy of his utmost effort throughout his life. He initially became convinced of the necessity for constitutional change during his campaign for the legislature in 1798. "Upon that occasion by the consent of all parties concerned," he declared of his own Harrison County, "every free white was permitted to vote," although the state constitution clearly imposed a property qualification for the suffrage. Jackson believed that the restriction violated the Virginia Bill of Rights, which set forth the principle that citizens with a "permanent common interest in the community" had the right to vote. Because of the restriction, Jackson regularly observed "many persons *voting* [illegally and] by courtesy alone." One of his first actions as a young legislator was the presentation of a petition of Harrison County citizens, which he perhaps inspired, calling for a convention to amend the constitution, particularly portions relating to the suffrage and representation in the General Assembly. The legislature rejected the petition, and for the next quarter of a century Jackson struggled in vain to secure legislative authorization for a convention.[1]

On 15 January 1800 a motion in the House of Delegates called for a constitutional convention with representation based upon white population, but it was tabled. The records do not show who made the motion; very likely it was Jackson, who later stated that at that session of the legislature he presented compelling reasons for the revision of the constitution. Richard Brent, an opponent of Jackson, however, argued that with war raging abroad, the French "making wild experiments in the science of free government," and the American domestic scene troubled with party strife over the Alien and Sedition Acts, the time was not propitious for major changes in the constitution.[2] Jackson yielded to these arguments and did not press the fight for reform at that time, but he "considered the reasons then given against calling a convention, as a pledge that when these causes ceased, there would be a common effort to effect it."[3]

Jackson undoubtedly supported a more inclusive resolution that was offered on 7 January 1801 by Delegate James Breckenridge of Botetourt County. The resolution, which failed of adoption, declared that "the constitution of this state, is radically defective, that the representation in both houses of the legislature is unequal and unjust, whereby the people, in many counties and senatorial districts, possess much more legislative power, than their fellow citizens of equal numbers, in other parts of the state, thus vitally destroying the fundamental principle of republicanism, that the majority shall control, and not be subservient of the minority." Breckenridge's resolution also contended that the state had an excessive number of legislative and executive officers and that reforms would effect economy in government.[4]

The time for constitutional change was not at hand, but Jackson did not allow the question of reform to die. Unable to make progress in the legislature, he set forth his views in the Richmond *Examiner* under the pseudonym "A Mountaineer." The two most glaring defects in the constitution,

---

[1]Clarksburg *Intelligencer*, 15 May 1824.

[2]Virginia, House of Delegates, *Journal, 1799*, 8.

[3]Clarksburg *Intelligencer*, 15 May 1824.

[4]Virginia, House of Delegates, *Journal, 1800*, 58.

which he considered violations of the Bill of Rights, related to the property qualification for voting and inequities in the representation in the legislature. With respect to the suffrage, he declared that "the disfranchisement of all the freemen of Virginia, except those possessing lands, is so impolitic a measure, and so subversive of natural right, that if the constitution were perfect in every other part, it would demand a prompt interference, and a decisive change."

Jackson drew attention to the sixth section of the Bill of Rights and its declaration that "all men having sufficient evidence of permanent common interest with, and attachment to the community have the right of suffrage, and cannot be taxed or deprived of their property for public uses, without their own consent, or that of their Representatives so elected, nor bound by any law to which they have not *in like manner, assented* for the public good." He pointed out that Virginia derived a great part of her tax revenue from levies on slaves, horses, taverns, and peddlers' licenses and that persons paying taxes in these forms were not necessarily represented in the legislature that laid the taxes. Those who paid taxes on property other than real estate and were denied the vote were taxed without their consent in violation of the Bill of Rights.

According to Jackson, the most serious flaw in the constitution, which made others "dwindle into insignificance" and reared its "hideous crest above them like the summit of the majestic Alps over the cottages that surround its base," was the system of representation in the legislature. The provision of the constitution that allowed small Warwick County to have the same number of delegates as Frederick County could only be compared to allowing Delaware to have a representation equal to Virginia in the United States House of Representatives.[5]

Quite apart from its undemocratic features, Jackson saw the state constitution as the source of numerous problems for western Virginia. He blamed its defects for the economic retardation of the trans-Allegheny re-

---

[5]Richmond *Examiner*, 15 January 1803. That Jackson was "A Mountaineer" is supported by the similarity of their arguments and phraseology and a statement of John Prunty to George Jackson, the father of John G., that the latter's anonymous letter had appeared in the *Examiner* a few days previously. George Jackson to John G. Jackson, 21 January 1803, John George Jackson Papers, Lilly Library, Indiana University, Bloomington.

gion and contended, with more asperity than truth, that it accounted for the unattractiveness of Virginia to immigrants. In support of the latter point he cited the example of his own Harrison County, which after fifty years of settlement remained essentially a wilderness where wolves and other wild animals were common.[6]

During the years from 1803 to 1810 Jackson's service in Congress and the demands of his personal affairs left little time for pressing the cause of constitutional reform. He heartily approved petitions presented in 1802, 1803, 1805, 1807, and 1810 by the residents of the western counties calling upon the legislature to devise ways of amending the constitution or to poll qualified voters on the question of a convention. He experienced keen disappointment when the Senate in 1806 rejected a House resolution authorizing an expression of popular opinion on a constitutional convention. During the War of 1812 the General Assembly appeared even less inclined to consider petitions presented by residents of western counties with predictable regularity. Perhaps Jackson himself slackened his efforts, for, as a brigadier general in the Virginia militia, he was preoccupied for several months with essential military affairs.[7]

The postwar clamor for constitutional reform in Virginia was based upon economic necessity as well as upon political principle. Both Republicans and Federalists recognized the need to promote domestic manufacturing, provide adequate transportation facilities, and establish sound banking institutions. Constitutional changes seemed imperative in order to remove restrictions on the franchise that would discourage the attraction of free, but propertyless, laborers, provide a system of representation in the legislature that would reflect anticipated increases in industrialized western areas, make possible legislation designed specifically to stimulate industry, and break the power of the agrarian gentry of eastern Virginia over state government. With his various industries, his banking interests, and his efforts to construct a slackwater navigation in the West Fork of the

---

[6]Clarksburg *Intelligencer*, 15 May 1824.

[7]Virginia, House of Delegates, *Journal, 1816*, 86; Ohio County Legislative Petition, 15 December 1812, Virginia State Library, Richmond.

Monongahela, Jackson had compelling personal reasons to continue and even intensify the struggle for constitutional reform.[8]

In late 1815 western counties again presented petitions requesting that sheriffs be required to take the sense of the people on the question of a constitutional convention. A bill to that effect passed the House of Delegates 89 to 83 but failed of Senate approval. It had the support of Philip Doddridge, a Federalist from Brooke County and a major spokesman for the trans-Allegheny region, and Edward B. Jackson, then a first-term delegate from Harrison County.[9]

Following the adjournment of the General Assembly in 1816, members of the committee of the House of Delegates who had favored ascertaining popular sentiment regarding a convention addressed a statement to the people of the commonwealth. They declared that the legislators who supported a convention represented a majority of the free white population of Virginia, the only constitutionally just basis of representation. They called upon each county or corporation to appoint an agent to poll the voters in the next general election on the question of a constitutional convention and to certify the results to the next General Assembly.[10]

Sentiment for a convention continued to mount in western Virginia. In early June, twenty-two prominent residents of Valley and trans-Allegheny counties met at Winchester and published an address in which they declared that constitutional provisions regarding representation had produced such disproportions in the Virginia General Assembly as to make "an absolute mockery of the principles of free government." The House of Delegates, made up of two members from each county, irrespective of their population, was controlled by forty-nine eastern and southern counties, which contained less than half the total population of the commonwealth. Similarly, the population of the country west of the Blue Ridge entitled parts

---

[8]For Western dissatisfaction with the Virginia constitution, see Charles Henry Ambler, *Sectionalism in Virginia from 1776 to 1861* (Chicago: University of Chicago Press, 1910) 82-86, 93-99; Otis K. Rice, *The Allegheny Frontier: West Virginia Beginnings, 1730-1830* (Lexington: University Press of Kentucky, 1970) 359-65.

[9]Virginia, House of Delegates, *Journal, 1815*, 37, 60, 63, 109-10, 165.

[10]Charles Town *Farmer's Repository*, 21 March 1816.

of the state to nine of the twenty-four senators, but a law of 1792 allocated it only four senatorial seats.

The authors of the address took a constitutionally high ground. They reminded the people that "their right to assemble in convention is not derived from the *Legislature*, but from a higher source. It is derived from the almighty governor of the universe, who created them free, and has given them the will and the power to assert their rights. It is moreover guaranteed, if such guarantees were necessary, by the declaration of rights, which the framers of the constitution, in the abundance of their caution, thought it proper to make."[11] The Winchester address called upon persons who subscribed to its views to hold county meetings on 4 July 1816, or as soon thereafter as practicable, and name two delegates to meet at Staunton on 19 August "for the purpose of devising and adopting measures for effecting a convention of the people of this Commonwealth." The signers of the address hoped for cooperation from eastern and southern counties, but they made their principal appeal to the people of the northern and western sections, for whom a "regeneration" of the state's political institutions would bring recovery of their rights and the opportunity of transmitting them unimpaired to their children.[12]

Even in the East some political leaders and newspaper editors called for conciliation of the West. In a famous letter to Samuel Kercheval in July 1816, Thomas Jefferson called for representation based upon white population, free white suffrage, and the popular election of most state and local officials. Thomas Ritchie of the Richmond *Enquirer* warned conservatives that the "clamors and complaints" of the people could not be stilled and called upon them to bow to the destiny that awaited them. The Richmond *Virginia Argus* advocated that the "great point, of equal representation be first settled," with later consideration of "other subjects, such as the extension of the right of suffrage, [and] the greater independence of the judiciary."[13]

---

[11]Ibid., 5 June 1816.

[12]Ibid., 21 March 1816.

[13]Ambler, *Sectionalism in Virginia*, 95-96; Richmond *Virginia Argus*, 8 and 16 June 1816.

Western leaders were by no means united as to either the powers to be conferred upon any constitutional convention or the procedures by which it should be assembled. One former legislator urged each of Virginia's congressional districts to elect ten representatives to a convention that would meet in Richmond on 1 November 1816 while the legislature was in session, so that "this subordinate Body should behold the majority of the sovereign People in supreme convention." He declared, "Republicanism, morally speaking is the synonyme [*sic*] of christianity."[14]

John G. Jackson was a Harrison County delegate to the Staunton Convention, which assembled on 19 August with sixty-nine delegates representing thirty-six counties. Following the election of Congressman James Breckenridge as the convention's president, Jackson, also a member of Congress, offered the first significant resolution. His proposal stated, ". . . it is expedient at this time to adopt measures for a General Convention of the people of the Commonwealth, to amend the Constitution of the State; which Convention shall meet during the present year."[15]

On 22 August the committee of the whole, to which Jackson's resolution had been referred, reported it with two amendments, both designed, as Jackson desired, to give any constitutional convention broad power to effect reforms. The first amendment "resolved that this Convention do consider the existing inequality in the representation in the two Houses of the General Assembly of Virginia, as a grievance, and as derogating from the rights of a large portion of the good people of the Commonwealth." Jackson immediately moved to insert "unanimously" after "resolved." His motion carried. The second amendment provided that "a committee . . . be appointed to prepare on the part of the convention, a memorial to the Legislature of the State, to be presented at their next session, requesting them to recommend to the people of the State the formation, on fair and equal principles, of a general convention, empowered to amend the constitution, on every point on which it shall be found to be defective." Chapman Johnson of Augusta County, one of those favoring a convention with limited powers, moved to strike out the second amendment. He offered a substitute that would limit any constitutional conven-

---

[14]Charles Town *Farmer's Repository*, 19 June 1816.

[15]For the journal of the Staunton Convention, see ibid., 11 September 1816.

tion to amendments that would "give a fair and equal representation to every part of the state in both branches of the Legislature, and . . . provide for subsequent amendments from time to time as the good people of this commonwealth may think expedient." Johnson's amendment failed of passage by a vote of 28 to 40.

Following the defeat of Johnson's amendment, William H. Fitzhugh of Fairfax County moved to set the number of members to draft the memorial to the General Assembly at seven and to strike the words "on every point on which it shall be found to be defective" in the second amendment proposed by the committee. His motions carried, the second by a vote of 57 to 11. All of the eleven members, including Jackson, who opposed the amendment, which limited the scope of any convention, represented trans-Allegheny counties. The convention approved the version as amended, 59 to 9, with Jackson voting with the majority.

Jackson then moved that the convention recommend to the people of Virginia the presentation of a memorial, based upon the principles set forth in the second amendment, to the next session of the General Assembly. The committee, appointed by the chairman, consisted of Jackson, Fitzhugh, George Tucker of Pittsylvania County, William A. Burwell of Franklin County, John Love of Prince William County, Henry St. George Tucker of Frederick County, and Elisha Boyd of Berkeley County.

The memorial, which the committee presented, emphasized inequities in representation. It declared that while "passing over many lesser evils," members chose to devote their attention "exclusively to one, not doubting that the same remedy which will be applied to it, will at the same time be extended to every principle in the constitution inimical to the rights and happiness of an independent people." Asserting that "the government of the commonwealth is actually . . . in the hands of a minority, inhabiting a particular section of the state," it called upon the General Assembly to provide for a convention to amend the constitution.

The convention decisively defeated a motion by Johnson to table Jackson's resolution and the memorial, but it adopted a proposal by Burwell calling upon the legislature to solicit the sentiments of the people at the elections in April 1817 if it did not deem itself competent to act upon the question of a convention. In accordance with Burwell's resolution, Jackson, Burwell, Boyd, Love, George Tucker, Henry St. George Tucker, and William F. Gordon of Albermarle County were appointed a standing committee to recommend a plan for selecting delegates to the constitutional convention if the people expressed a desire for one. The original resolution then passed by a vote of 61 to 7.

Six members of the Staunton Convention filed a minority report. They included Johnson, Breckenridge, Allan Taylor of Botetourt County, Henry Edmundson of Montgomery County, and James McDowell and John Leyburn of Rockbridge County. Although applauding "the calmness, temper and dignity which have characterized the conduct of the majority," they held that any change in the constitution "should be approached with the most prudent caution, and touched with trembling timidity." They insisted that changes in representation be coupled with a constitutional provision securing every part of the state from an undue portion of taxes. Moreover, they believed that provisions for future changes should be made without "unnecessarily agitating the public mind, or endangering the public tranquility." They expressed a willingness to support a constitutional convention for specified objects, but they were not ready "to commit the whole constitution, with all its consecrated principles, to untried hands."

The convention ended on a note of harmony, with the dissidents pledging to "unite their best efforts, with those of the majority, in securing the great object for which this convention was assembled, by those means, which appear to them, best suited to the end—by means of a limited convention." Jackson offered a resolution thanking Breckenridge "for the ability and impartiality with which he had performed the arduous duties of President of this convention."[16]

On 16 November 1816 the memorial of the Staunton Convention, with a cover letter from Breckenridge, was presented to the House of Delegates. On motion of Philip Doddridge, a delegate from Brooke County, the House referred it to a select committee, ultimately made up of thirty-three members. It also referred to the committee additional petitions of western counties calling for a constitutional convention.[17]

Doddridge delivered the report of the select committee on 12 December. It set forth the grievances of the West in forceful terms. Yet, despite the strong feelings expressed at the Staunton Convention and overwhelm-

---

[16]Material in the preceding paragraphs is drawn from the Charles Town *Farmer's Repository*, 11 September 1816.

[17]Virginia, House of Delegates, *Journal, 1816*, 28, 31-33.

ing support for a convention in those counties in which the sense of the people was diligently taken, the committee report declared that "the fundamental principles of government should not be subjected to alteration, until the disapprobation of the people is express and unequivocal." It also called for ascertaining the will of the voters regarding a convention at the next election. If they approved, the governor should immediately arrange for election of delegates from each congressional district, with the number to be determined on the basis of white population. Finally, any constitutional convention should be authorized to deal only with questions of representation and equality of taxation, and provision should be made "for such alterations as experience, the only sure test of political theory, shall suggest."[18]

Jackson was not a member of the House of Delegates, but the votes of his brother, Edward B., who represented Harrison County, clearly reflected his views. Edward B. Jackson stood with the minority in an unsuccessful effort to enable all free white male citizens over twenty-one years old to vote on the question of holding a convention. He opposed an amendment to empower the proposed convention to extend the "right of suffrage," but he voted for an amendment to grant it "to all persons having sufficient evidence of a permanent common interest with, and attachment to, the community." Delegate Jackson voted for the final measure, which passed the House of Delegates by the narrow margin of 79 to 73 and then failed of approval in the Senate.[19]

Deeply disappointed, John G. Jackson believed that the main cause for the failure of efforts for constitutional reform could be traced "as well to a want of concert between the friends of reform as to the united energies of those interested in perpeuating [*sic*] existing abuses." He maintained that alleged fears of universal suffrage were unjustified since even the reformers believed that voters should give "sufficient evidence of a common interest in or attachment to the community." He did not regard subsequent actions of the legislature in equalizing the land tax and altering representation in the Senate as adequate substitutes for genuine constitutional revision, even

---

[18]Ibid., 86-87.

[19]For the progress of the proposal in the House of Delegates, as well as Jackson's votes on various amendments to it, see ibid., 166-70, 180-84.

though those measures temporarily allayed some of the popular unrest in the West. The situation, Jackson contended, "demands further efforts by a united people to remedy the enormous evils of their present defective system." He believed that there was no more likelihood of "a wise, efficient & uniform system of Laws, where the Constitution is radically defective" than of "mature & luxuriant fruits when the roots & trunk of the tree are decayed & rotten & its branches sickly & diseased."[20]

Jackson continued to hope that somehow a convention might soon be held and that he might be a member.[21] He was almost certainly the author of a pro-convention communication, signed "Anti-Monarchist," to the Clarksburg *Republican Compiler*. The writer maintained that according to principles of government by the consent of the governed, set forth in the Declaration of Independence and the Virginia Bill of Rights, two out of three adult white males in Virginia were not bound to respect and obey the laws of the state. He contended that "working the roads, serving as jurors, paying taxes, living three, five, ten, fifteen or more years in the commonwealth and fighting for the liberty of the country" were "sufficient evidence of permanent common interest with, and attachment to, the community." The government of Virginia, the writer continued, "savours so much of monarchy" that, unless a constitutional convention extended the franchise to all free men without distinction of freehold, a century would be required to wipe away the stigma. The letter drew approving comments from the editor of the *Republican Compiler* and endorsement by the editor of the Wheeling *Va. North-Western Gazette*, who commended its author for his effort to change a political system that continued to "shackle and cramp" the energies of the state.[22]

In his comments Jackson evinced little appreciation for the economic woes of the East, with its loss in land values, declining production, dwindling exports, and minimal population growth. Nor did he have any pa-

---

[20]Undated manuscript, Meigs-Jackson Papers, Blennerhassett Historical Park Commission, Parkersburg, West Virginia (hereinafter cited as Meigs-Jackson Papers, BHPC).

[21]Jackson to Mary S. Jackson, 27 January 1817, John George Jackson Papers.

[22]The letter of "Anti-Monarchist" is noted in the Wheeling *Va. North-Western Gazette*, 29 August 1816.

tience with Eastern determination to counteract these misfortunes by retaining the political advantages that the section had enjoyed for so many years. Regardless of the influence of economic considerations upon his thinking, throughout his career Jackson rather consistently predicated his arguments for reform upon political principles rather than economic necessity.[23]

As the years passed, Jackson grew increasingly dissatisfied with the constitution of Virginia and reflected bitterly upon the failures of 1816. From both public and private experience he became convinced that constitutional restrictions contributed significantly to the arrested economic development of the western sections of the state and that adequate roads, river improvements, banking facilities, educational institutions, and political attractions would never be attainable as long as political power remained in the hands of an Eastern minority.

Jackson chose the occasion of a militia muster at Clarksburg in the spring of 1824 to deliver rather wide-ranging remarks on the question of constitutional revision. He sent a copy of his address, later published in the Clarksburg *Intelligencer*, to Henry Clay, who voiced "entire concurrence" with his views "on most of the great points of government, and especially that which relates to the Elective franchise." Clay declared that Kentucky, which had removed all property qualifications for the franchise, had experienced "no inconvenience whatever from the most extended exercise of it."[24]

In his address, one of the most cogent and informed ever made regarding the need for constitutional revision, Jackson excoriated legislative efforts to restrain the people from the exercise of their legitimate powers recognized in the Declaration of Independence and the Virginia Bill of Rights. Such attempts, he asserted, served to "affirm with all the solemnities of a deliberative assembly, the monstrous doctrine, that the *People* were unfit to be trusted with self-government, . . . and must be guarded against themselves as their own worst enemies." He charged that placatory

---

[23]For economic difficulties that underlay in part the struggle for constitutional reform, see, for example, Ambler, *Sectionalism in Virginia*, 100-27; Rice, *Allegheny Frontier*, 309-41.

[24]Clarksburg *Intelligencer*, 15 May 1824; Henry Clay to John G. Jackson, 19 June 1824, John George Jackson Papers.

moves toward the West in the form of equalization of representation in the Senate were intended to subvert constitutional revision and that those responsible for them had "violated the Constitution themselves, to preserve it inviolate by the people."

One of the most glaring flaws in the existing frame of government, Jackson contended, lay in its violation of the principle of separation of executive, legislative, and judicial powers. He cited the exercise of judicial powers by the county courts, members of which, he declared, at all times constituted a majority in the legislature. He disavowed any intention of disparaging "that excellent and patriotic corps, the Justices of the Peace," but he believed that even they would admit that in their organization and habits they were not "well calculated to perform Judicial functions" and that justice in their courts was "proverbially slow."

Turning to legislative defects, Jackson concentrated attention upon the provision of the constitution by which each county, irrespective of population, was entitled to two members in the House of Delegates. He found intolerable a system in which Warwick County, with 650 white inhabitants, had the same number of delegates as his own Harrison County, with about 10,000 white residents. Jackson also favored giving the Senate power, equal with that of the House of Delegates, to originate bills—except money bills, a right denied it under the existing constitution.

The executive department, Jackson believed, was "if possible worse organized than the Legislative." He regarded the governor's council as "a dead load upon the department" and "as useless as eight extra wheels would be to a farmer's waggon [*sic*]." Jackson declared that when "a justly censurable act is committed, each one can cry out with Macbeth, 'Thou canst not say 'twas I that did it.' " He favored a stronger executive upon whom responsibility for actions could clearly be fixed.

Jackson then reverted to one of his favorite themes in his arguments for reform, the question of suffrage. Once again he drew attention to the sixth article of the Virginia Bill of Rights, which conferred the right of suffrage upon men with sufficient evidence of permanent common interest in the affairs of the state. Yet, he noted, the constitution required that a voter must have a freehold of twenty-five acres of improved land, fifty acres of unimproved land, or a house and lot in town. Thus, it denied a man with twenty-four acres of highly improved land the right to vote but conferred the franchise upon the owner of fifty acres of wild land worth less than "one of the deer . . . bounding over them." Jackson noted the case of a late chancellor of the Supreme Court, who did not exercise the right of suffrage at Winchester because his fine lands near the town contained less than twenty-five acres, while twenty other voters, whose combined property was of less value, exercised the franchise freely.

Even though Jackson believed that the provision in the constitution relating to suffrage was "at war with all the dictates of reason and enlightened experience," he did not advocate universal suffrage in the sense in which that term was commonly used. He would not, for instance, "allow that privilege to an iternerant [*sic*] oar [*sic*] digger or collier, who are [*sic*] here today with their pick and shovel, intermeddling with our elections, and marching off tomorrow, with these implements of their trades to the state of Ohio, to control theirs." On the other hand, he would not deny the right to vote to "the tenant, for years residing on his leasehold estate, and earning an honest subsistance [*sic*], or the industrious mechanic who raises up his family amongst us in credit and respectability." The latter, he declared, should not be classed with "the aforementioned citizens of the world, who have no country nor home, for which they feel attachment." Although Jackson did not attempt to "define the proper limits of this invaluable privilege" of voting, he did not hesitate to declare that "wealth is of all others, the most fallacious & unsatisfactory criterion, for if wealth furnishes a fit rule, it follows that the overgrown rich should have numerous votes, in proportion to that wealth, like the holders of stock in incorporated companies."

Jackson also found objectionable a provision in the constitution that prevented ministers from serving in the legislature. He attributed their debarment to a belief that the established clergy in 1776 were hostile to the Revolution, a feeling that the political controversies of that day were out of keeping with the role of "ministers of our holy religion," and a desire to effect separation of church and state. Disqualification of ministers, Jackson declared, was wrong in principle, and framers of the United States Constitution had wisely omitted such a restriction.

Noting that his own father had been an officer in the army, a member of the Virginia convention that ratified the federal constitution, a legislator, and a congressman, Jackson declared that he himself had also been "rocked in the cradle of the revolution." Although he revered its framers, he had little sympathy for those who called upon the people "to be a little blind to the faults of the Constitution, and to preserve it, if not for its intrinsic merits[,] for the sake of its patriotic framers and defenders." He believed, instead, that "if we maintain the principles which they have declared sacred, . . . we shall render a fitter testimony of that reverence, than by shutting our eyes upon the lights of experience, & the demonstrations of political truths." He contended that the founding fathers "knew that all sciences were progressive, and none more so, than the science of free government." Referring to Jefferson and others, Jackson maintained that many of those founding fathers yet living favored reform. For himself, he would "revise the Constitution now, more especially that we might have the lights of their wisdom and reflections."

Although Jackson conceded that the original Virginia constitution had carried the state through the Revolutionary War, he held that "a common danger, a common cause, and common efforts bound us together more than the wisdom of its articles," and "when Peace came it was found to be a rope of sand wholly inadequate to secure the blessings of liberty." Its framers, he declared, "hastily built for us a convenient cabbin [*sic*]" that sheltered the people "from the winds and the rain for that eventful period," but which no longer sufficed. Jackson believed that the time had come to "examine every log in the old cabbin [*sic*] from the foundation to the top" and to "retain for the new building only such as were sound and strong[,] rejecting all the rest." Pleading for a constitutional convention "unfettered and unlimited," he asserted that he was "not afraid to trust the people" and would not "adopt the solecism that they are unfit for self government."

Jackson advanced no new procedures for effecting constitutional changes. He denied the authority of the legislature to call a constitutional convention on its own initiative, but he held that it should forthwith instruct the sheriffs in the various counties to take a poll of the people on the question. If the legislature refused to authorize such a poll, the people should act independently, for they could "change the fundamental law, without obtaining or even soliciting the assent of their public servants, erroneously called their masters." Jackson disclaimed any thought of personal benefit from constitutional change, desiring only the prosperity and glory of Virginia, "the land of my birth, the land in which I expect to repose when I am gathered to my Fathers, and where I hope my children will live after me joint-heirs to the happiness and welfare of a renovated and improved system of liberty and prosperity founded in equal rights and equal laws."[25]

---

[25]Clarksburg *Intelligencer*, 15 May 1824. For similar views, see also an undated draft petition to the Virginia legislature, in Jackson's handwriting, Meigs-Jackson Papers, BHPC.

During the early part of 1825 Western hopes for a constitutional convention rose again. The House of Delegates passed enabling legislation by a vote of 105 to 98, but the Senate, by a vote of 13 to 11, once more refused its assent. Western disappointment knew no bounds. The Martinsburg *Gazette* declared that "men frequently 'feel power and forget right.' "[26] Out of these new frustrations came the Staunton Convention of July 1825, which took up the cause of reform where the convention of 1816 had left off, but with no more success than its predecessor.[27] Finally, in 1829-1830 a convention was held, with the authorization and approval of the General Assembly. With all its distinguished personnel and its national attractions, it proved totally disappointing to the West. Not for another twenty years, in the Reform Convention of 1850-1851, did the West gain most of the political principles for which it had fought so tenaciously for half a century, and for which Jackson had spoken so eloquently.

John G. Jackson never lived to see the victory of the democratic political principles for which he had fought nearly all of his public life. His death in March 1825 spared him the disappointment of observing the failure of the second Staunton Convention, the Constitutional Convention of 1829-1830, and subsequent efforts to effect genuine reform in the fundamental law. The achievement in 1850, however, was in some respects no less a tribute to Jackson's own efforts than to those who lived to witness the final victory.

---

[26]Martinsburg *Gazette*, 17 February 1825.

[27]Ambler, *Sectionalism in Virginia*, 142-43; Rice, *Allegheny Frontier*, 365-66.

12 THE FINAL YEARS

The demands of his expanding industries and his preoccupation with the affairs of the Monongalia Navigation Company never extinguished John G. Jackson's interest in politics and public affairs. Less than a year after he left Washington in April 1817, he began to consider the possibility of returning to the House of Representatives. Among those who gave him encouragement was John C. Calhoun, who expressed delight that Jackson might resume a place in public life. Calhoun wrote him, "Our country has need of the services of her most experienced and able statesmen. It is a subject much to be deplored, that the changes in Congress are so frequent as to prevent that accumulation of experience there, which is necessary to the proper management of the affairs of our national government."[1]

During the summer of 1818 Jackson began to test the political climate of his congressional district. William McKinley, his longtime political ally in Ohio County, informed Jackson that he had discussed the possibility of Jackson's candidacy with numerous Republicans and that, with few exceptions, they had promised to vote for Jackson. McKinley believed, nevertheless, that some prominent Republicans would object to him because of his vote in favor of the United States Bank, which "has already done great mischief and . . . will finally destroy the liberties of these states," the unpopular Compensation Act, and legislation that permitted running the mail stages and keeping the post offices open on Sundays. Despite "all these bad things," McKinley urged Jackson to announce his candidacy without de-

---

[1]John C. Calhoun to Jackson, 31 March 1818, John George Jackson Papers, Lilly Library, Indiana University, Bloomington.

lay, for "[i]f you cannot be Elected no other on the republican side can in my opinion be Elected." He advised Jackson to seek the support of editors in Morgantown, Charlestown, and Wheeling, but to personally "keep out of sight" and allow his friends to be more active in the promotion of his cause.[2]

In February 1819 the Clarksburg *Republican Compiler*, a perennial supporter of Jackson, launched his campaign with a vigorous attack upon the views James Pindall, the incumbent congressman, had expressed on the question of expatriation. Jackson, who had spoken forcefully while in Congress for an expatriation law, almost certainly inspired, if he did not actually write, the article in the *Republican Compiler*. Pindall had declared that Congress had the power of naturalization but that only the "sovereign" states had the power of expatriation. He further noted that only one state, Virginia, had enacted an expatriation law and that its law would "serve better as an ornament to a museum, than a legislative precedent."[3]

The Federalists struck back by charging that while Jackson was in Congress he had opposed the appropriation of federal funds for the construction of the Cumberland Road. The Morgantown *Monongalia Spectator* accused him of speaking against the road in remarks made at Uniontown, Pennsylvania, and declared that "he must get out of the scrape as well as he can." The Wheeling *Va. North-Western Gazette*, however, refuted the allegations and quoted Colonel David Shepherd of Ohio County, who heard Jackson's remarks in Congress in 1816, as stating that the Western country owed the appropriation for the road to the exertions of Jackson.[4]

The contest between Jackson and his Federalist opponent took a personal turn. "Vindex," in the *Monongalia Spectator*, accused Jackson of writing two articles in the Clarksburg *Republican Compiler* that alleged Pindall had

---

[2]McKinley to Jackson, 17 July 1818, Jackson Family Papers, Virginia Historical Society, Richmond.

[3]The position of the Clarksburg *Republican Compiler* is noted in the Wheeling *Va. North-Western Gazette*, 11 February 1819. For the views of Jackson and Pindall, see *Annals of Congress*, 13th Cong., 2d sess., 1094-95, 1097; *Annals of Congress*, 15th Cong., 1st sess., 1045-50.

[4]Morgantown *Monongalia Spectator*, 13 February 1819; Wheeling *Va. North-Western Gazette*, 25 February 1819.

resorted to legal technicalities to avoid repayment of $2,500 he had received from the Bank of Marietta. The editor of the Morgantown newspaper inquired whether Jackson was "willing to risque the fate of the Election upon the comparative honesty of yourself & your opponent" and asserted that Jackson would certainly be the "loser by the investigation."[5]

On 27 February a number of freeholders of Ohio and Brooke counties met at West Liberty to consider the election of a congressman. With McKinley presiding and Robert I. Curtis, later editor of the Wheeling *Va. North-Western Gazette*, acting as secretary, the assembly agreed to support Jackson and to circulate handbills and resolutions in his behalf.[6] Within less than two weeks, however, Jackson received notification of his appointment as a federal judge for the newly created District of Virginia West of the Allegheny Mountains.[7] Upon receiving his judicial appointment, Jackson withdrew as a candidate for the House of Representatives, and McKinley consented to enter the race against Pindall. Pindall won the election, although McKinley received nearly twice as many votes in Wheeling.[8] Whether Jackson could have been elected had he remained in the contest is uncertain, but he almost certainly would have failed to amass the sizable margins he had received in his earlier campaigns.

Jackson's appointment as judge of the new Virginia district, although by no means assured, came as no great surprise. On 20 December 1818 Richard Mentor Johnson called upon Return Jonathan Meigs, Jr., the post-

---

[5]Morgantown *Monongalia Spectator*, 13 February 1819.

[6]Wheeling *Va. North-Western Gazette*, 4 March 1819.

[7]Jackson's commission as federal judge, dated 24 February 1819 and signed by President James Monroe and Secretary of State John Quincy Adams, is in the John George Jackson Papers. The commission was enclosed in an official notification of Adams to Jackson, 3 March 1819, John Quincy Adams Papers, National Archives, Washington, D.C. Jackson received unofficial information that he had been confirmed by unanimous vote of the Senate in a letter from John W. Eppes, 24 February 1819, Jackson Family Papers. Earlier the same day, however, Richard Mentor Johnson had advised Jackson against relaxing "as to the Election on account of the prospect of a judgeship that is uncertain as to the passage of the Bill[.]" Johnson to Jackson, 24 February 1819, John George Jackson Papers.

[8]Wheeling *Va. North-Western Gazette*, 18 March 1819, 8 April 1819.

master general and Jackson's father-in-law, and together the two visited John W. Eppes to discuss Jackson's expressed interest in the new post. All agreed that Jackson deserved the position on the basis of his "capacity, integrity, acquirements [and] faithful service."[9] Moreover, incumbent congressman James Pindall favored Jackson's appointment, not only as a means of removing a formidable rival in the congressional race, but because his own legal attainments enabled him to appreciate Jackson's qualifications. Eppes, a longtime friend, wrote Jackson that he believed Jackson could serve his country better in some other sphere, presumably in Congress, and that he reluctantly recommended him for the judgeship.[10]

In accepting the nomination, Jackson wrote Secretary of State John Quincy Adams, saying, ". . . altho I am diffident of my capacity to perform the functions of this new & important office with adequate ability, I have been induced by the solicitation of my friends to determine on its acceptance." To President James Monroe he expressed reservations about the propriety of accepting the appointment because of his "apprehensions that a state of things may arise in the nation, wherein I would better serve my country by being its Representative in Congress." He told the president that he would reassess the situation after he had served two years, and, if necessary, he would "relinquish the position I now accept, & lend my feeble aid to support the great cause espoused in 1798, & of which I have never ceased to be the zealous advocate." Jackson also sought to smooth over past differences with Monroe by declaring that, contrary to appearances, he had not opposed President James Madison's desire to appoint Monroe secretary of state in 1809 but had merely pointed out that considerable opposition to Monroe existed in Virginia at the time.[11]

Jackson took the oath of office as judge of the new district of Virginia on 20 March 1819 before Justice of the Peace Daniel Kincheloe, his brother-in-law. His debut as judge excited general approbation. In his remarks to

---

[9]Johnson to Jackson, 20 December 1818, John George Jackson Papers.

[10]Eppes to Jackson, 24 February 1819, Jackson Family Papers.

[11]Jackson to Adams, 11 March 1819, John Quincy Adams Papers; Jackson to Monroe, 11 March 1819, James Monroe Papers, Library of Congress, Washington, D.C. A copy of the letter to Monroe is also in the John George Jackson Papers.

his first grand jury he set forth his philosophy of government and of the role of the judiciary. Drawing upon the social contract theory, he declared that before governments existed man was so insecure in his person and property that "his sleepless nights [were] succeeded by days of gloomy melancholy" and the "worst conditions of savage barbarism." To free himself from this state, man instituted government resting upon the consent of the governed. Jackson declared that "the best preservative of this freedom is to be found in the wisdom with which the laws are adapted to the conditions of society, and the fidelity with which they are executed."

Turning to the role of the judicial system in assuring the freedoms that government should promote and protect, Jackson traced the development of the grand jury. He declared that the Constitution required him, "as one of the public functionaries, to take care that no person shall be held to answer *here* for a capital or otherwise infamous crime, without the presentment or indictment of a Grand jury." He instructed the jurors that they had a duty to indict the criminal, but he warned them to base their charges only upon unimpeachable evidence. He expressed the humanistic view that "Our laws seek rather to reform than to chastise; and where *they require* that the blood of the criminal shall be shed, it is more for the sake of example than for punishment."[12]

Throughout his judicial career Jackson continued to stress to grand juries the seriousness of their responsibilities. In 1822 he reminded the grand jurors that they should "present no person, through fear, favor, or affection." He ranged beyond their own responsibilities to express his firm conviction that the United States government had attained "the highest degree of perfection, of which any form is susceptible, & thus [had] solved the great enigma, whether man is capable of self government, without the 'divine aid of Kings to rule over him.'" Jackson alluded to the Greek struggle for freedom and voiced the hope that "the Country of Laonidas [*sic*], & Demosthenes, & Homer, will be redeemed from the despotism of the haughty

---

[12]For Jackson's oath of office, see U.S. District Court, District of Virginia West of the Allegheny Mountains, Order Book No. 1, 1819-1831, 2, Record Group 21, National Archives Record Center, Suitland, Maryland (hereinafter cited as U.S. District Court, Western Virginia, Order Book No. 1). Jackson's charge to the grand jury is recorded in the Clarksburg *Republican Compiler*, 1 October 1819; Wheeling *Va. North-Western Gazette*, 7 October 1819.

Turk, by whom it has been enslaved for Centuries." He drew attention to the great exertions of the nations of the western hemisphere for freedom and the price at which the liberty of the United States had been purchased. In conclusion, Jackson declared that "the majesty of the Laws [should] be inviolate" and that while they existed, even though they be impolitic, they should be administered "with scrupulous fidelity, without favor, & without malice."[13]

The rules of the new court provided that it should maintain its records at Clarksburg, Lewisburg, and Wythe Court House—now Wytheville, Virginia—the three places where Jackson's court sat. Jackson heard cases originating in Monongalia, Harrison, Ohio, Wood, Brooke, Randolph, Tyler, Lewis, and Preston counties at Clarksburg; those having their origins in Kanawha, Greenbrier, Mason, Cabell, Nicholas, and Monroe counties and part of Pendleton County at Lewisburg; and those emanating from Wythe, Lee, Grayson, Washington, Montgomery, Russell, Scott, Giles, and Tazewell counties at Wythe Court House.[14]

The records of the courts held at Clarksburg provide some insight into the nature of the cases that came before Jackson and his interpretations of the law. Court sessions were usually short, lasting from three to six days. The grand jurors usually made no presentments, and the cases in which they made presentments were of a routine nature, such as those of George D. Barns for forgery and Solomon Collett for forcibly resisting an officer of the United States.[15]

Most of the cases brought before Jackson involved ejectment suits and arose from the confused land situation in western Virginia. The most noted of the ejectment suits related to the French Creek area of present Upshur County, West Virginia, where immigrants from Massachusetts, Connecticut, and Vermont had settled between 1808 and 1816. These settlers in-

---

[13]Draft of Address to "Gentlemen of the Grand Jury," May 1822, Meigs-Jackson Papers, Blennerhassett Historical Park Commission, Parkersburg, West Virginia (hereinafter cited as Meigs-Jackson Papers, BHPC).

[14]U.S. District Court, Western Virginia, Order Book No. 1, 3. The records of the courts held by Jackson at Lewisburg and Wythe Court House are apparently no longer extant.

[15]Ibid., 6, 8, 18, 34, 50, 66, 102, 127, 145.

cluded members of the prominent Phillips, Young, Gould, Alden, and Gilbert families. After residing on their lands for several years, they discovered that their titles were not clear and that they might be required to repurchase their property and even the improvements they had made from nonresident claimants previously unknown to them. Robert Young, one of their leaders, instituted legal proceedings designed to clarify their titles.[16]

One of the claimants to the French Creek lands, Daniel Boardman of New York, who in 1806 had retained Jackson as his attorney, engaged James Pindall, Jackson's close friend and political rival, as his attorney.[17] On 22 May 1820 Pindall entered an ejectment suit in the federal court, which, in accordance with the custom of using fictitious names, was styled *Tom Hungryful, lessee of Daniel Boardman and Robert Means* v. *Dick Starvation*. Jackson's court summoned Robert Young and Elijah Phillips, residents of French Creek, to appear as defendants at the next session of court "in the room of Dick Starvation." Unless they appeared, Jackson declared, the court would award judgment and United States writs of possession to the plaintiff. Pindall informed Boardman, however, that no decision could be made in the case at that time because of the lack of a surveyor's report on the lands.[18]

Meanwhile, the defendants in the French Creek ejectment suit attempted to show that Boardman's claim was part of a larger patent held by Archibald McCall of Philadelphia but originally granted to Standish Ford

---

[16]For an account of the land disputes involving the French Creek residents, see Otis K. Rice, *The Allegheny Frontier: West Virginia Beginnings, 1730-1830* (Lexington: University Press of Kentucky, 1970) 146-47. The interest of the Jackson family in lands and the relationship of land ownership to political leadership are brought out also in John Alexander Williams, *West Virginia: A Bicentennial History* (New York: W. W. Norton & Company, Inc., for the American Association for State and Local History, 1976) 38-47.

[17]Pindall to Boardman, 4 April 1820, Daniel Boardman Papers, West Virginia Collection, West Virginia University Library, Morgantown.

[18]U.S. District Court, Western Virginia, Order Book No. 1, 9. For case papers concerning the suit, see U.S. District Court, District of Virginia West of the Allegheny Mountains, Record Book, 79-91, Record Group 21, National Archives Records Center, Suitland, Maryland (hereinafter cited as U.S. District Court, Western Virginia, Record Book); James Pindall to Daniel Boardman, 5 September 1821, Boardman Papers.

and John Reed, also of Philadelphia, on the basis of a forged plat. The suit, designated as *John Ousthimoff, lessee of Archibald McCall, Standish Ford, and John Reed* v. *Bill Letsmealone,* also came before Jackson's court. It, too, was continued, but it was docketed ahead of Boardman's suit. After several continuations, the McCall, Ford, and Reed case received consideration at the spring term, 1822, of Jackson's court, with Robert Simpson and Levi Hopkins appearing in the place of Bill Letsmealone. In keeping with the findings of the jury, Jackson ruled that the plaintiff should recover from Hopkins the unexpired term of his lease in both land and appurtenances, but that he should receive nothing and recover no costs in the suit against Robert Simpson.[19]

The suit brought by Boardman did not come up until 27 October 1823. The jury returned a verdict in favor of Boardman, and Jackson ruled that he should recover possession of the property and the costs of the suit.[20] Boardman emerged the victor in the suit against the French Creek residents, but the claims of Ford and Reed remained to be settled. On 22 October 1821 a suit to decide their claims had been entered under the designation of *John Doe, lessee of Standish Ford and John Reed* v. *Richard Roe.* Defendants in the place of Richard Roe included thirteen residents of French Creek represented by James Pindall. In order to determine whether the Ford and Reed patent derived from a forgery, Jackson issued a *subpoena duces tecum* to James Robertson, the register of the Virginia land office, to appear at the next term of court. Robertson failed to appear, and Jackson cited him for contempt of court unless he provided a satisfactory explanation. At the spring term of court in 1824, William Seddon, the new register of the land office, was subpoenaed. Whether he appeared is doubtful, but when the case finally went to the jury on 26 October 1824, the jurors rendered a decision in favor of the defendants.[21]

A very different type of case brought before Jackson involved the *United States of America* v. *Jonathan Jackson, John Jackson, James McCally, and Edward*

---

[19]James Pindall to Daniel Boardman, 11 August 1823, Boardman Papers; U.S. District Court, Western Virginia, Order Book No. 1, 10, 26, 38, 72. Case papers in the suit are in U.S. District Court, Western Virginia, Record Book, 361-89.

[20]U.S. District Court, Western Virginia, Order Book No. 1, 131, 133.

[21]Ibid., 53, 94, 112, 151, 171, 179.

Jackson. This suit, docketed for 25 October 1820, originated in the failure of Jonathan Jackson to settle his accounts, as collector of internal revenue for western Virginia, with the Comptroller of the Treasury. With the assent of the plaintiff, the court decided that the government should recover from the four defendants the sum of $5,000 and costs of the suit, but the parties agreed to a stay of judgment until the next term of court.[22]

At the last term of court at which Jackson presided, another suit involved close relatives. In that case, heard on 30 October 1824, the United States government sought to recover money from the estate of Jackson's grandparents, John and Elizabeth Jackson. He ruled in favor of the government, with the stipulation that $5,000 and costs should be levied on the goods and chattels of the deceased.[23]

In January 1824 several prominent members of the bar in the Valley of Virginia launched a move to enlarge Jackson's circuit to include a court at Staunton. Jackson expressed to John Brown, their leader, a willingness to add a court at Staunton. Opposition arose in several places, most notably from William Smith of Greenbrier County, who feared that Lewisburg might be eliminated from the circuit, and from some attorneys in Frederick and Berkeley counties who favored Woodstock over Staunton as the location of any new court. Jackson worked through Joseph Johnson, his close friend who then represented the First Virginia District in Congress, to obtain a bill that enlarged his circuit to include a court at Staunton.[24]

Even as a jurist, Jackson wielded considerable political influence and found difficulty in remaining aloof from politics in his congressional district. Following the decision of Jackson's brother, Edward B., not to seek reelection to Congress in 1823, the Jacksons endorsed the candidacy of Joseph Johnson, a protégé who later became the first popularly elected governor of Virginia and the first from west of the Allegheny Mountains. Jackson's endorsement of Johnson stirred Philip Doddridge, a perennial Federalist adversary, to raise questions about Jackson's political activities. Doddridge reminded Jackson of an agreement they had made in April 1823

---

[22]Ibid., 27.

[23]Ibid., 186.

[24]Brown to Jackson, 6 January 1824, John George Jackson Papers; Brown to Jackson, 10 February 1824, ibid.; Johnson to Jackson, 17 January 1825, ibid.

"to bury our past differences" and added that before Jackson had left Congress in 1817, "I had become so far satisfied with your public course in that body, that I had determined not to aid in any further opposition to your election." Doddridge admonished Jackson that, aside from voting, judges should take no part in politics. Electioneering, he declared, fostered strife that often survived long after elections, and persons who appeared before a judge who had been active in politics might question the impartiality of his decisions.

Doddridge, himself a candidate for the congressional seat vacated by Edward B. Jackson, hoped to run without the opposition of the powerful Clarksburg family. He expressed amazement that John G. Jackson had characterized a speech by Johnson at the Harrison County polls as the ablest that he had ever heard and told Jackson that "those who could judge of this and knew your judgment, and attainments could not believe you sincere in that declaration." Doddridge declared that Johnson was totally incapable of advancing the cause of internal improvements, which both he and Jackson so ardently desired, since he "has to depend on others for the smallest operation in arithmetic and [is] destitute of all general information."[25] Despite Doddridge's bitter condemnations, Johnson, with the aid of the Jacksons, won the congressional seat.

Jackson's opposition to the party caucus system of nominating candidates for president and vice-president of the United States also had political overtones. In December 1823 Jackson published a series of three articles, which he signed "Virginius," in the Clarksburg *Intelligencer*. He declared that "the right of the people to choose their own rulers is one of the fundamental principles of a free government" and that any departure from that system was "dangerous to the extreme." The caucus system, he maintained, "virtually place[s] the election of the principal executive officer in the hands of the legislature, . . . an event never contemplated in a Representative Government, but as a *dernier* resort," when the choice could be made in no other way.[26]

The "Virginius" articles were directed against the candidacy of William H. Crawford, who had been nominated by party caucus. Jackson acknowl-

---

[25]Doddridge to Jackson, 29 November 1824, ibid.

[26]Clarksburg *Intelligencer*, 6 December 1823.

edged that many Republicans, including John C. Calhoun and Henry Clay, had participated in party caucuses in previous elections when no serious divisions existed regarding candidates. Yet, he insisted, no one would deny that they were "men too high minded to be deliberately and voluntarily engaged with factious demagogues in support of unconstitutional doctrines and practices."[27] Reverting to what he regarded as the true principles of the party, Jackson declared that he well remembered "the time, when the mere mention of the name, *Caucus*, would have produced a feeling of alarm in the bosoms of honest republicans." He was convinced that "to an *honest* Republican, it produces the same effect at the present day."[28]

Evidently Jackson sent several copies of his "Virginius" articles to Calhoun. In response to an accompanying letter from Jackson, Calhoun, a presidential aspirant, wrote that "we have indeed an important crisis before us, which in many respects resembles at bottom, the great struggle of '98" and that it, too, represented "a great conflict of principles." Calhoun declared that a party had grown up that hoped to control the government "not through the confidence and attachment of the people, but by a dexterous use of what is called party machinery." Its leaders said nothing about the Constitution, but considered "adhesion to the decision of a caucus . . . the only test of pure Republicanism." Calhoun wrote that the radicals who pressed decision by caucus had great strength in Virginia and in the New York Regency, but he believed that his own prospects were generally good. He informed Jackson that he needed to be very discreet in letters he sent out, but assured him that he had so many coming in that his enemies could not possibly read all of them.[29]

Jackson gave his assessment of the candidates for president in 1824 to his friend Caesar A. Rodney, who was then serving at a diplomatic post in Buenos Aires. He confessed to Rodney that he felt "decidedly hostile to Crawford," whom he regarded as the favorite of Virginia. He reported to Rodney that Andrew Jackson had "risen astonishingly since the last year," largely through his service in the Senate, where he had exhibited to "an eminent degree the character of a mild[,] liberal & accomplished gentle-

---

[27]Ibid., 20 December 1823.

[28]Ibid., 13 December 1823.

[29]Calhoun to Jackson, 19 December 1823, John George Jackson Papers.

man—no cutting off of ears, no military despotism. His enemies were confounded, his friends delighted." Judge Jackson, however, did not believe that the Tennessean could be elected. Since Andrew Jackson had no "partiality for Mr. Clay," who had censured him for the hanging of two British "renegadoes" in Florida, John Quincy Adams hoped to win the Tennessee senator's support by assuring him the votes of the Adamsites for the vice-presidency. Jackson also believed that Calhoun would settle for the vice-presidency, by arrangement with either Adams or Jackson.

John G. Jackson himself preferred Clay. Of the Kentuckian, he declared, "I am delighted with Clay's career, upon South American independence, the tariff, & Internal Improvement, & if it were not for the temper of Europe, which renders justice tributary to Policy, I would add the Greek question also." Jackson believed that Clay would provide strong competition for Adams and that he would not accept any office from Adams. In fact, he predicted that the election would go into the House of Representatives, where Clay, with strong support, would emerge the victor.[30]

Events proved Jackson right in predicting that the presidential contest would reach the House of Representatives, but they left him wide of the mark in foretelling the winner or judging Clay's willingness to serve in an Adams administration. When the question reached the House, Jackson sought the opinion of Congressman Richard Mentor Johnson of Kentucky on its outcome. Johnson informed Jackson that Andrew Jackson, Clay, and Crawford were all optimistic. Johnson believed, however, that Adams would win, although Andrew Jackson had more popular support. He gave a clue to John G. Jackson's own thinking at this time by stating, "I am like you[;] I can support either & be satisfied with either."[31]

During the years following his retirement from the House of Representatives Jackson maintained his deep interest in both domestic and foreign affairs. He privately criticized the action of President Monroe, who during the Adams-Onís negotiations concerning the acquisition of Florida, took possession of Amelia Island, an outpost near the Georgia border that had slipped away from Spanish control. In the words of Jackson's close friend John W. Eppes, Monroe chose to consider the persons in control of

---

[30]Jackson to Rodney, May 1824[?], ibid.

[31]Johnson to Jackson, 11 and 17 January 1825, ibid.

the island "as pirates [and not] as a Foreign power [and] turned them out with as little ceremony as a farmer would the hogs of his neighbor who were destroying his crops." Eppes told Jackson, "Some few old fashioned fellows like yourself talk about the constitution[,] letters of marque & reprisal and captures by land and Sea vested in Congress and deny the Presidents [*sic*] right to have so conducted" the occupation.[32] On the other hand, with respect to the acquisition of Florida in 1819, Jackson wrote Monroe, ". . . there is as far as I can learn an unexampled unanimity. This last atchievement [*sic*] constitutes the proudest trophy in your career of auspicious administration."[33]

Among domestic matters the tariff retained a place of special importance in Jackson's mind. His experience with manufacturing and the pressing needs for industry in the West had long since made him a firm protectionist. In May 1824 he congratulated Henry Clay, the foremost advocate of protectionism, upon his "truly great Speech upon the Tariff." "To my mind," he wrote Clay, "your previous exhibitions have established upon the most solid basis, your unquestionable claims to the reputation of a great debater (&, what is of more value) of a great Statesman." Jackson departed from "the fastidiousness of custom" to tell Clay that if he had had any doubts of Clay's stature as a statesman, "this last great effort of a great mind would have fixed my opinion, & forever." Clay received Jackson's opinion "with particular satisfaction, as giving strength and confidence in my own."[34]

As the years passed, Jackson became increasingly appreciative of the work of the founding fathers. In July 1823 he observed to Thomas Jefferson that the nation had just witnessed another anniversary of independence and that it brought into "splendid review" the contributions of "the immortal dead" and the "few survivors" remaining. Noting that "the Declaration of Independance [*sic*], alike the immortal monument of the nations [*sic*] glory & the fame of its authors[,] has been ascribed by the concurrent testimony of all contemporaries to your pen," he declared to Jefferson, ". . . as a post revolutionary man enjoying all its benefits . . . I tender you

---

[32]Eppes to Jackson, 18 January 1818, ibid.

[33]Jackson to Monroe, 11 March 1819, ibid. See also Richard Mentor Johnson to Jackson, 24 February 1819, ibid.

[34]Jackson to Clay, 15 May 1824, ibid.; Clay to Jackson, 24 May 1824, ibid.

the homage of sincere gratitude." He wished Jefferson an end "as happy & glorious as your life has been illustrious & beneficial to your country & to the whole human family."[35]

At the same time Jackson also addressed a letter to Lafayette, declaring that the principles on which the United States had been founded had become "as firm as the foundation of our ever lasting mountains" and that the nation experienced "supreme gratification" in seeing them taking root and expanding everywhere. Jackson expressed regret, however, in seeing France, which "at one time boldly espoused the rights of man[,] receding from its proud position & returning to ignoble servility." He asserted that as a legislator and congressman, he had always favored a course in foreign affairs that "was long reproached with undue partiality to France." Although he was disappointed that France under Louis XVIII had not settled down "into a form of comparative freedom" after the foreign wars were over, he told Lafayette, "I will say that *you* have fulfilled our highest expectations—that we continue to be proud of you & offer up our daily prayers for your happiness."[36]

Jackson's interest in the formative years of the nation extended to the preservation of significant records. On 9 December 1821 he confessed to James Madison that he had "indulged a constant desire" to correspond with him on the question of publication of Madison's notes on the Constitutional Convention of 1787. He believed that "the period has arrived when a publication of the debates &c of the Federal convention, which you are known to possess in manuscript, is demanded by a regard to justice & expediency." The printing of the notes of Robert Yates, he declared, had "excited a laudable curiosity & interest common to all your friends to know the real facts."[37]

In regard to government power, Jackson wrote Madison that if he had proposed "to infuse more vigor & strength into the national government than it possesses," he had shown remarkable foresight. "I will frankly own," Jackson admitted, "that an attentive observation of its progress for more

---

[35]Jackson to Jefferson, 12 July 1823, ibid.

[36]Jackson to Marquis de Lafayette, 12 July 1823, ibid.

[37]Jackson to Madison, 9 December 1821, ibid.

than 20 years has convinced me (contrary to my first impressions) that the Union has more to fear from inadequacy of power in the head & anarchy in the members than from every other danger combined," a view confirmed, he believed, by the experiences of the War of 1812.[38]

In response to Jackson's letter, Madison asserted that newspaper extracts of Yates's published notes convinced him that he should consider publication of his own notes, since the Yates volume constituted "not only a very mutilated but a very erroneous edition of the matter to which it relates." The former president acknowledged the value of his own notes in tracing the development of the institutions of government and as a source for the study of the science of government, but he believed that they could not serve as a guide in applying the Constitution. Jackson must have found special gratification in Madison's assertion that "if a key is to be sought elsewhere, it must not be in the opinions or intentions of the Body which planned & proposed the Constitution, but in the sense attached to it by the people in their respective state conventions where it received all the authority which it possesses."[39]

Jackson's interest in recording firsthand information concerning the nation's history included the preservation of accounts of local events. In 1819 the Virginia legislature enacted legislation requiring the drafting of an accurate map of the state, along with data on each section. Among those designated to collect data was Hugh Paul Taylor of Covington, whose newspaper sketches in the Fincastle, Virginia, *Mirror* were later used by Alexander Scott Withers in his noted *Chronicles of Border Warfare*. Taylor asked Jackson to provide information on geographical and climatic conditions, Indian tribes and antiquities, early settlers, place names, population, manners and modes of life, literature and science, commerce and manufacturing, religion, lawyers and physicians, and other matters of general interest. Jackson's reply to Taylor is no longer extant, and when Withers finally compiled his *Chronicles*, he drew much of his information on the early his-

---

[38]Ibid.

[39]Madison to Jackson, 15 September 1821, Jeffress Collection, Alderman Library, University of Virginia, Charlottesville.

tory of the upper Monongahela Valley from notes and data provided by Edwin S. Duncan.[40]

Jackson's light judicial duties left him considerable time for his personal interests and for state and local political affairs. In 1818 he accepted the post of treasurer of the school commissioners of Harrison County, who had the responsibility of administering money provided by the Literary Fund of Virginia for the education of poor children. In 1819 the Harrison County Court appointed Jackson and Edwin S. Duncan as inspectors of the public buildings of the county.[41] Jackson and his brother Edward pressed for the appointment of Daniel Kincheloe, their brother-in-law, for principal assessor of Virginia, and in 1820 they supported him in his successful election to the Virginia House of Delegates.[42]

On 18 March 1818 the governor of Virginia appointed Jackson to a twenty-one-member commission to make plans for the proposed University of Virginia. Meeting at a tavern in Rockfish Gap on 4 August, the commission considered Lexington, Staunton, and Charlottesville as sites for the institution. Jackson and a majority of the other commissioners joined Thomas Jefferson in recommending Charlottesville to the General Assembly as the best location. The commission also proposed that professorships be established in languages, both ancient and modern, mathematics, physico-mathematics, physics or natural philosophy, botany, anatomy, government, law, and ideology.[43]

---

[40]Taylor to Jackson, 15 August 1823, John George Jackson Papers. For Taylor's newspaper sketches and the sources used by Withers for his *Chronicles of Border Warfare*, see "Memoir of the Author" by Lyman Copeland Draper in Alexander Scott Withers, *Chronicles of Border Warfare*, new ed. (Cincinnati: Stewart and Kidd Company, 1895) viii-xii.

[41]Harrison County Court Minute Book, 1818-1820, 70, 226, Harrison County Courthouse, Clarksburg, West Virginia.

[42]Jackson to James P. Preston, 22 September 1819, Virginia, Executive Papers, Virginia State Library, Richmond; Edward B. Jackson to Robert G. Scott and James Heath, 23 September 1819, ibid.

[43]Nathaniel Francis Cabell, *Early History of the University of Virginia* (Richmond: J. W. Randolph, 1856) 437-38, 447. See also Wheeling *Va. North-Western Gazette*, 14 January 1819.

Upon his return home, Jackson urged representatives from northwestern Virginia in the General Assembly to locate the university at Charlottesville. His efforts proved significant and successful. Joseph C. Cabell, a strong advocate of Charlottesville in the legislature, reported to Jackson that George I. Davisson, a delegate from Harrison County, had assured him of the votes of twenty-two delegates from northwestern Virginia. Cabell told Jackson that their support would enable him to "penetrate the designs of the opposition and . . . break their combination."[44]

Jackson continued to look after the interests of personal and political friends. In 1819, when the discontinuance of the Morgantown *Monongalia Spectator,* published by William McGranaghan, left no designated printer of the laws in Jackson's section of the state, he recommended his friend, Gideon Butler, the editor of the Clarksburg *Republican Compiler,* to fill the place. Jackson wrote Secretary of State John Quincy Adams that many citizens in his district had already contemplated a remonstrance against McGranaghan, who "had grossly abused our State institutions, the governor & other prominent men in it, & proposed our annexation to Pennsylvania, & by such conduct rendered himself highly obnoxious." He also maintained that Clarksburg, as the seat of two courts embracing large districts and "central to a numerous population," should be the place at which the public laws were printed.[45]

Other federal appointments excited Jackson's interest. In 1819 he recommended James Prunty for the post of United States marshal.[46] When his close friend, United States District Attorney Jacob Beeson, died, Jackson recommended another friend, James Pindall, often a political rival, as a man whose "eminent talents, & popularity" qualified him for the place. In case Pindall should not receive the appointment, Jackson proposed that Lewis Maxwell, a representative of Lewis County in the Virginia legislature, be offered the position.[47]

Family matters continued to demand much of Jackson's attention. Following his departure from Congress in 1817, he and his wife agreed that

---

[44]Cabell, *Early History of the University of Virginia,* 141.

[45]Jackson to Adams, 15 July 1819, John Quincy Adams Papers.

[46]Jackson to James Monroe, 11 March 1819, John George Jackson Papers.

[47]Jackson to James Madison, 11 September 1823, ibid.

Jackson's daughter Mary should continue her education in Washington, where she could be under the watchful eye of Sophia Meigs.[48] In 1820 a daughter, Eugenia, died, and the following year two other children also died. In December 1821 Jackson wrote James Madison, ". . . we have been visited in the past six months with great & distressing sickness[;] our most lovely child Madisonia 6 years old & an infant son 9 months old fell victims to it." He told Madison that he then had surviving a daughter, Sophia, who was eight years old, and a son, James Madison, who was four years old. Mary, his daughter by Mary Payne Jackson, was then at home.[49] Of Jackson's ten legitimate children who had been born by the end of 1821, eight had died before reaching maturity.[50]

The year 1822 brought happier times for the Jacksons. On 23 September they became the parents of a daughter, whom they named Columbia. The following month Jackson's son, John Jay, returned home after serving as adjutant of the Fourth Infantry at Montpelier, Alabama, and Pensacola, Florida. John Jay had decided to resign from the army and read law, with a view to entering practice at Parkersburg, which appeared to offer better opportunities than Clarksburg.[51] Sometime in late 1824 the last of Jackson's children, a daughter named Floride, was born. Her birth, however, was overshadowed by the marriage of Jackson's eldest daughter, Mary, to John James Allen, a young Clarksburg attorney, who had already become a friend of the family.[52]

During 1823 and 1824 Jackson suffered the loss of two of his closest friends. John W. Eppes, whom he had known for more than a score of years,

---

[48]See, for example, Sophia Meigs to Mary S. Jackson, 11 May 1820, Meigs-Jackson Papers, BHPC.

[49]Jackson to Madison, 9 December 1821, John George Jackson Papers; Dorothy Davis, *John George Jackson* (Parsons WV: McClain Printing Company, 1976) 293. See also Madison to Jackson, 28 December 1821, Jeffress Collection.

[50]See, for instance, Jackson to Caesar A. Rodney, 8 January 1823, Gratz Collection, Historical Society of Pennsylvania, Philadelphia; Davis, *John George Jackson*, Genealogical Chart of Jackson Family, following page 340.

[51]Davis, *John George Jackson*, 302.

[52]Ibid., 318-21; Dolley Madison to Jackson, 27 November 1824, John George Jackson Papers.

died on 15 September 1823. Jackson described Eppes as "one of my elect cut off in the zenith of his usefulness and in the vigor of intellectual fame."[53] The following year another friend, Caesar A. Rodney, suffered steadily declining health. During his illness Jackson wrote him, ". . . it has been my fortune . . . to form, considering the extent of my acquaintance, but few friendships; but they make up in their ardent character, for their paucity." Despite his knowledge of Rodney's condition, Jackson was unprepared for the shock when a letter he addressed to Rodney in Buenos Aires by way of the State Department was returned to him by John Quincy Adams with a note that Rodney had died a few days previously.[54]

The losses of his children and close friends, together with the anxieties over affairs of the Monongalia Navigation Company, probably contributed to periods of melancholy that marked the closing months of Jackson's life. One night, when he could not sleep, he composed some lines, which he entitled "Song" and which he gave to his brother William on the morning of 8 January 1825.[55]

When the autumnal rains descend upon Mount Alto & scatter the yellow
leaves that cast a sickly hue upon its summit,
think of me & of the days gone by;
for there I hunted the wild buck which delighted to gaze down upon our
village.

When the hoar frost & early snows drive the shivering husbandman
within his cottage,
think of me, & of the pursuits at such seasons;
for then I was wont to launch into the deepest recesses of the forest
in pursuit of its wild game.
Think of me.

---

[53]For the death of Eppes and its effects on Jackson, see Jackson to Caesar A. Rodney, May 1824[?], ibid. The closeness of the friendship is also suggested in Eppes to Jackson, 18 January 1818, ibid.

[54]Jackson to Rodney, May 1824[?], ibid.; Adams to Jackson, 19 August 1824, ibid.

[55]The "Song" is in Meigs-Jackson Papers, BHPC. On the back of the copy is written, "Given me by my dear J[ackson]—Jany 8th 1825. Died March 28, 1825. W. Jackson."

The sorrows and troubles that surrounded Jackson's last years may have influenced him to consider a diplomatic post. Richard Mentor Johnson approached President Monroe with the suggestion that he appoint Jackson minister to Mexico. Joseph Johnson wrote that he had made inquiries about the post in Buenos Aires, but he believed that Monroe would make no appointment. Moreover, Joel R. Poinsett and William Henry Harrison were under consideration for the Mexican position. If, as rumored, Harrison should be elected to the United States Senate, Johnson believed that he could procure for Jackson "a very strong recommendation from the Members of Congress." Johnson's request that Jackson be "more explicit on the subject," however, suggests that Jackson had not reached any firm decision.[56]

Toward the end of 1824 Jackson's health became a matter of increasing concern. Dolley Madison wrote him that she regretted his "want of health" and hoped that he would soon be well again.[57] In succeeding weeks Jackson did not regain his customary vitality. Early in March 1825 he suffered a mild stroke, but even then his physician and brother-in-law, Dr. William Williams, did not "apprehend any danger."[58] Williams prescribed calomel, and Jackson showed signs of recovery, but he cancelled the spring terms of court at Staunton and Wythe Court House. On 24 March Jackson decided to ride out to Mile's End. At the iron furnace "his mouth began to run," and he returned home to his bed. Perhaps sensing the gravity of his situation, he implored Williams and his brother Edward, also a physician, not to "deceive" him. About nine o'clock on Monday evening, 28 March 1825, Jackson said that he wanted to make a statement. Those who were in the room with him, with the exception of his wife and Edward, left the room. By the time they left he was unable to speak, an indication that he had suffered another stroke. Two hours later he died.[59]

---

[56]Richard Mentor Johnson to Jackson, 11 January 1825, John George Jackson Papers; Joseph Johnson to Jackson, 17 January 1825, ibid.

[57]Dolley Madison to Jackson, 27 November 1824, ibid.

[58]Mary E. P. Jackson Allen to Sophia Meigs, 4 April 1825, Meigs-Jackson Papers, BHPC; Clarksburg *Intelligencer*, 26 March 1825.

[59]Mary E. P. Jackson Allen to Sophia Meigs, 4 April 1825, Meigs-Jackson Papers. Jackson died within seven hours of Return Jonathan Meigs, Jr., his father-in-law.

On 29 March Jackson's son-in-law, John J. Allen, assumed the duty of informing the Meigs family that Jackson had died at eleven o'clock the previous night. Allen told them that their daughter, exhausted by fatigue and anxiety, had fainted shortly before Jackson's death. Sleep had refreshed her, but she was "still overwhelmed with grief." Allen expressed the hope that, "soothed by the kind attentions of her friends, time . . . will moderate her grief; and in the performance of her duties to the children of him she mourns, she will find some consolation for her loss."[60]

Following funeral services conducted by the Reverend George Brown of Clarksburg, Jackson was buried in the family cemetery in the Orchard Place, about half a mile from his residence. There, within the shadows of Pinnickinnick, a mountain peak overlooking his estate, he found rest beside Mary Payne Jackson and his departed children.[61]

The Clarksburg *Intelligencer*, in a widely copied obituary, traced Jackson's achievements and characterized him as "an accomplished scholar, an eminent statesman, an able jurist, and patriotic citizen." His death, it asserted, produced "a chasm in society, which his acquaintances may hope for but cannot see filled."[62] The final tribute was recognition of the unique place that Jackson had held in the political, economic, and cultural life of western Virginia and of the nation.

---

[60]Allen to Sophia Meigs, 29 March 1825, ibid.

[61]George Brown to John J. Allen, 30 March 1825, Allen Family Papers, Virginia Historical Society, Richmond; Davis, *John George Jackson*, 328.

[62]Clarksburg *Intelligencer*, 2 April 1825. Among other newspapers that carried notices of Jackson's death was the Richmond *Enquirer*, 15 April 1825.

BIBLIOGRAPHY

PRIMARY SOURCES

MANUSCRIPTS

Adams, John Quincy. Papers. National Archives, Washington, D.C.

Allen Family. Papers. Virginia Historical Society, Richmond.

Boardman, Daniel. Papers. West Virginia Collection, West Virginia University Library, Morgantown.

Breckenridge-Watts. Papers. Alderman Library, University of Virginia, Charlottesville.

Cassady, Mary Allen. Collection. Fincastle, Virginia.

Cook, Roy Bird. Collection. West Virginia Collection, West Virginia University Library, Morgantown.

Dabney-Jackson. Collection. Virginia State Library, Richmond.

Gallatin, Albert. Papers. New-York Historical Society, New York.

Gratz Alphabetical Collection. Historical Society of Pennsylvania, Philadelphia.

Gratz Collection. Historical Society of Pennsylvania, Philadelphia.

Jackson, John George. Papers. Lilly Library, Indiana University, Bloomington.

Jackson Family. Papers. Virginia Historical Society, Richmond.

Jeffress Collection. Alderman Library, University of Virginia, Charlottesville.

Kentucky Papers. Draper Manuscripts. State Historical Society of Wisconsin, Madison.

Madison, James. Papers. Alderman Library, University of Virginia, Charlottesville.

Madison, James. Papers. Library of Congress, Washington, D.C.

Madison, James. Papers. New York Public Library, New York.

Manuscript Collection VFM #14. Ohio Historical Society, Columbus.

Marietta College. Manuscript Collection. Dawes Memorial Library, Marietta, Ohio.

Meigs-Jackson. Papers. Blennerhassett Historical Park Commission, Parkersburg, West Virginia.

Meigs-Jackson. Papers. Ohio Historical Society, Campus Martius Museum, Marietta, Ohio.

Monroe, James. Papers. Library of Congress, Washington D.C.

Morgan, Charles S. Papers. West Virginia Department of Archives and History, Charleston.

PUBLIC ARCHIVES

Harrison County. Legislative Petitions. Virginia State Library, Richmond.

Harrison County. Personal Property Tax Lists, 1801-1814. Virginia State Library, Richmond.

Harrison County. Records. Harrison County Courthouse, Clarksburg, West Virginia.

Circuit Court Records.
County Court Minute Books, 1792-1820.
Deed Books 3, 6, 7, 21.
Land Books, 1801-1819.
Land Book, Lower District, 1821.
Land Book, Upper District, 1821.
Tithable Lists, 1812-1814.
Will Book 3.

Monongalia County. Legislative Petitions. Virginia State Library, Richmond.

Ohio County. Legislative Petitions. Virginia State Library, Richmond.

Ohio. Records. Office of the Auditor, Land Office, Columbus.

Randolph Academy. Minutes of the Board of Trustees, 1803-1851. Typescript. West Virginia Collection, West Virginia University Library, Morgantown.

United States. Adjutant General's Office. Records, 1780s-1917. Application Papers to the United States Military Academy, 1815/20. National Archives, Washington, D.C.

United States. Court. District of Virginia West of the Allegheny Mountains. Order Book No. 1, 1819-1831. Record Group 21. National Archives Records Center, Suitland, Maryland.

United States. Court. District of Virginia West of the Allegheny Mountains. Record Book. Record Group 21. National Archives Records Center, Suitland, Maryland.

United States. Treasury Department. Miscellaneous Treasury Accounts. General Accounting Office. 1st Auditor's Office. National Archives, Washington, D.C.

United States. War Department. Letters Received. Registered Series. National Archives, Washington, D.C.

Virginia. Board of Public Works. Records. Virginia State Library, Richmond.
Journals B, C, D, E.
Letterbook A.
Monongalia Navigation Company Records.

Virginia. District Court. Records. Monongalia County Records. West Virginia Collection, West Virginia University Library, Morgantown.

Virginia. Eleventh Circuit Court. Chancery Orders No. 2. Harrison County Circuit Court Records. Harrison County Courthouse, Clarksburg, West Virginia.

Virginia. Executive Papers. Virginia State Library, Richmond.

Virginia. Executive Papers. Militia. Virginia State Library, Richmond.

Virginia. Executive Papers. Pardon Papers. Virginia State Library, Richmond.

Virginia. Superior Court. Fourth District. Chancery Orders No. 3. Harrison County Courthouse, Clarksburg, West Virginia.

Virginia. Supreme Court of Appeals. Order Book No. 4. Virginia State Library, Richmond.

Washington County, Ohio. Probate Court Records. Marriage Records. Volume 1. Washington County Courthouse, Marietta.

GOVERNMENT DOCUMENTS

Carter, Clarence Edwin, ed. *The Territorial Papers of the United States; The Territory Northwest of the Ohio River, 1787-1803.* 2 vols. Washington DC: Government Printing Office, 1934.

Lowrie, Walter, and Walter S. Franklin, eds. *American State Papers: Documents, Legislative and Executive, of the Congress of the United States . . . 1809-1823.* 7 vols. 1832-1861. Reprint. Wilmington DE: Scholarly Resources, 1972.

Palmer, W. P., et al., eds. *Calendar of Virginia State Papers and Other Manuscripts.* 11 vols. Richmond VA: Virginia State Library, 1875-1893.

Richardson, James D., comp. *A Compilation of the Messages and Papers of the Presidents of the United States, 1789-1897.* 10 vols. Washington DC: Government Printing Office, 1896-1907.

Shepherd, Samuel, comp. *The Statutes at Large of Virginia, from the October Session 1792 to the December Session 1806, Inclusive.* 3 vols. 1835. Reprint. New York: AMS Press, Inc., 1970.

U.S., Congress. *Annals of Congress of the United States, 1789-1825.* 42 vols. Washington DC: Gales and Seaton, 1834-1856.

Virginia. *Acts Passed at a General Assembly of the Commonwealth of Virginia, . . . 1798-1825.* Richmond VA: Publisher varies, 1798-1826.

Virginia. Board of Public Works. *Annual Report . . . to the General Assembly, 1820-1826.* Richmond VA: Publisher varies, 1820-1826.

Virginia. *A Collection of All Laws and Resolutions of the General Assembly of Virginia, Relating to the Board of Public Works; The Report of the Commissioners Appointed to View Certain Rivers Within the Commonwealth in 1812; The Reports of 1814-15, from the Committee on Roads and Internal Navigation, to the Legislature; and the Several Annual Reports of the Board of Public Works to the General Assembly of Virginia, up to 1819*. Richmond VA: Shepherd and Pollard, 1819.

Virginia. *Journal of the House of Delegates of the Commonwealth of Virginia, . . . 1797-1825*. Richmond VA: Publisher varies, 1797-1826.

Virginia. *Proceedings and Debates of the Virginia State Convention of 1829-1830*. 1831. Reprint. New York: Da Capo Press, 1971.

Virginia. *The Virginia Report of 1799-1800, Touching the Alien and Sedition Laws; Together with the Virginia Resolutions of December 21, 1798*. Richmond VA: J. W. Randolph, 1850.

CONTEMPORARY SOURCES

Adams, Charles Francis, ed. *Memoirs of John Quincy Adams, Comprising Portions of His Diary from 1795 to 1848*. 12 vols. New York: J. B. Lippincott & Co., 1874-1877.

[Asbury, Francis]. *The Journal of the Reverend Francis Asbury, Bishop of the Methodist Episcopal Church, from August 7, 1771, to December 7, 1815*. 3 vols. New York: N. Bangs and T. Mason for the Methodist Episcopal Church, 1821.

[Cutts, Lucia B., ed.] *Memoirs and Letters of Dolly Madison, Wife of James Madison, President of the United States*. Boston: Houghton, Mifflin and Company, 1886.

Doddridge, Joseph. *Notes, on the Settlement and Indian Wars, of the Western Parts of Virginia & Pennsylvania, from the Year 1763 until the Year 1783 Inclusive, together with a View, of the State of Society, and Manners of the First Settlers of the Western Country*. Wellsburgh [W]V: Printed for the author, 1824.

Gerry, Elbridge, Jr. *The Diary of Elbridge Gerry, Jr*. New York: Brentano's, 1927.

Hopkins, James F., Mary W. M. Hargreaves, and Robert Seager, eds. *The Papers of Henry Clay*. 7 vols. Lexington: University Press of Kentucky, 1959- .

Jackson, John G. *Oration Pronounced in Clarksburg, on the Fourth Day of July, 1812, and Thirty-Seventh Year of American Independence*. Clarksburg [W]V: F. & A. Britton, 1812.

Wagstaff, H. M., ed. *The Papers of John Steele*. 2 vols. Raleigh NC: North Carolina Historical Commission, 1924.

Withers, Alexander Scott. *Chronicles of Border Welfare*. Edited by Reuben Gold Thwaites. New ed. Cincinnati: Stewart and Kidd Company, 1895.

NEWSPAPERS

Baltimore (MD) *Federal Republican and Commercial Gazette*. 1809.

Charles Town *Farmer's Repository*. 1816.

Clarksburg *Bye-Stander*. 1810.

Clarksburg *Independent Virginian*. 1819.

Clarksburg *Intelligencer*. 1823-1825.

Clarksburg *News*. 1886.

Clarksburg *Republican Compiler*. 1819-1820.

Clarksburg *Telegram*. 1876.
Marietta (OH) *American Friend, & Marietta Gazette*. 1830.
Martinsburg *Gazette*. 1825.
Morgantown *Monongalia Gazette*. 1809.
Morgantown *Monongalia Spectator*. 1819.
Raleigh (NC) *Minerva*. 1809.
Raleigh (NC) *Register*. 1809.
Raleigh (NC) *Star*. 1809.
Richmond (VA) *Enquirer*. 1815-1816.
Richmond (VA) *Examiner*. 1816.
St. Clairsville (OH) *Ohio Federalist*. 1813.
Washington (DC) *National Intelligencer*. 1807-1825.
Wheeling *Register*. 1890.
Wheeling Repository. 1807-1808.
Wheeling *Va. North-Western Gazette*. 1819.

SECONDARY SOURCES

BIOGRAPHICAL

Atkinson, Geo[rge] W., ed. *Bench and Bar of West Virginia*. Charleston WV: Virginian Law Book Company, 1919.

Brant, Irving. *James Madison, Commander-in-Chief, 1812-1836*. New York: The Bobbs-Merrill Company, Inc., 1961.

______________. *James Madison, Father of the Constitution, 1787-1800*. Indianapolis: The Bobbs-Merrill Company, Inc., 1950.

______________. *James Madison, Secretary of State, 1801-1809*. Indianapolis: The Bobbs-Merrill Company, Inc., 1953.

Clark, Allen C. *Life and Letters of Dolly Madison*. Washington DC: W. F. Roberts Company, 1914.

Cook, Roy Bird. *The Family and Early Life of Stonewall Jackson*. 4th ed., rev. Charleston WV: Education Foundation, Inc., 1963.

______________. "John George Jackson." *West Virginia Review* 12 (April 1935): 208-10, 221.

Davis, Dorothy. *John George Jackson*. Parsons WV: McClain Printing Company, 1976.

"Edwin S. Duncan." *West Virginia Historical Magazine* 2 (April 1902): 74-76.

Gittings, John G. *Personal Recollections of Stonewall Jackson; Also Sketches and Stories*. Cincinnati: The Editor Publishing Company, 1899.

Ketcham, Ralph. *James Madison: A Biography*. New York: The Macmillan Company, 1971.

Malone, Dumas. *Jefferson and the Ordeal of Liberty*. Boston: Little, Brown and Company, 1962.

______________. *Jefferson, the President: First Term, 1801-1805*. Boston: Little, Brown and Company, 1970.

MONOGRAPHS AND GENERAL WORKS

Abernethy, Thomas Perkins. *The Burr Conspiracy*. New York: Oxford University Press, 1954.

Adams, Henry. *History of the United States of America*. 9 vols. New York: Charles Scribner's Sons, 1909-1911.

Ambler, Charles H. *A History of Education in West Virginia from Early Colonial Times to 1949*. Huntington WV: Standard Printing and Publishing Company, 1951.

______________. *Sectionalism in Virginia from 1776 to 1861*. Chicago: University of Chicago Press, 1910.

Ambler, Charles H., and F. P. Summers. *West Virginia, the Mountain State*. 2d ed. Englewood Cliffs NJ: Prentice-Hall, Inc., 1958.

Babcock, Kendric C. *The Rise of American Nationality, 1811-1819*. Vol. 13 of *The American Nation: A History*. 28 vols. Edited by A. B. Hart. New York: Harper & Brothers, 1904-1918.

Bailey, Thomas A. *A Diplomatic History of the American People*. 8th ed. New York: Appleton-Century-Crofts, 1969.

Beeman, Richard R. *The Old Dominion and the New Nation, 1788-1801*. Lexington: University Press of Kentucky, 1972.

Bemis, Samuel Flagg. *A Diplomatic History of the United States*. 5th ed. New York: Holt, Rinehart and Winston, Inc., 1965.

Broussard, James H. "Party and Partisanship in American Legislatures: The South Atlantic States, 1800-1812." *Journal of Southern History* 43 (February 1977): 39-58.

Brown, Stephen W. "Congressman John George Jackson and Republican Nationalism, 1813-1817." *West Virginia History* 38 (January 1977): 93-125.

______________. "Satisfaction at Bladensburg: The Pearson-Jackson Duel of 1809." *North Carolina Historical Review* 58 (January 1981): 23-43.

Cabell, Nathaniel Francis. *Early History of the University of Virginia*. Richmond VA: J. W. Randolph, 1856.

Callahan, James Morton. *Semi-Centennial History of West Virginia*. [Charleston]: Semi-Centennial Commission of West Virginia, 1913.

Channing, Edward. *The Jeffersonian System, 1801-1809*. Vol. 12 of *The American Nation: A History*. 28 vols. Edited by A. B. Hart. New York: Harper & Brothers, 1904-1918.

Cunningham, Noble E., Jr. *The Jeffersonian Republicans: The Formation of Party Organization, 1789-1801*. Chapel Hill: University of North Carolina Press for the Institute of Early American History and Culture, 1957.

______________. *The Jeffersonian Republicans in Power: Party Operations, 1801-1809*. Chapel Hill: University of North Carolina Press for the Institute of Early American History and Culture, 1963.

Davis, Dorothy. *History of Harrison County, West Virginia*. Clarksburg WV: American Association of University Women, 1970.

Doherty, William Thomas. *Berkeley County, U.S.A.: A Bicentennial History of a Virginia and West Virginia County, 1772-1972*. Parsons WV: McClain Printing Company, 1972.

Harmer, Harvey. *Old Grist Mills of Harrison County*. Charleston WV: Charleston Printing Company, 1940.

Haymond, Henry. *History of Harrison County, West Virginia, from the Early Days of Northwestern Virginia to the Present*. Morgantown WV: Acme Publishing Company, 1910.

Horsman, Reginald. *The Frontier in the Formative Years, 1783-1815*. New York: Holt, Rinehart and Winston, 1970.

_______________. *The War of 1812*. New York: Alfred A. Knopf, 1969.

Jordan, Daniel P., ed. "Congressional Electioneering in Early West Virginia: A Mini-War in Broadsides, 1809." *West Virginia History* 33 (October 1971): 61-78.

Jordan, Philip D. *The National Road*. Indianapolis, 1948; Gloucester MA: Peter Smith, 1966.

Lewis, Virgil A. *Second Biennial Report of the Department of Archives and History of the State of West Virginia*. Charleston WV: n. p., 1908.

McDonald, Forrest. *We the People: The Economic Origins of the Constitution*. Chicago: University of Chicago Press, 1958.

Magrath, C. Peter. *Yazoo: Law and Politics in the New Republic; The Case of Fletcher v. Peck*. New York: W. W. Norton & Company, 1966.

Mahon, John K. *The War of 1812*. Gainesville: University of Florida Press, 1972.

Miller, Thomas Condit, and Hu Maxwell. *West Virginia and Its People*. 3 vols. New York: Lewis Historical Publishing Company, 1913.

Rice, Otis K. *The Allegheny Frontier: West Virginia Beginnings, 1730-1830*. Lexington: University Press of Kentucky, 1970.

Risjord, Norman K. *The Old Republicans: Southern Conservatives in the Age of Jefferson*. New York: Columbia University Press, 1965.

Smelser, Marshall. *The Democratic Republic, 1801-1812*. In *New American Nation Series*. 33 vols. to date. Edited by Henry Steele Commager and Richard B. Morris. New York: Harper & Row, 1954- .

Stevens, Abel. *A History of the Methodist Episcopal Church in the United States of America*. 3 vols. New York: Eaton and Mains, 1864.

Stutler, Boyd B. "Money Is What You Make It." *West Virginia Review* 10 (May 1933): 226-28.

Tyler, Alice Felt. *Freedom's Ferment: Phases of American Social History from the Colonial Period to the Outbreak of the Civil War*. Minneapolis: University of Minnesota Press, 1944.

Williams, John Alexander. *West Virginia: A Bicentennial History*. New York: W. W. Norton & Company, Inc., for American Association for State and Local History, 1976.

Young, James Sterling. *The Washington Community: Eighteen Hundred–Eighteen Twenty-Eight*. New York: Columbia University Press, 1966.

THESES, DISSERTATIONS, OTHER UNPUBLISHED MATERIALS

Brown, Stephen W. "John George Jackson: A Biography." Ph.D. dissertation, West Virginia University, 1977.

______________. "John George Jackson, Frontier Jeffersonian." Master's thesis, Marshall University, 1973.

Jordan, Daniel Porter, Jr. "Virginia Congressmen, 1801-1825." Ph.D. dissertation, University of Virginia, 1970.

Tazeski, Stanley P. Letter to author, 5 March 1973.

Index